CUPBOARDS of CURIOSITY

*© 2007 Duke University Press*
*All rights reserved*
*Designed by C. H. Westmoreland*
*Typeset in Adobe Janson with MT Bulmer*
*display by Tseng Information Systems, Inc.*
*Library of Congress Cataloging-in-Publication*
*Data and republication acknowledgments*
*appear on the last printed pages of this book.*

AMELIE HASTIE

# CUPBOARDS *of* CURIOSITY

*women, recollection, and film history*

DUKE UNIVERSITY PRESS

*Durham & London*   2007

*For my mother, father, and stepfather*

*And in loving memory of my grandmothers Frieda Emily Horton, Cécile Amélie Hastie, and Virginia Beahrs*

Sometimes timing really is everything, or at least it makes a kind of luck. Five heroes swept in to help me at perfect moments in this book's production. Scott Higgins read the introduction and chapter 2 with such care that he actually found typos in the footnotes; Raiford Guins lent me his brain for the introduction when mine wasn't up to par. Pat Mellencamp reappeared in my life just in time to read a draft of chapter 4; her very presence and then her speedy yet thorough read sustained some of the last stages of this work. Most of all, I want to thank Patty White, whose attentive and early reading shaped chapter 1 (and much of the book as a whole). "Theorize," she said. And to Lee Grieveson, who cheered me to the finish line on blind faith, I look forward to your role as my ideal reader. Though this book didn't have the benefit of his eyes, I know that everything will be better after this because of him.

My readers for Duke University Press, most particularly Judith Mayne, led me to sharpen the argument and the project overall. For the freedom of time and then the reminding of it, I want to thank my editor Ken Wissoker, who encouraged the project from way back and who gently worked through its end with me. Thanks also to the staff at Duke University Press, especially Katie Courtland, Judith Hoover, Pam Morrison, and the very sweet Courtney Berger.

This work benefited from my study of collections lodged in The Academy of Motion Pictures Arts and Sciences, the George Eastman House, the Library of Congress, the University of Southern California, and the University of Wisconsin, Madison. Thanks in particular to Barbara Hall at the Herrick Library; to John Horne at the Hearst Castle archives; to Anthony L'Abbate, Barbara Galasso, and Dan Wagner at the Eastman House; and to Joseph Yranksi, a private collector who generously shared his materials and his knowledge concerning Colleen Moore. At my home base of University of California, Santa Cruz, I would also like to thank the librarians Greg Careaga, Chela Lucas, Paul Machlis, and the inimitable David Kirk. Matt Tierney was the perfect research assistant in the final throes of this work, embodying the ideal combination of affability and intelligence.

My colleagues in the Film and Digital Media Department at the University of California, Santa Cruz, have been a constant source of patient encouragement and cheerful enthusiasm. Thanks in particular to longtime supporter David Crane, Sharon Daniel, Irene Gustafson, Peter Limbrick, Chip Lord, Margaret Morse, Lynda Potzus, and especially Shelley Stamp, an exemplar of intellectual grace. Rosa-Linda Fregoso, Jennifer Gonzalez, and Catherine Ramirez, and my writing coach-gourmand Nancy Chen have also been excellent models and friends—I thank my lucky stars that I am in a community with such vibrant and brilliant women. For their support of my work, I thank also Jody Greene, Herman Gray, David Marriott, and Eric Porter, as well as Chris Connery and Gail Hershatter at the Center for Cultural Studies. My community extends well beyond Santa Cruz; for ongoing and very timely support, I would also like to acknowledge Susan Courtney, Kay Dickinson, Anne Friedberg (for the book's main title!), Jane Gaines, Judith Mayne, Anna McCarthy, Edward O'Neill, Sara Ross, Jacqueline Stewart, Dan Streible, Haidee Wasson, Mark Williams, and especially Mary Desjardins. To the uncategorizable Tara McPherson, thank you for sharing your family and your intellectual life with me in the final stages of this process. Even now I can't properly articulate my appreciation to Alan Dorosin, whose resolute faith in my brain helped to heal it. Dirk Westphal's photographic work has been an ineffable inspiration to me, as have Barbara Epler's amazing mind, Claudia Steinberg's work ethic (and fashion sense), Marti Noxon's ability to produce something beautiful out of a painful world, and Arlo Hastie's expertise in the art of relaxation.

I am also grateful for the camaraderie of the *Camera Obscura* editorial collective, which has sustained me intellectually and emotionally over the past several years. My thanks especially to collective members Lynne Joyrich, Sasha Torres, Patricia White, and Sharon Willis. Our work together has surely informed my understanding of (and insistence on) intellectual collaboration throughout this project.

To my friends, my colleagues, and my family—thank you.

Research for this book was supported by grants from the Arts Division and the Committee on Research at the University of California, Santa Cruz.

CONTENTS

*Acknowledgments* ix

*Introduction*
    THE COLLABORATOR
        At the Cupboards of Film History 1

1   THE COLLECTOR
        Material Histories, Colleen Moore's Dollhouse, and Ephemeral Recollection 19

2   THE HISTORIAN
        Autobiography, Memory, and Film Form 72

3   THE CRITIC
        Louise Brooks, Star Witness 104

4   THE EXPERT
        Celebrity Knowledge and the How-tos of Film Studies 155

*Notes* 195

*Bibliography* 225

*Index* 239

ACKNOWLEDGMENTS

All scholarly works spring from a subjective position, however easy or difficult to map. In media studies we write about the films we love, the institutions we hate, the histories that have excluded us, the spaces of identification with whatever subject we are in the process of discovering, uncovering, recovering. When I think about what has (subjectively) driven my own work here and what also drives my dedication, in part, to the memory of my grandma (Frieda Emily Gaensslen Horton), I think about the nooks and crannies of her house. My grandma was a pack rat, and I would hazard to say that all pack rats are historians of a sort, their collections endeavoring to stop time, to hold ephemerality in abeyance, to sustain a present life for the past. Some of my grandma's collections were displayed, others categorized and tucked away, some packed in boxes in the basement, others in the cupboards and shelves lining the basement stairs. I spent much of my visits with her in a state of investigation and discovery, sometimes with her at my side to narrate this or that history and sometimes ensconced in semisecrecy, ever seeking clues to my family history.

The acknowledgments therefore map a personal and professional history of a work, and much of this history (and mapping) is indebted to my family. First and foremost, I would like to thank my mom, Claudette Hastie Beahrs, for her unconditional support of my work. My dad, Frank B. Hastie Jr., and my stepdad, John Beahrs, also had an encouraging enthusiasm and belief in this work. My brother Matt built both a wing on his house and a perfectly scaled dollhouse for his daughter Katie in the time it took me to finish one chapter; my brother Bow produced a body of art and wrote a book over the years of my own production. Both of them inspired and sustained me. With thanks also to the Hardy family, to David Crane—who led me to Moore in the first place—and to his immediate family, to Virginia and John V. Beahrs—all of whom offered encouraging networks of support—and to Katrine deWitt, whose generous gift helped me to focus on my writing and teaching as I was finishing graduate school.

Gaston Bachelard sees the house as a metaphorical and actual site for where memories are lodged, and this is in part why I am drawn to his work. So I see this work also in terms of where it was written, enabled by those friends who have given me a place to write. Barbara Epler has turned over her own apartment in New York, time and again, complete with chocolates on the pillow and flowers in the window. Chapter 1 was largely produced in the comfort of the home of my friend Aline Akelis, chapter 4 drafted at Wendy West's Upper West Side apartment, revisions on every chapter made in the visiting scholar suite at the home of Tara McPherson and Rob Knaack, the introduction, at long last, I finished in a luxurious room at the Montage in Laguna Beach, in the company of the Noxon-Bynum family, and the copy editing I completed in a comfy hammock on the lanai at the home of Nancy Chen and Dru Gladney.

The most formative space for the beginning of this work was, of course, the graduate program in modern studies at the University of Wisconsin, Milwaukee. I was lucky to work with three professors in particular, Lynne Joyrich, Patricia Mellencamp, and Kathleen Woodward, who were models, however distinct, of intellectual generosity, collegiality, and pedagogy. No matter what was the subject of my work, it was met with the same keen eye of my dissertation advisor Lynne Joyrich, who read every word I wrote, more than once. Her teaching drew me to UWM, and her kindness, as well as her unflagging sense of responsibility, got me through it. My thanks to other teachers as well: Herbert Blau, Bernard Gendron, Kristie Hamilton, and Patrice Petro. My luck in my studies extended to my cohort, especially James Castonguay, Elana Crane, Mary Elliott, Gretchen Papazian, Sarah Sharpe, and, most of all, Nicole Cunningham. A special thanks also to Mary Kriofske and Carl Bogner. And though we didn't go to the same programs, I feel I went to graduate school with two of my best friends, Nicole Cooley and Lisa Nakamura, who unfailingly supported me in all my studies and in all of my work since. They have each been with me for close to twenty years, and I can't do without them.

## INTRODUCTION: THE COLLABORATOR

### *at the cupboards of film history*

*Re*-create.
I want to re-create some of the women it has been my good fortune to know. Who would have known Cleopatra or Mary Magdalene or Barbara Fritchie or Betsy Ross or even the Blessed Mother herself if somebody hadn't re-created them in the time-space continuum. They *continue*, because of what others have said or written of them, as do the senators in John Kennedy's *Profiles in Courage*.
—ADELA ROGERS ST. JOHNS, *Some Are Born Great*

Feminist curiosity can constitute a political, critical and creative drive.—LAURA MULVEY, *Feminism and Curiosity*

Colleen Moore's memoir, *Silent Star*, begins with dueling histories of early Hollywood: one is a dry account that traces the industry's origins through real estate speculation and fair weather; the other suggests that Hollywood was born when unlicensed companies fled the arm of the Motion Picture Patents Corporation. Moore claims that she prefers this second version: "It has a serial thriller touch to it that sounds like Hollywood." She follows these stories of the origins of Hollywood with tales of the origins of her own stardom. Here she recollects an experience with her first scrapbook; an avowed fan of the movies, like many girls of her day (and like fans of later eras), she kept a book with clippings of her favorite film stars. But she also left one spot blank: an opening where she would place a photograph of herself as a star. As she writes, "The only difference between my movie scrapbook and those of my friends was that I left a blank page in mine for my own picture after I became a movie star. Because I didn't just hope to go to Hollywood. I intended to."[1] Told retrospectively, this anecdote appears as a prophecy of her stardom. And the prophecy is all the more fantastic when one considers that she went on to compile thirty-six scrapbooks detailing her work in Hollywood. But more important, the function of this story is consistent with the structure of all of her written and otherwise collected works: it points to the star's investment both in stardom and her place in film history, and it exhibits her fascination with and reflection on herself as a visual image. Indeed, as this little anecdote shows, Colleen Moore comes to represent her own best fan—and, in later years, her own best historian.

## AN OPEN BOOK

This trope—of a woman contemplating her own image on- and off-screen—inevitably persists across the memoirs of women who worked in film production and later wrote about their experiences. As they tell the stories of their lives, often depending on narratives of both progress and decline, stars such as Louise Brooks, Lillian Gish, Gloria Swanson, and Ethel Waters reflect upon themselves as images. Such reflection occurs even in less conventional narratives set in how-to manuals like Moore's *How Women Can Make Money in the Stock Market*, *Marlene Dietrich's ABC*, and Zasu Pitts's *Candy Hits*. These works produce and display knowledge outside of film culture, but they also rely on their authors' roles in film history to reveal this knowledge; film culture and history thus become a platform for other displays or embodiments of knowledge and expertise, often entangled with a kind of expert self-reflection. As this thread—of the female star or director looking at herself on-screen or behind the camera—winds across works as diverse as memoirs and cookbooks, we can track the inherent compatibility between autobiography and the subject's expertise in her field, whether that's the production of films or of stardom, the hobby of making fudge, or, as is more often the case, some combination of practices. So, if the early cinema can be said to derive from a cabinet of curiosities, given its impulse toward display, then perhaps we might think of these works as the cupboards: an interior, usually domestic space over which women often hold sway, with the enclosed items awaiting their necessity, their discovery enabled by what Laura Mulvey calls "feminist curiosity."[2] Usually lodged therein, the woman's expertise concerning her own life's story and her place of labor ultimately manifests itself in a kind of knowledge about the production of history, one that inherently intertwines fact and fiction, reminiscence and prophesy, the temporality and structure of film forms.

Surely such acts of introspection, or self-reflection, are the essence of any autobiography, whoever the subject. But the production and exhibition of self-reflection takes on new meaning when the subject of the memoir is a woman who worked in the production of cinematic fictions. These acts of self-reflection usually include a simultaneous speculation on the seemingly opposite poles of film production and reception. Acting as a "fan" of herself, as Moore does, the star models a kind of consumerism for other fans and readers. In fact, Moore goes on to claim that the "girl who lived across the street" also "left a blank page in her scrapbook for me!"[3] These blank spots mark a future space for history to be made, and they signify also an active construction of it; that is, they point to the making of history by the subject herself. Therefore, the star's consumerism is already tied to acts of production, which might allow future readers to rethink the divide between these two arenas. In consuming her image on the screen and on the page, the silent star especially, who often functions as pure image on screen, becomes the producer of her image in history.

Thus, in the same breath, this act of self-reflection becomes a reflection on the medium of film and its history. Stars such as Moore, Brooks, and Dietrich, early directors such as Alice Guy-Blaché and Nell Shipman, and others working in the industry as writers, journalists, or designers each utilize a variety of autobiographical forms to reflect on stardom, film industries, film history, and film form. Put somewhat differently, they draw on this form not only to reflect on their own lives but also often to produce their own theoretical and historical models about their work and the industries they have been engaged in. In this way, these writers function both as models for their fans and as models for the scholar who re-collects their work years later. And through this design for a future recollection, these subjects become collaborators with the scholars who turn to their works. It is in part through this relationship (and the women's own anticipation of being re-collected in the future) that is sketched a nonlinear temporality akin to the archive, to memory, and to film form.

Another instance in which the same breath of memory and history, collection and recollection is shared, therefore revealing a breadth of historical relations and reading practices, occurs in the very materiality of a book. Moore produced first her scrapbooks in childhood and then, upon her seemingly prophesied successful career, those detailing her stardom. Louise Brooks, an avid reader, wrote a series of critical essays about film culture, but she also wrote *in* books. She donated her own library to the George Eastman House in Rochester, New York; her books are full of her penned jottings in the margins. Her marginalia have the effect of a palimpsest, or perhaps the near simultaneity produced by moving-image media, as one page of Brooks's work displays multiple histories and multiple critical practices. This is historiography writ not large but in the margins, and in the object to be potentially held in our hands decades later, pulled from the cupboards of feminist curiosity.

So, on the same page, history is read, written, and read again. For instance, Brooks takes a copy of Francis Steegmuller's *Cocteau: A Biography* and makes notes throughout regarding how one can articulate a public history of a gay man. This is clearly a book she read very closely, one with which she was intimately engaged as reader and writer; this intimacy is revealed in her own hand, alongside the copy on the pages. In Fred Lawrence Guiles's biography of Marion Davies, she explicitly notes in the frontmatter, "This book studied and researched up to page 292 with a library copy, 2 June 1973 L.B. to 23 June 1973," noting "reading time" under these dates (Brooks was notorious for marking up books in her local library as well). Her ideas sprinkled throughout the Cocteau biography and her factual descriptions of reading time are the more sober evidence of her practices as a reader and writer; usually her comments are fairly cantankerous. For instance, Brooks refutes claims made about Frances Marion's accuracy as a historian with the following cranky (and notably arguable) commentary: "Frances Marion dies in 1973 leaving all film history polluted with her unresearched lies, inventions, and non-facts received as gospel."[4] Though her very obsession with truth is significant, I am less interested in debating Brooks's own accuracy here and more concerned in mulling over the literal and metaphorical significance of her words in the margins. In her marked-up copies, then, we see layers of historical production colliding: Guiles's biography of Davies, Brooks's reading and response to this historical construction, the future (or present) moment of reading Brooks's notes. In my own act of reading Brooks's markings I am struck with the remembered impression, a delayed afterimage effect, of making my own notes in her book of essays or in biographical works about her. In each case, we collaboratively recreate history on the already inscribable surface of the page. These are books we hold, touch, read, write in; they literalize and signify the knowledge we might embody about the object of history and its very writing.

Brooks's act of writing in her books also inscribes metaphorically the ways many histories and forms of critical production are formed in the margins. This is what interests me in these jottings: they display a place of relegation, but a space that can be reoccupied, recollected, recreated. Like Moore, Brooks, Dietrich, and many since, women who have worked in film production also act as critics, historians, and theorists, albeit often in surprising and sometimes indirect ways. In granting their own intellectual labor this status, I am placing works that often seem tangential to film study and film history at the core of my excavation: memoirs and cookbooks, ephemera and collections. My cupboards. These genres and forms display the linkages between women and the margins of history into which they are often placed. Because many of the women whose work I discuss were kept out of histories of the era (both popular and scholarly), this collaboration seeks in part to retrieve their work, to remove the genres and forms they produced and accumulated from the margins of film history and film culture. Surely part of a larger renaissance in film studies, this retrieval is merely a valuable starting point and a means of organizing this study overall: I look at the works of these women to show how they appropriate a variety of personal or domestic forms to make their lives public, to reveal their presence in history, and to display their theoretical insights. Indeed, their histories, ideas, and expertise are made known again through the publication of their writings years after their work in film, and they are retrieved, or recollected, further by scholars decades later. Thus, we can expand an act of retrieval with the practices of history and fantasy merged together—what we newly imagine as "history" and those fantasies of fictional production.⁵

## RECREATED AUTHORS, RECREATING HISTORIES

In his exegesis on the work of remembrance, "A Berlin Chronicle," Walter Benjamin describes the inherent multidimensional temporal nature of memory. Emphasizing, for instance, that a "shock" experienced in the present lays the groundwork for a future excavation of a memory, he notes how present implantations of experience impend toward the future: "There are memories that are especially well preserved because, although not themselves affected, they are isolated by a shock from all that followed." He ends this extended essay by considering how one such memory—his father's narration of a relative's death—was rooted for future retrieval in relation to the space of his childhood bedroom: "But that evening I must have memorized my room and my bed, as one observes exactly a place where one feels dimly that one will later have to search for something one has forgotten there."⁶ The fact that Benjamin imagines mining domestic spaces for his memories is suggestive of the intimacy of memory work and its potential as a model for an understanding of the ways histories can be told. As Gaston Bachelard tells us, "Thanks to the house, a great many of our memories are housed, and if the house is a bit elaborate, if it has a cellar and a garret, nooks and corridors, our memories have refuges that are all the more clearly delineated."⁷ Although Benjamin is describing a deeply personal and subjective phenomenon, his understanding of this temporal work of domestic memory—that a present moment reaches to the future, and the present that future becomes reaches back to the past—could easily be understood in a collective cultural and spatial framework as well. It is this complex temporality that I am able to describe in part through a focus on texts by women who worked in the silent era but took up writing later in life. In fact, most of the women on whose work I focus wrote their memoirs and other volumes in the 1960s, therefore allowing for a collective experience of retrieval.

My own emphasis on this triple temporal framework—the film work in the silent period, the written work decades later, and the scholarly recollection even decades after that—underscores the very structure of memory that I address throughout this book. But my turn to women who worked in the silent era is significant for other reasons as well. For one, the silent era is a clearly formative moment in film history: not only does it mark the nascence and the quickly developing period of film production, but it also was a period that offered an abundance of roles for women that essentially remains unmatched today. To draw on Benjamin's understanding of memory, the very prodigality of this period, cut short by changes to the studio system and the coming of sound, marked a shock that imprinted it in the minds of the women who recollected their experiences later. The range of their work recollected years later also offers a model for my own study: in my reconsideration of their multiple roles as authors, I am in part duplicating and in part expanding this model. Finally, my turn to the silent period enables a creative rethinking of the relationship between women and image, as well as between visuality and writing. Although these issues that spring from a particular set of historical contexts are indeed important to my study, I am also interested in moving beyond this period to broaden the ways we see contemporary productions of history and to complicate the theoretical and visual models from which we might approach this history. Thus, in my final chapter, I look at the writing of contemporary celebrities as well, such as Sophia Loren, Yoko Ono, Isabella Rossellini, and Christy Turlington. These contemporary writers—some teachers, some students, some both—also tell us how to do things. With an eye for self-analysis and the world of icon production, for instance, Rossellini seems as much a descendant of Louise Brooks as she is of Ingrid Bergman and Roberto Rossellini (her "marginalia" are even printed in her memoirs); her book full of family photographs is like Moore's scrapbook, yet designed to enter into the collections of her readers and fans. To paraphrase Bachelard, her most personal recollections can come and live in her house and then in her books, which take their places in our own cupboards and shelves, in our own houses.[8]

As my own method of interpretation is partly a result of the awareness of the encounters between the critic and the objects of her or his study—an opportunity, in fact, to see these objects as subjects and authors in their own right—the methods of the authors I examine also spring from the objects they produce. These objects—films, writings, collections—are reformulated through acts of recollection. It is thus through their writings and objects that these authors and collectors perform as theorists and historians; moreover, in these works we can see embedded theoretical and historical practices forged through the relationships between these writings and collections, film form, and the processes of memory. Such relations might be most apparent in the fact that the autobiography and memoir are forms that spring directly from the subject's memory (or her rendering of it). In the case of many stars' memoirs, their writings concern their labor in industries that produced cinematic fictions. As Bachelard might say, the universe comes to inhabit their houses.[9] Their writings therefore invariably deal with these fictional productions, often typically linking the stars' "real" lives to fictional film: drawing on a narrative structure similar to the fictional film to tell their stories or utilizing visual and cinematic metaphors to describe their experiences. In this way, facts and fictions, private and public lives, written and cinematic forms become fundamentally intertwined.

But there is another dimension to these linkages through film form's delineation of these very ideas. Like autobiographies and memoirs, various cinematic texts invariably enact the process of remembering, both explicitly and implicitly. First, documentaries about women who worked in film production often draw on both their subjects' memories (even in absentia) and their fictional films to tell the complex stories of their lives. Hence, these cinematic texts have a double historical function: the fictional films take on a historical design, and the documentaries more directly sketch a relatively linear biographical history.[10] But second, and perhaps more important, film form, whether documentary, fictional, or experimental in nature, can itself be akin to memory, as Hugo Münsterberg, Maya Deren, and Gilles Deleuze have all theorized, albeit from different angles.[11] As the complex system of remembering can be likened to spatial and cartographical design (as in Benjamin's extended essay)—which might be circular, cylindrical, or gridlike, with many points of intersection—it can also be likened to film form. Deren proclaims, for instance, "The celluloid memory of the camera can function, as our memory, not merely to reconstruct or to measure an original chronology. It can place together in immediate temporal sequence, events actually distant, and achieve, through such relationships a peculiarly filmic reality."[12] To Deren, the very reality of film is based on recollective processes.

Because written autobiographies and cinematic auto/biographical films follow the narrative and formal structure of the films their subjects helped to make, they, too, can be read through theories of both memory and film form. This is not to suggest that we read the histories of narrative film production and reception in terms of the very same narrative structure of these films, particularly that of a classical, linear, fictional framework. Such a structure might suggest a teleological practice antithetical to a more complicated understanding of historical practices and recollective processes. I suggest, instead, that avant-garde theories and practices of film form (represented, in part, by Deren's statement earlier), which invite us to approach "story" and narrative differently, might be applied to thinking about the histories of film as well. This approach can be further amplified by an understanding of the role and structure of the processes of recollecting. For the purposes of my work, recollection becomes a historiographical method: it is a tool by which we make history. Implicitly tied to acts of remembering, recollecting is also, most certainly, linked to acts of collecting. Historians and theorists, indeed, collect the works of our subjects. The figures and their writings become part of my own recollection in this volume, underscoring the collaborative nature of this and other scholarly projects with the very subjects we investigate.

In taking seriously this amalgam of autobiographical works—and their subsequent models—as objects of film history and theory, I am attempting in part to rethink the divisions between writing and film. I am interested in the visual quality of these works, whether they are objects in a dollhouse, pages in a scrapbook, the layout of a cookbook, or writings in the margins. The visual quality also gives way to the tactile; in so doing, it reveals the subject's investment in and invention of history and theory as an active, palpable construction. Paying attention to these multiple and tangible forms of construction, we can inevitably rethink our understanding of authorship in cinematic production and history. This reevaluation stems in part from conjoining the form of the written memoir to the cinematic object via the processes and form of memory itself. I am interested in a history whose structure resembles not a simple linear narrative but an archive or collection, like Colleen Moore's thirty-six scrapbooks or Marlene Dietrich's eccentric encyclopedia. Through the collection itself and subsequent acts of re-collection, many parts can meet together to produce multiple reflections on this history—and the subjects of history. This production takes place at an intersection between visual and written texts, between ethereal and material objects. At this intersection, in fact, we can understand written works through visual forms, ephemeral images or objects through materiality. Such reflections in turn directly impact our understanding of authorship in film and film history.

Looking at a range of writings—theoretical works, surely, and histories that spring from academic film studies, but also autobiographies and biographies, popular criticism, advice manuals, cookbooks, newspaper columns, and scrapbooks—I reassess both what makes up a historical text as well as what makes for a critical one. In recognizing these works as historical and theoretical texts, I am also recognizing their writers as *authors* and thus granting them a certain authority befitting this role. Indeed, their various writings and collections significantly call attention to the multiple roles women play as authors both in the production of film and in the production of our knowledge of film theory and history. To flesh out this production of knowledge, I read the writings of the women I consider alongside some of their filmic output and especially through other cinematic sites. This investigation entails yet another attempt at a bridge between filmic and written discourses, for I also bring together the two media, or the study of the two media, through my interpretive and historical models. Specifically, my analysis is informed by both filmic and literary models. This mingling of media is perhaps best represented by my interest in Maya Deren's theory of the anagram:

> An anagram is a combination of letters in such a relationship that each and every one is simultaneously an element in more than one linear series. This simultaneity is real, and independent of the fact that it is usually perceived in succession. Each element of an anagram is so related to the whole that no one of them may be changed without affecting its series and so effecting the whole. And, conversely, the whole is so related to every part that whether one reads horizontally, vertically, diagonally or even in reverse, the logic of the whole is not disrupted, but remains intact.[13]

The notion of the anagram is, of course, what ultimately sets up Deren's likening of film form to memory.[14] Furthermore, by offering the anagram as a way to understand film form, Deren suggests a certain interdisciplinarity inherent in the production of visual arts. Allowing these various texts, theories, and histories to mingle in my own project, we can add to our understanding of how history—and indeed knowledge—have been authored in film studies. In introducing new texts into this anagrammatic site, I hope to rearrange our conceptions of authorship, textual production, and the role of writing in film studies.

In his critique of "la politique des auteurs," André Bazin suggests that "the auteur is a subject to himself"; he then writes, "Jacques Rivette has said that an auteur is someone who speaks in the first person. It's a good definition. Let's adopt it."[15] Although Bazin's discussion is not entirely applicable to my own textual investigation, I would like to "adopt" this notion in some form. That is, what if we took this statement quite literally? How might it alter first our perception of authors and then our perception of the "subject" in films and in film history? This book does not seek to revive tired debates over who or what is a film's auteur, but drawing on such questions, it is still a "politique" regarding authorship. However, as I've suggested, this is an authorship not of film texts but of film history, or the recollections of film history. In fact, the notions of the collection and the recollection guide the authorship of women's histories of the silent period, especially as these authors reveal themselves as the subjects of their own work.

Surely debates around authorship are inherently linked to issues of authority. As even the barest etymology would show, the two words spring from the same origins. Specifically, they are each derived from the Latin *auctor* (creator) and *augere* (to create, increase). Thus, whereas *author* can mean, typically, a "writer," it also means "originator." Moreover, authority means not only the "right and power to command," but also "an accepted source of expert information." An authority, obviously, can be an author, and an author carries with her or him a certain authority. In this project, then, I define *author* in both a traditional sense, as a writer, and also in the broad sense of one with authority or power over the origination of not just texts but also information or knowledge. I therefore see my project as part of recent feminist courses of study, especially as I look at women's labor, particularly the labor of authorship, in both the production of cinematic texts and the production of cinematic histories.

I briefly rehearse these questions not to offer a final word on them. Indeed, how could one attempt to do so? The debates are already simultaneously "dead," like Barthes's author, and forever immortal. Like the study of genre, author studies have provided a useful frame for the dissemination of knowledge about film history in scholarship and in teaching. As Claire Johnston argues, in fact:

> The development of the auteur theory marked an important intervention in film criticism: its polemics challenged the entrenched view of Hollywood as monolithic, and stripped of its normative aspects the classification of films by director has proved an extremely productive way of ordering our experience of the cinemas. In demonstrating that Hollywood was at least as interesting as the art cinema, it marked an important step forward. The test of any theory should be the degree to which it produces new knowledge: the auteur theory has certainly achieved this.[16]

Rather than celebrate either the author's death or its incessant rebirth, I suggest considering authorship itself in a different form so as to continue to produce "new" knowledge. Informed by ongoing debates regarding authorship, my investigation considers how film history itself is authored through the intertextual work of writings, films, and other visual and ephemeral collections.

The convergence of authorship, writing, and history is particularly manifest in studies of the various roles women have played in these intersecting fields. Giuliana Bruno suggests that writing is itself a significant form of authorship in film studies as "women, historically excluded from authorship, have become authors by writing about other women.... The female reader is now effectively engaged in a double construction of the female authorial subject."[17] Likewise, explicitly linking writing and film through an examination of the film work of the poet H.D., Anne Friedberg offers a similar proposition: "In film studies we have to begin to question, at its very premise, the mechanism of writing women *into* history. It is not just to chart the uncharted, and colonize the dark continent with names, but rather, to investigate sexual difference of 'subjects' in history: both how this difference is written *into* or *out of* history and how this written history is used."[18] As women have been written into or out of film history, they have become authors not only by writing about other women, but also by writing about themselves and about cinematic experiences in one form or another. My study arises out of what may initially appear to be simply a return to a basic historical definition of an author as a composer of written text. But from this basic premise I seek to expand our definition of the author and our understanding of her or his place in history. My conception of authorship thus differs from some of the traditional models in film studies, though, arguably, past conceptions of auteurs and authors have much to do with questions of power, whether artistic, economic, or historical.

I therefore meet this seemingly originary definition with the competing and complicating conceptions of authorship that have been offered in film history and film studies. Historically, I argue, women have played a number of roles as authors: directors, screenwriters, and stars; historians, commentators, and theorists. And not only have they authored their own texts, but they are also "authored" by other written and visual texts that consider them. As I imagine and investigate central textual figures in the first three chapters—Colleen Moore, early director Alice Guy-Blaché, and Louise Brooks—I do so under the rubric of the generic figures they represent and also, of course, in relation to other women and their written and material works. As "textual figures," these women are configured through a complex network of texts that include their own memoirs, histories, theoretical writings, films, photographs, and other collectible or ephemeral objects. Moreover, their written works and their "images" (their personal histories and their popular personas) have been further circulated and collected in film studies and in cinematic works, in theoretical essays, popular biographies, and traditional and experimental documentary films. As "generic" figures they represent the particular roles they play as writers: historians, critics, collectors, and experts. The historical and textual movement I am engaged in throughout the book allows me to trace these multiple levels of authorship. It shows, too, the expanded boundaries of film history and film culture that *Cupboards of Curiosity* envisions.

## RECOLLECTION AND RE-CREATION

In many ways, film histories, especially star histories, work against a chronology or linearity. As a film image is timeless, the past lives on, seemingly without change, yet this past, as history has evinced, is also ephemeral. In this way, our very history of film is produced, in effect, by cinematic time—or at least the time of the image.[19] We therefore need other material models for our histories. Carolyn Steedman muses on the relationships among memory, history, and the archive in *Dust: The Archive and Cultural History*: "In the Archive . . . many historians have discovered that they do have *somewhere to put what they find.* . . . The place where what is found may be put, is History. It is in this way, and outside the walls of the Archive, that History has become the place where quite ordinarily and by remembering, we can find things where we have already put them."[20] In what might at first glance seem a circular logic, Steedman's eloquent reverie is ultimately an analysis of the ways that the space of the archive can transform memories (or acts of remembering) into histories. In so doing, we can broaden what we actually think of as history. My goal, through the objects and subjects I consider, is to expand the space of the film archive to deepen the space of film history.

With a reconsideration of authorship, its attendant authority, and the authoring of film history as the general instigation and core of my focus, each of the chapters that follow map a textual history through memory, fiction, ephemera, and other visual, written, and cultural forms. To create a study that acknowledges the subjects' own authority in the production of film culture and the production of our knowledge about it, my work posits a recollection of their texts—written and cinematic, factual and fantastic, tangible and ephemeral. So, although their respective work in film and writing links the figures in my study, each defines or clarifies a different relationship between the production of filmic texts and the production of our knowledge about her. To highlight these relationships, chapters are organized in terms of generic textual figures: "The Collector," "The Historian," "The Critic," and "The Expert." This structure allows me to explore particular modes of written work and epistemological production but also to move between written genres and particular historical figures. Most important, it allows me to emphasize how these women also speak for themselves, often contemplating the very role their own writings play in the construction of a "real" or "true" history.

The first three chapters essentially have a central case study, but they also make links between that figure and others who have played similar roles through their written work; the fourth chapter builds on those that precede it and also brings in fresh material about a variety of other figures. Therefore, the chapters are not restricted to biographical case studies; rather, I examine how various women are textually rendered in film, writings, and other objects—by themselves and by others. Moreover, the primary chapters are organized so as to build on the genres these women produced in order to create a dialectical understanding of what makes up a historical or theoretical or critical text. Obviously, I do not follow a strict chronological line, either by the dates the women lived or when they worked in film, but this shaping itself might reflect on the arrangement of both history and memory. The chapters might even be read in various orders (as we usually tend to do anyway, I think), much like Deren's anagram, to create other chronologies of history and theory.

Chapter 1, "The Collector: Material Histories, Colleen Moore's Dollhouse, and Ephemeral Recollection," considers works ranging from star scrapbooks to silent star Colleen Moore's dollhouse, to ephemera produced in tandem with silent features that later take on a historicizing function. Although my emphasis is on texts concerning Moore, I link her case to that of other stars and to other collections (such as scrapbooks for figures like Mary Pickford, Joan Crawford, and Louella Parsons, and collections like the San Simeon oral history project). On the surface, Moore does not appear to have the same concern over the recovery of her place in film history as do Guy-Blaché and Louise Brooks; on the other hand, she seems the most invested in preserving her history from the beginning of her career. Of the central figures I investigate, Moore is the least well-known. This may be, paradoxically, a result of the fact that she continued to find success in other ways and spaces after her work in Hollywood. These successes might have displaced her early investments and therefore curtailed their later realization. Or perhaps her work as a comedienne has provoked less interest for historians until quite recently.[21] Whatever the reasons for her relative disappearance from Hollywood histories, Moore functions as a formative figure for this study; her collections of writings, photographs, and objects, alongside other like collections, are the most diverse of the cases I look at. As such, they suggest provocative models for an understanding of these various histories and our relationship to them. This chapter therefore examines the relations between these kinds of collections, with Moore's own dollhouse at the center of the study. I argue that history is embedded in forms ranging from a star's writings to her scrapbooks to material objects and ephemera. The female celebrity herself often inaugurates these collections, and we as scholars recollect them to produce new histories that might highlight their work as cultural archivists.

Chapter 2, "The Historian: Autobiography, Memory, and Film Form," examines the role of the memoir as both a form and a product of film history. I consider works by director Nell Shipman and stars Linda Arvidson, Lillian Gish, Colleen Moore, Gloria Swanson, and Ethel Waters, but my focus is particularly on the memoirs of director Alice Guy-Blaché. This chapter especially attempts to set in motion a clearer understanding of the relationship forged between history, memory, and cinematic and written forms through close attention to the memoirs of Guy-Blaché and other stars and directors. Thus informed by writings on film form, memory, autobiography, and nineteenth-century women's writings, my study of Guy-Blaché delineates the relationship between history and memory in the construction of texts by and about her. Both the rediscovery and the production of alternative histories have been an important part of feminist scholarship, as this work seeks to bring to light new knowledge about women's lives that has been forgotten or made invisible; however, I caution that explicitly elevating Guy-Blaché and her contemporaries to the status of historians might seem to be risky work, considering the fallibility or fictionalizing function of memory. But in doing so, our knowledge of history, historiographical processes, and film culture can be valuably transformed. Through recognizing how memoirs by early directors and stars function as histories, we can not only recognize the fallibility of institutionalized histories (at this point in time, this seems common knowledge), but we can consider how active such women have always been in the production of histories. Moreover, these works particularly reveal how narrative films and the histories of those films together recombine fact and fiction, reality and fantasy. This juggling is perhaps inevitable when we consider that the histories these women write also concern the production of fantasy.

Chapter 3, "The Critic: Louise Brooks, Star Witness," examines the written works by silent film star Brooks and their subsequent circulation in popular and scholarly arenas. The dual emphasis in this chapter considers the links between image and word as well as Brooks's function as a critic of film and film history. Broadly speaking, her writings exemplify two key points: first, she was in part responsible for the circulation—indeed, the authorship—of her image (as Lulu) in film history; second, her image as "Lulu," far from being just a silent icon, is produced in written and cinematic forms. Finally, although I emphasize how Brooks acts as a theorist of film and stardom, I bear in mind also how her work as a critic is often curtailed—even by

Brooks herself—in the dominant representation of her as pure image and through the focus on her ambiguous sexuality.

My final chapter, "The Expert: Celebrity Knowledge and the How-tos of Film Studies," concludes my work through an analysis of a range of how-to manuals authored by silent and sound stars as well as contemporary celebrities of visual culture. Considering works from *Candy Hits* by Zasu Pitts to *Marlene Dietrich's ABC* to Christy Turlington's *Living Yoga*, I am interested in what histories and what epistemological practices are lodged in these writings and in the objects they describe. By investigating this further miscellany of film history, I look to how these extracinematic texts might remark on our critical understanding of the figures they represent, on stardom, on film production, and on film studies more broadly. Surely the logic of ephemera and the collectible together inform an understanding of film culture and film history: history, like films, has a fleeting experiential quality, yet by definition it is also a "collectible" of sorts. We might watch a certain film repeatedly, store up on objects that mark (and market) our favorite movies, or even follow a star's recipe for fudge in order to prolong and expand our experience of a film. This expansion of the experience is also a form of embodiment, perhaps most peculiarly evident through our rehearsals of the advice (on cooking, cleaning, glamour, sex, exercise, religion, and so on) proffered by celebrities. These acts of repetition, rehearsal, and embodiment, moreover, are also akin to our desire to produce historical knowledge. Is not this production, after all, another way to stem the ephemerality of experience, through the embodiment of knowledge?

In this compilation of materials and ideas, *Cupboards of Curiosity* has several interlocking aims. First, I am attempting to rethink the category of authorship, displacing the emphasis in film studies on the director (though still linking my consideration to that role). Of particular importance, I seek to emphasize the authority inherent in authorship, especially in the authorship of history. Reading these texts seriously grants an authority to their authors. With this authority thus granted, I also want to consider the roles these women play for contemporary film scholars; that is, are we not the mediums for retelling their stories today? Do they anticipate our work to come years after theirs? Moreover, what relationships do these writings therefore produce between, for instance, stars and fans or fans and scholars? These questions most explicitly suggest the inherent relations between the collector and recollector, especially pointing to the ways these roles are often interchangeable. Finally, this book itself expands —or at least comments on—the range of objects of study in the discipline of film and media scholarship. Throughout my own collection, I am making central those objects or texts that are often marginalized, hidden, or simply set aside in order to underscore their historicizing function; I am filling my cupboards with written texts alongside visual productions (from fictional films to documentaries), material objects, and ephemera to produce both an interdisciplinary study and an intertextual reading. But most important, I see these reflections as another beginning, so that other works might in turn be recreated from it, perhaps even starting with notes etched in the margins of this page.

# 1

THE COLLECTOR

*material histories, Colleen Moore's dollhouse, and ephemeral recollection*

> Objects that decorate my house have a history; they aren't just there to look pretty. — ISABELLA ROSSELLINI, *Some of Me*

> The objects in our lives, as distinct from the way we make use of them at a given moment, represent something much more, something profoundly related to subjectivity: for while the object is a resistant material body, it is also, simultaneously, a mental realm over which I hold sway, a thing whose meaning is governed by myself alone. It is all my own, the object of my passion. — JEAN BAUDRILLARD, "The System of Collecting"

To offer a definition of the collector and the collection and the importance of each to this project, I want to begin with an image. This image articulates at once a number of issues central to my study of silent star Colleen Moore and other figures having to do with collections and collectibles, loss and recovery, the historian and her or his subject of inquiry. It is a photograph of Moore taken around 1927, surely as a publicity shot, which is part of a collection of photographs now housed at the library of the Academy of Motion Pictures archives

**1** The consuming star: Colleen Moore eats her chocolates.
*Photo courtesy of the Academy of Motion Picture Arts and Sciences.*

in Los Angeles. It is not a still from a film but an image apparently taken in her own home; in a sense, it is part of a series promoting a film in production (one of the series shows her reading a script for a contemporaneous film). More than that, as a publicity shot and with the objects it includes, this photograph seems to be promoting *Moore herself* as a star. The image is of Moore eating from a box of chocolates as she lounges in her home. On closer inspection, we can see that the chocolates themselves bear Moore's signature, metaphorically and literally. These chocolates are wedded to Moore's image: the box has her picture on it, the interior includes a poem ascribed to her, and one piece of chocolate actually has her signature embossed on it. As such, they were clearly collectibles produced for consumption—along with Moore's image itself. But here, of course, is the problem: How long can one actually "collect" the chocolates? By definition they won't last: they will be eaten, or they will go bad. One could, then, make a metaphorical link between the chocolates and the star: they are produced for consumption, and they can't last. In this way, they are the perfect sign of the seeming ephemerality of Moore's star image.

But this is where the photograph comes in. This picture is one of approximately two hundred that were rediscovered about fifteen years ago in Moore's former residence by the recent owners, Mr. and Mrs. Robert Stack. One story is that they were found in a wall when the new residents were redoing the place. The Stacks donated them to the academy, and they are now part of a fairly substantial collection of photographs of Moore at the library, mixed in with ones donated from other sources. All basically similar, most are 8 x 10 (though some run larger) and appear to be professionally shot. Many were clearly taken at Moore's home (they show her cooking, showing off her garden, lounging at home, displaying collectibles, and so forth); others, especially the substantial number of head shots and fashion photos, were clearly taken in a studio. Few, however, are credited, and none in the Stack collection has any explanation. But all document Moore as a star (and all that stardom entails, from making her perform "ordinary life" to displaying her as glamorous).

The fact that these photographs were discovered in Moore's former home invites a couple of ways of thinking about Moore's own role in their very re-collection. First, they were obviously originally part of Moore's own collection (or potentially that of her first husband,

**2** Colleen Moore's display of chocolates. *Photo courtesy of the Academy of Motion Picture Arts and Sciences.*

John McCormick, as he was largely responsible for many of her promotional strategies). Thus left in the house as a collection of sorts, we might consider these photographs as predicting a moment of rediscovery at some point in the future, as they surely offer clues to Moore's history of stardom. Moreover, the subsequent moments of discovery—after that by the new tenants in her home, and therefore by the historian in the library (the archivist or the visiting scholar or fan)—invite a pleasure in themselves, which I will discuss by way of the collector, the collection, and the moment of recollection.

In all of these ways—pointing to ephemerality, collectibility, rediscovery, and the multiple layers of a star's image in history—this photograph opens up many of the primary points that I argue throughout this work. This image and its subsequent recollection present Colleen Moore in a dual role: as historical object of inquiry and as a historian herself. And there is no doubt about it: Colleen Moore was a collector. She amassed, stored, and invested in everything from miniatures to money to the ephemera of film fame. She produced or contributed to a significant number of histories of Hollywood in the teens and twenties: her autobiography, entitled *Silent Star* (1968); thirty-six scrapbooks kept in the Special Collections Library at the Motion Picture Archives, as well as the substantial photograph collection housed there; Kevin Brownlow and David Gill's 1980 *Hollywood* documentary series (in which Brooks also briefly appears); a collection of unpublished oral histories of William Randolph Hearst's San Simeon estate;[1] the advice manual *How Women Can Make Money in the Stock Market* (1969); the companion to her collection of miniatures, *Colleen Moore's Doll House* (published shortly after the other two volumes);[2] and even, I would maintain, the collection of miniatures, the dollhouse itself, as well as other collectibles produced during her heyday as a star.

As a savvy businesswoman, Moore appeared to see history itself as a kind of business: one makes investments and watches them come to fruition. Or perhaps she understood the historian's role as like a detective's and so left clues to her own celebrity that would later be rediscovered if necessary. Indeed, I would argue that Moore's particular acts of collecting anticipated and therefore attempted to preserve against a future loss in history. She never squandered her money—as did many of her contemporaries in Hollywood—and she attempted also to save her own position in history as one of the biggest box office stars in the 1920s. Yet, although she seemed to anticipate it and attempted to forestall it, her relative disappearance from history did eventually come—even if that loss itself, too, was ephemeral.

With Moore as a central case study, read alongside a number of other celebrities who were involved in similar archival projects, I define the collector who has a peculiar temporal and affective relation to the production of history. She collects objects and materials of the present so that her history may be retrieved and guarded in a future time. This is an affective investment: it signifies a love for oneself, a love for one's past (her family, her memories, her work), and a fear of loss. I pursue this definition and phenomenon of the collector by looking at a variety of collections kept by or about Moore and other stars. To inquire into the function of collecting, I turn to several different sorts of objects: a variety of star scrapbooks, a collection of oral histories concerning the Hearst Castle, Colleen Moore's dollhouse, and a series of collectibles mostly related to Moore. Although Colleen Moore acts as the central figure in this study, I set her works in relation to other stars' collections, thus showcasing how this chapter, like the project as a whole, is a kind of re/collection itself.

## INVESTING IN HISTORY

Much contemporary writing in cultural studies that concerns nostalgia, souvenirs, and collecting turns to Susan Stewart's groundbreaking work *On Longing: Narratives of the Miniature, the Gigantic, the Souvenir, the Collection*. Stewart mines a variety of texts and objects to explore their temporal and epistemological structure as well as their function as commodities. Given her focus, *On Longing* potentially has much to bear on my own objects of study. However, though it is unquestionably an elegiac work that has inspired many further investigations, Stewart's text is ultimately an incomplete exegesis on collecting, in large part because of the rigid distinctions she marks between the souvenir and the collection. I briefly trace these points here, drawing also on Walter Benjamin's own theory of collecting in his essay "Unpacking My Library," as well as several essays included in *The Cultures of Collecting* (some of which themselves draw on the works of Stewart and Benjamin, as well as Jean Baudrillard and Sigmund Freud), to move beyond Stewart's text and thus offer another theory of the collection that we might read alongside her foundational interpretation. As a test case of sorts, I then look to celebrity scrapbooks to redefine the collection as a memorializing and historicizing text.

In *On Longing*, Stewart claims that the scrapbook "must properly be seen as [a] souvenir rather than as [a] collection." She distinguishes between the two in regard to what she sees as their respective relationships with the past. "The souvenir," she writes, "is not simply an object appearing out of context, an object from the past incongruously surviving in the present; rather, its function is to envelop the present within the past." This definition seems implicitly to link the souvenir with acts of remembering (which is, of course, highly justified, considering the origin of the term): the souvenir, Stewart argues, allows one to return to the past via the object and, seemingly, the memories it invokes. Its relationship to the past is in part predicated on its function as a private object and those narratives associated with private memory. The souvenir exemplifies the "capacity of objects to serve as traces of authentic experience." Incomplete, as it is only a sample or metonym of an experience because it is essentially tied to nostalgia, the souvenir is necessarily "supplemented by a narrative discourse." Although the souvenir is tied to this authentic experience, Stewart notes that it "moves history into private time." She thus rightfully points out that the souvenir marks a private yet "partial" lived experience, so that the souvenir itself must be supplemented by narrative.[3]

On the other hand, claims Stewart, the collection exists out of time, either historical or private:

> The collection offers example rather than sample, metaphor rather than metonymy. The collection does not displace attention to the past; rather, the past is at the service of the collection, for whereas the souvenir lends authenticity to the past, the past lends authenticity to the collection. The collection seeks a form of self-enclosure which is possible because of its ahistoricism. The collection replaces history with *classification*, with order beyond the realm of temporality. In the collection, time is not something to be restored to an origin; rather, all time is made simultaneous or synchronous within the collection's world.[4]

Certainly this definition is in part accurate. Collections are often defined by a form of classification that might overtake their historicizing, temporal, or private qualities. Jean Baudrillard, on whose work Stewart in part draws, notes that in a collection, "all objects become equivalents of one another."[5] This equivalency is in part what sets the collection out of time, as Stewart argues. Given this emphasis on classification over historicization, Stewart suggests that the souvenir and the collection are mutually exclusive textual objects. She even marks certain forms of collections, such as the scrapbook, as souvenirs instead, to maintain this clear distinction. In her essay "Collecting Paris," Naomi Schor duplicates this logic, also drawing on the work of Baudrillard in her reading of Benjamin's essay on book collecting.

In his eloquent rumination on collecting, "Unpacking My Library," Benjamin emphasizes the relation between collecting and remembering. Regarding his own process of acquiring (and then re-viewing) books, he notes, "This or any other procedure is merely a dam against the spring tide of memories which surges toward any collector as he contemplates his possessions. Every passion borders on the chaotic, but the collector's passion borders on the chaos of memories." He goes on, "Everything remembered and thought, everything conscious, becomes the pedestal, the frame, the base, the lock of his property."[6] In what appears to be drawn from an implicitly incongruous logic, Schor suggests that Benjamin's understanding of the collection expressed here is lacking because he doesn't take into account its difference from the souvenir that Stewart traces decades later. Preferring Stewart's distinctions over Benjamin's reading, Schor suggests that Benjamin bears some "confusion or failure to distinguish between what Susan Stewart has described as the souvenir and the collection, two closely linked but radically different assemblages of objects. According to Stewart, then, Benjamin's books function more as souvenirs than as parts of a collection." Again drawing on "Stewart's paradigmatic opposition," Schor continues: "Benjamin's collection is not in fact a collection, but a collection of souvenirs. His library *qua* souvenir overrides and very nearly cancels out its nature as a collection."[7]

Although I agree that the sorts of distinctions Stewart makes between the souvenir and the collection are often operative, they are perhaps just as often not, particularly in the case of private collections or collections that are themselves based on private or personal forms. Indeed, Benjamin's "confusion" between the souvenir and the collection is hardly a failure: rather, he points to the explicit relationship that the collection itself may have to memory, subjectivity, and, by extension, history. Schor implies this possibility by suggesting that his collection is a "collection of souvenirs"; I would argue, contra Schor and Stewart, that such a case does not cancel out the two phenomena, but suggests instead an intimate relationship between them.

In taking advantage of Benjamin's "confusion"—he does, after all, see memories as "chaotic"—I would precisely define the kinds of collections I am looking at here (scrapbooks, oral histories, Colleen Moore's dollhouse, and various paracinematic collectibles) as having a memorializing *and* historicizing function. Thus, I do not see the souvenir and the collection as opposites or mutually exclusive; rather, I contest that they not only can coexist but can also inform one another. Each gives the other a new context—through memory, through narrative, through history—rather than destroys or erases the context of the other. Specifically, for instance, as with Benjamin's various books, the individual objects in a collection (we could indeed mark them as souvenirs) function to invoke memories and histories. The materiality of these collectibles comments on the historicizing function of objects: they embody both history and fantasy, and they lend a materiality to that history and fantasy. Thus, explicitly set in relationship to one another through the structure of the collection, the narrative they tell becomes richer as it builds between objects. Whereas Schor (again, drawing on Baudrillard and Stewart) sees this narrative structure as a kind of "seriality," I maintain a slightly more chaotic reading that instead allows for multiple interpretations and histories to be produced. Given this complicated narrative structure which is necessarily built on the "chaos of memories," the collection has a temporality that is not necessarily out of real time, as Stewart suggests. Rather, the collection has a precise, if complex, temporal order. Specifically, the collection is always at once an investment in the future and in history. It looks forward to a moment in the future when it will gain greater value, not just economically but historically. Any collection is thus an investment in the importance of history, whether a personal and private or an institutional history. Baudrillard himself would at least partially agree with this point; he argues that "objects in our daily lives" that we collect and therefore possess contain a "quotient of invested affect . . . in no way inferior to that of any other variety of human passion."[8]

Such investments—in history, of affect—are particularly apparent in scrapbooks. Interestingly, Stewart classifies the (generic) scrapbook not as a collection but as a souvenir. She asserts that it is a souvenir because "the whole dissolves into parts, each of which refers metonymically to a context of origin or acquisition. . . . In contrast, each element within the collection is representative and works in combination toward the creation of a new whole that is the context of the collection itself. The spatial whole of the collection supersedes the individual narratives that 'lie behind it.' "[9] Yet, in the case of many celebrity scrapbooks, which function to chronicle a history, "each element" does "work in combination toward the creation of a new whole," such as a story of a star's career, her marriage, or her work off-screen. Moreover, it is through the relation between the parts (which is to say, the collected clippings contained therein) with one another and the parts with the whole that we see more specific impressions emerge than just those expressed in the singular clippings alone. Often such items are, in fact, structured as a sort of historical collage—or a collage of history—which demands a reading of their arrangement as well as of the information offered by them individually. Roger Cardinal, in fact, defines certain of artist Kurt Schwitters's collages as an "attempt to create a new whole out of disparate elements." He notes, as well, that "the collage is in fact a collection."[10] In the case of many celebrity scrapbooks, the inverse is true. Given this, we can see how many different art and textual forms are themselves present in this particular history making: the souvenir, the collection, the collage, the book. And each form has some relation to the other: each scrapbook is a collection of souvenirs both catalogued and arrayed in a collage-like structure, yet assembled in the pages of a book.

## THE COLLECTION'S AUTHOR, THE FAN'S SUBJECT

Some collections are inevitably bound and defined by categorization (such as stamps, butterflies, figurines, dinnerware, and furniture); for others, the category itself is looser. The latter is surely the case of Colleen Moore's dollhouse, which I discuss later in this chapter, and it is also the case with celebrity scrapbooks. In the case of these scrapbooks, the category of classification is simply "Mary Pickford" or "Colleen Moore" or "Louella Parsons"—that is, the subject or object of the scrapbook itself. As Jean Baudrillard writes, "The image of the self is extended to the very limits of the collection. Here, indeed, lies the whole miracle of collecting. For it is invariably *oneself* that one collects."[11] Nowhere but in a scrapbook or a photo album is it therefore more true that "it is invariably *oneself* that one collects." But this is complicated by the circumstances and structures of such collections. Publicly housed in places such as the Margaret Herrick Library, the University of Southern California, the Billy Rose Collection at the New York Public Library, the George Eastman House, and other universities and archives, these scrapbooks indicate suggestive relations to history, authorship, and subjectivity. The variety of ways the books have been constructed and kept raise some important questions about these relations: Who, for instance, is the subject of the scrapbook? Who is the scrapbook's author? What bearing does this authorship and subjectivity have on the definition of a collector? What does each reveal about historiographical practices?

Who constructed the scrapbooks and how many were put together for each figure varies among the celebrities represented across collections.[12] In the case of some, it is unclear who kept the scrapbooks, but most were largely organized either by a family member, a personal assistant, or a fan. Moore's, for instance, do not have a clear author, but it seems likely that the majority of them were constructed by an assistant (potentially an unnamed woman pictured in some of the photos in the Stack collection at the Herrick and who apparently dealt with Moore's fan mail), whereas Pickford's were kept and then offered by a variety of fans to Pickford herself, who then donated the books to the Academy of Motion Picture Arts and Science. Silent star Claire Windsor's scrapbooks were designed by fan Al Bahrer well after her career and obviously with Windsor's input and own materials. It is difficult to determine who produced Louella Parson's sixty-one scrapbooks; the "authors" are not noted, yet the style of organization differs across the books. Richard Barthelmess's fifty scrapbooks, on the other hand, appear to have been kept by his mother, and those of the stars Fay Wray and Billie Burke are even more evidently lovingly constructed, each resembling a more traditional scrapbook than many of the other celebrity models, with each page devoted to just one image or piece of text.

Either in content or in construct, those scrapbooks that appear to be largely professional records—such as Moore's, Parsons's, and Barthelmess's—follow a similar structure of order and disarray. These books primarily include clippings and publicity photos reproduced in newspapers and magazines which review both the celebrity's career and public statements about her or his private life. These clippings run the gamut of film reviews, columns penned by the celebrity, stories about the star's career, and pieces about major and minor events, from weddings to puff pieces on the celebrity's home or charitable acts. They are set in the pages of the scrapbooks in a way that often resembles a newspaper, with multiple columns of stories that begin and end at various levels of the page. But they are also more scattered than the pages of a newspaper, and often long, one-column stories are folded up within the scrapbook, which creates an even greater sense of disarray. Moreover, the contents are arranged in a variety of books designed for some other purpose; their covers imprinted with the word "Invoices," many of both Louella Parsons's and Colleen Moore's earlier books, for instance, are actually transformed ledgers. Given the arrangement of individual pages and that of the books as a whole, these sorts of scrapbooks are relatively disorganized, unlike other forms of collections more bound by a systematic and orderly classification. Hence, in the books of Moore and Norma Shearer, for instance, the same story will repeat throughout; we often see a review or a planted publicity piece from a variety of newspapers, and these appear to be arranged in order of receipt of the clipping, rather than in order of the date of publication or even by topic. This form of repetition itself produces an odd temporal order to the books, which has bearing also on its narrative function. For instance, in book 6 of the Moore collection, a story concerning the term "flapper" recurs throughout the volume. Announcing that the Camp Fire Girls are inviting Moore to join them against the word being used to describe young girls, and making the plea that the word "moderns" be used instead, this story was clearly spun from one original source, but it is printed in a variety of newspapers across the country and is collected in the scrapbook at random intervals.[13] This kind of temporal and visual arrangement is not serial in nature (which is why critics like Stewart claim that the scrapbook is not, in fact, a collection), and it challenges a conventional narrative form as well. Working through some of the same questions, Stephen Bann notes that "we can look at certain forms of visual communication—more exactly, 'mixed' forms, involving both image and text—as establishing a historical series, within our period. The fact that they do so without being able to rely, except indirectly, on narrative strategies does not preclude them from having some role to play in the rediscovery of the past."[14] In the case of this scrapbook, it creates a narrative about Moore's omnipresence and importance.

Although the scrapbooks together form histories of their subjects through the compilation of materials, however much in disarray, the dominant story they tell is that the subject of the scrapbook is always a star.[15] Of course, she is the star of her collection, but she is also a star in history, given the profusion of materials about her collected therein. To discern the depth of a particular figure's stardom, in fact, one must read each collection of scrapbooks in relation to one another. (Hence, an examination of Mary Pickford's books against Colleen Moore's, or Colleen Moore's against Claire Windsor's, ultimately reveals the relative significance of the figure. Whereas Moore's books contain studio plants on stories about Camp Fire Girls, for instance, Pickford's books show much larger-scale spreads about the enormity of her popularity throughout the world. Similarly, whereas Windsor's books essentially carry the same few stories throughout—such as her "disappearance" while horseback riding, itself revealed potentially to be a publicity stunt—Moore's stories are more varied and have endured for many more years.) But, of course, the purpose of these individual collections is not to produce cross-readings between scrapbooks of various stars; rather, they engender a reading across the individual pages and books themselves to produce a sense of the figure's significance to her public and to history.

Given this nearly inevitable conclusion of the scrapbooks, it might also seem that the "subject" of the books and the subjectivity they produce are inevitable as well. However, the subject of the books, the "oneself" to which Baudrillard points, is challenged both by the authorship and the sometimes differing focus of the volumes. To flesh this notion out further, I want to first pay special attention to the scrapbooks of columnist Louella Parsons, but in some relation to the volumes for Pickford, Moore, and Windsor as well. Parsons's books are a particularly interesting case in relation to other scrapbooks kept by figures involved in film production. Though she eventually became more and more of a celebrity herself, her work in Hollywood had to do with documenting the celebrity and stardom of others. Hence, many of her earlier scrapbooks simply record her columns on Hollywood, detailing the lives and work of stars of the silent (and then the sound) period. In this way, there are dueling subjects (and authors) of her scrapbooks. Because her columns deal with many different stars—Marion Davies, of course (Parsons was a Hearst columnist, after all), as well as figures like Charlie Chaplin, Pola Negri, and Rudolph Valentino—there is not one particular subject of the books in the same way as with Moore's or Pickford's collections. Parsons herself is not the subject of the books in a conventional way: her columns are not about her own doings, though they surely document her knowledge of Hollywood life. Thus, her scrapbooks do chronicle the role she plays as subject in a certain sense: Parsons is the subject who knows from experience, as well as the one who is the "I" of the columns (and the image in the photograph that often accompanies them).[16] This particular subjectivity is that of the author herself: more than anything, perhaps, her scrapbooks record Parsons *as author*. Yet this is an authorship that is also precarious, as she is probably not the author of the scrapbooks themselves; more than likely, as with the scrapbooks of other celebrities, someone other than Parsons constructed these books. Her history and subjectivity as chronicled in the scrapbooks is necessarily collectively forged.

This sort of dueling authorship and subjectivity is also apparent in those books that were designed by fans and offered as tokens or a form of homage. In some cases—especially in Moore's, and most markedly in the story she recounts in her memoirs of her first scrapbook—the star herself appears to identify as the fan and subject at once; yet in other cases, these two roles are more discrete. For Claire Windsor's books, compiled by fan Al Bahrer decades after her film career was over, the subject of the books is simultaneously the star and her fan. That is, these works document Windsor's career, but they also document the affective relation Bahrer has to Windsor. Similarly, many of Pickford's books kept at the Herrick were constructed by a variety of fans. These books are far more eccentric than those that Bahrer designed. Whereas the Windsor books essentially eliminate repetition of articles from multiple sources and largely create a narrative about her career (including director Lois Weber's creation of her as a "star"), some of the Pickford books more clearly narrate the fan's fascination with the celebrity whose life she or he is documenting. This is particularly true of a book compiled for Pickford by a fan, Jame J. Shanahan of Toronto.[17] Compiled in 1951, it chronicles Pickford's postfilm life, including her plans to buy her birthplace and her trip to Canada. And although the book is marked as "especially assembled for Mary Pickford, Sweetheart of Toronto," it includes other, miscellaneous clippings as well, such as stories about bizarre maladies, magic tricks, Pilaga Indians, and even Colleen Moore's dollhouse tour in Toronto. In its peculiarities, this volume crystallizes how it is "oneself that one collects" in a scrapbook, thus complicating the subject of the book through the intrusion of the subjectivity of its author, Shanahan.

These scrapbooks are, finally, epistemological collections, invested with affect and history and designed for rediscovery either by the subject herself or by a future reader. Though not a scrapbook per se, but instead an assortment of the sorts of materials one might keep in a scrapbook (or a box or a drawer or even a cupboard or the pages of a book), Mercedes de Acosta's correspondence, objects, and ephemera regarding her relationships with Marlene Dietrich and Greta Garbo and housed at the Rosenbach Museum and Library in Philadelphia is a collection that precisely designs such a moment of rediscovery. Patricia White describes her experience with this collection in "Black and White: Mercedes de Acosta's Glorious Enthusiasms": "De Acosta's cache of fan-magazine and newspaper clippings—any fan could have one like it; my crumpled obituaries of Garbo and Dietrich fell out of my picture books when I began this essay—is archived alongside her wonderful collection of letters from her wonderful collection of women."[18] Collecting herself along with her lovers, de Acosta manages the production of a personal history of public women that remains somewhat ethereal even as (or because) it produces a new affect in the scholar who finds it decades later. Thus, as peculiar epistemes, scrapbooks and dispersed collections like de Acosta's offer to us a history in fragments, ordered through a seemingly determinate yet ultimately elusive subject. Authored collectively and often indeterminately, they make stars out of their subjects and historians out of their authors; given that the subjects and authors themselves remain unfixed, so do the roles of star and historian. Perhaps appropriately, as the film star is predicated on her or his visual character or essence, these histories are as visual as they are rhetorical. That is, the scrapbooks can be read as histories aesthetically and formally, as well as through their points of origins (however partial). As I show below, they are useful for thinking about various ways of reading these different kinds of collections and recollections: through their very materiality of form, as visual constructions, and as written compilations.

## MARLENE SLEPT HERE

The celebrity home has long been made a source of fascination to movie fans. Crystallizing ways that a star is simultaneously like and unlike her or his "ordinary" fans, the celebrity home is itself a fantasy, a site for collecting, an embodiment of history, and a space of potential threat or loss. Colleen Moore's participation in multiple historical projects often included the production of a home and its history.

This trope is clearest in the execution of her stunning dollhouse, but it is also evident in the construction of her scrapbooks and her later contribution to the San Simeon oral history project. The scrapbook itself is a domestic art form, but it also often chronicles tales about domestic life for Moore.

As Moore's scrapbook 32 chronicles, 1935 was a very eventful year for the star. Her Fairy Castle was completed; her screen comeback, *The Power and the Glory*, with Spencer Tracy, debuted; her first book, *The Enchanted Castle* (a fairy tale for children that was about the dollhouse), was published; and both she and her Bel Air tenant, Marlene Dietrich, received widely publicized threatening phone calls.[19] Thus, between cheerful news clippings regarding the completion and cost of the Fairy Castle are the more ominous stories about threats targeted at the two stars. In early January 1935, callers threatened to kidnap Dietrich's daughter and steal the dollhouse. (From the news clippings, it is unclear if the same callers made both threats, and Moore does not discuss this experience in her memoirs.) The *Chicago Tribune* reported that Moore asked the police chief of Beverly Hills to assign a guard to her home after these anonymous threats. The star is quoted as saying, "I am in no fear for myself, but have asked to have my house watched while my $500,000 doll house is here."[20] Stories about Moore's and Dietrich's travails were printed in newspapers all over the country at the time of the threats: the scrapbook includes clippings from such cities as Elkart, Indiana; Lancaster, Pennsylvania; Birmingham, Alabama; and, later, St. Louis, Missouri.

One double-page spread in Moore's book offers an interesting spin on these events, highlighting the value of various Hollywood "properties." This collage includes three clippings, all of which concern Moore's Bel Air home.[21] On the left is a story with the headline "Film Stars Get 'Phone Threats'" from the Lancaster, Pennsylvania, *New Era* (January 8, 1935); it details threats made regarding Dietrich's daughter Maria and Moore's dollhouse and describes Moore's Bel Air residence as "an armed camp." The middle piece, which spans the two pages, is a photo spread on Moore's home (it has neither a date nor a citation of its origin). The photographs show her projection room, her "boudoir," and the downstairs "living porch." Finally, on the right side of the spread is another story on the threats, "Hollywood Highlights," from a South Norwalk, Connecticut, paper (January 10, 1935). It details the investigation of the threatening phone calls and adds a summary of some of the oft-repeated facts about the dollhouse (the labor involved in its construction, its insurance cost, objects contained in it, and so forth).

The individual stories, of course, offer information (albeit rather sketchy information) regarding the events taking place in early January 1935, Moore's now famous dollhouse, and her actual California home. But they also inherently suggest a certain anxiety—and even danger—that accompanies wealth and fame. These anxieties infect the home: in this case, both the real home in which Dietrich and her family live, and Moore's fanciful, yet extremely valuable, Fairy Castle. Moreover, their inclusion in the scrapbook and their particular arrangement illustrates how the scrapbooks function as documents of and narratives about Moore's history. They also exemplify Moore's authorship (or coauthorship) of her history and the larger history that enveloped her. As historical artifacts composed of many other "documentary" texts, they bear an interesting relation to acts of both collection and recollection. Understanding this relationship can help further highlight the implied links between the materials within the volumes.

Thus, we might read the scrapbooks in relation to another textual art form: film. For Moore's process of collection also bears some relation to montage, the cinematic rendering of collage. To borrow from Sergei Eisenstein's theories of montage, we can recognize further intertextual resonances in Moore's writings and collections; here we might consider those montage theories—how, for example, separate units within the books might "collide" to create new forms and new ideas—as well as Maya Deren's explication of the anagram in relation to film form. Deren describes the anagram this way: "Each element of an anagram is so related to the whole that no one of them may be changed without affecting its series and so affecting the whole. And, conversely, the whole is so related to every part that whether one reads horizontally, vertically, diagonally, or even in reverse, the logic of the whole is not disrupted, but remains intact."[22] The scrapbooks certainly re-collect and display many distinct elements throughout. Further, as provocative relationships might be suggested between the items in the scrapbooks, we also see a whole emerge within them: that is, of course, a history of Moore's stardom rendered in written and visual form.

Exhibiting their likeness to a collage, some segments of the scrapbooks typically appear almost in disarray, whereas others are more precisely organized.[23] The particular spread concerning the kidnapping threats and the dollhouse is pointedly arranged. If we read it through Eisenstein's and Deren's theories of montage, we can see links between the elements themselves and between the parts and the whole. First of all, in general, this spread works in tandem with the volume as a whole—and volumes 33 to 36 which follow it—to delineate a literal rendering of the relations between collection(s) and recollection. That is, these volumes recollect a collection of historical narratives (the newspaper clippings they hold), and specifically they recollect Moore's collection of miniatures. Second, this particular example issues interesting links between the home and the value of possessions that are contained within it. The photo spread of Moore's home stands as the scene of the threats made against the dollhouse and Dietrich's daughter. Yet, while the images give the other events a certain spatial context (they allow us to better visualize the events because we can see where they took place), they simultaneously produce other, contradictory impressions.

For instance, the inclusion of the lighthearted piece on the star's home potentially trivializes the threats. Read next to this piece, the threats are given a more mundane tone: the stories about them seem expressions of everyday Hollywood life. At the same time, we might read the spread on Moore's home through the stories on the threats: in this way, we might recognize a more foreboding element to the drive for knowledge about the star's everyday existence, especially fans' fascination with the stars' home lives. Other connections also appear through these pieces. Of course, the threats themselves reveal—and the arrangement of the stories in the book emphasize—a kind of equation between Dietrich's child and Moore's dollhouse. This equation is made both ways: the child is represented as a form of property that can be traded for money, and the dollhouse appears to be as emotionally valuable as a child. In a sense, the dollhouse even seems to function as Moore's child.

## HISTORY IN MINIATURE: COLLEEN MOORE'S DOLLHOUSE

These connections between real life and fantasy, the mundane and the extraordinary, are quite suggestive of the economics of consumer culture in general and what we see of Hollywood life in particular (that is, the community that is one of the greatest manufacturers of consumer culture in the United States and around the world). These connections are all invariably part of a historical discourse painted by Moore's collections and our recollections of them. As I've noted, Moore left a number of cinematic and historical legacies, and the dollhouse itself might stand as the greatest legacy of them all. Constructed over a period of seven years by expert Hollywood set designers under the direction of Moore and her father, Colleen Moore's Fairy Castle, as it is now called, traveled throughout the United States and Canada in the 1930s to raise money for children's charities and has long been a popular attraction at Chicago's Museum of Science and Industry. It is, to be sure, a lavish and beautiful work. The castle itself is bedecked with jewels, precious minerals, scenes from fairy tales, and reminiscences; the objects therein are exquisite treasures. They include furniture constructed from Moore's personal jewelry and other fine materials; tiny but functional things; paintings, tapestries, and other representational works; and even a library of one-inch books penned by famous authors. The castle is thus a veritable treasure trove for visual pleasure. But much of the pleasure involved in looking at it, I suggest, is in the interpretation that it invites. In its richness of detail, Moore's bountiful collection elicits our decipherment of the clues it (and, indeed, Moore) has left for film history.

It is quite clear that Colleen Moore's Fairy Castle is no average text. It begs to be read, both as a house and from the vantage of the film spectator. Like most collections, it does not have a clear linear structure or even a coherent narrative. Yet, as Gaston Bachelard has declared, a house can be read, particularly as a structure in which memories are lodged: "Of course, thanks to the house, a great many of our memories are housed, and if the house is a bit elaborate, if it has a cellar and a garret, nooks and corridors, our memories have refuges that are all the more clearly delineated." In other words, "Our most personal recollections can come and live here."[24] This sort of topography, with its implicit connection to memory, is what Svetlana Boym describes in *The Future of Nostalgia*. Drawing on the work of Frances Yates and Walter Benjamin, she declares, "This kind of mnemonic tradition recognizes the accidental and contiguous architecture of our memory and the connection between recollection and loss. Places are *contexts* for remembrance and debates about the future, not *symbols* of memory or nostalgia."[25] In the case of Moore's dollhouse, the structure and the objects therein guide our reading as artifacts of history and memory at once.

The topographical nature of this particular display, as well as its historical context, suggests that our viewing of the dollhouse might also be likened to the experience of watching a film. Because the dollhouse in its current installation is encased in a glass structure, we maintain a necessary distance from the actual image, and we see a series of images displayed as we move around the house. Yet, because of our own movement, we have less the vantage point of an immobile spectator in a theater seat and more the mobility of the camera itself. At the same time, looking at the dollhouse is akin to window shopping, especially as we can never purchase the actual items on display but can only imagine ownership and inhabitation. And this again leads to thinking about the space as the storehouse of images, of memory.

Looking at the dollhouse, like looking at the movies, therefore invites other forms of reflection, historical and theoretical. Specifically, the dollhouse narrates a history that is not only personal but also collective and that can be read from our various potential vantage points in relation to the cinema and to consumerism. Susan Stewart notes, "In writings on collecting, one constantly finds discussion of the collection as a mode of knowledge."[26] Stewart sees this knowledge as "contained" by the collection, and therefore ahistorical; I would argue that the mode of knowledge apparent in Moore's collection is indeed historical. In fact, at the turn of a new century (and since its making), the dollhouse stands as a nostalgic remnant of a particular time and place: Hollywood of the 1920s. But as the very notion of nostalgia hints, the knowledge and narration of history that Moore's collection invokes are also fundamentally bound to the construction of fantasy.[27] For everyday visitors and scholars alike, the dollhouse therefore offers an exciting proliferation not just of objects but also of relationships between objects, and therefore of ideas invoked by those relationships.

The castle's location at the Museum of Science and Industry nicely emphasizes its origins: under Moore's personal direction, it was created in the industrial town of Hollywood via the scientific and technological innovations of the film industry. As such, it offers evidence of a personal and a cultural history. With its companion book by the star, the castle unveils Moore's own autobiographical history, while it also implicitly discloses a history of Hollywood in the 1920s (the climax of Moore's career as a film star). This dual history is in part evident in its ties to fairy tales. While the stories of fairy tales influence the narrative of the dollhouse itself and the objects therein, they also play a prominent role in Moore's construction of her personal history as recounted in her memoirs, *Silent Star*, in which the actress invokes the specific narratives and general language of fairy tales, as well as Hollywood films, to tell her own life story. Moreover, as an extravagant, costly, and now almost priceless collection, the Fairy Castle displays the story of Moore's personal wealth as a movie star. It also points to the economics of Hollywood in general. The castle recalls both the lavishness of production and exhibition practices of the time, such as the great movie sets constructed for silent features in the 1920s and the movie palaces in which spectators saw the films, as well as the fascination with the private lives stars led in their own extravagant homes.

Thus, Moore's castle, in its own contexts of production and exhibition, reveals itself as a textual artifact that acts as a kind of visible evidence of the intertwinings of personal memory and cultural history, fact and fiction, collection and recollection. The particular histories Moore's works recall are inherently bound by fantasy, both in their narration through the fantastic and fabulous dollhouse and through the tellings of an industry defined by the production of fictions. To seek out and then reconstruct these sorts of relationships, I read the dollhouse from a variety of vantage points: through its own history (and the construction of it), through its connection to narrative, through its relation to other paracinematic works and film culture more broadly, and through the relation the scholar forges with it. I thus hope to respond to the seductive invitation the dollhouse offers in order to reawaken and re-present the relations that are preserved and made possible by this collection and its original author, the star.

## ARCHITECTURE OF HISTORY

Through the dollhouse and its attendant texts, such as her memoirs *Silent Star* and the tie-in *Colleen Moore's Doll House*, Moore narrates a story of Hollywood in which women have more relative control over their own historical destinies—even when that history is so directly connected to the fantasy of fairy tales and Hollywood film. Further, while Moore tells and retells the history of its origins and construction in her memoirs and her companion book to the dollhouse, her history is retold in another, less overt form: Terry Ann Neff's text composed for the 1997 edition of *Colleen Moore's Fairy Castle*. In this work, Moore's own words are lifted from her original volume and set in a new text, under new authorship. This sort of textual indebtedness to the star hints at the ways stars' authority over their own life stories is often displaced and simultaneously attests to Moore's primary role in the construction of the history of her life as well as the history of the dollhouse.

One aspect of Moore's history that is surely illuminated by the dollhouse is her own wealth and the surrounding luxury of Hollywood. Thus, like that envisioned in many of the extravagant sets of the silent films of the 1920s, the wealth displayed in Moore's castle is conspicuous (especially as it was undergoing construction during the era of the stock market crash and was displayed during the Depression that followed). To begin to bring these questions to the fore, let me first offer an abbreviated history of the castle. At the time of its construction, it was valued at $435,000. The labor alone would be almost impossible to reproduce. Writes Moore, "The castle was seven years in the building—from 1928, when the first plans were drawn, to 1935, when the landscaping was completed—and more than a hundred people worked on it during that time."[28] In *Silent Star*, she offers a different figure: "More than two hundred people worked on the house at one time or another."[29] This discrepancy suggests not only an inability to keep track of all the workers involved in the production of the castle but also the eventual disappearance of many of those individual laborers in history, with a few exceptions.[30] These numbers are hard to track, and so is the value of the possessions in the structure; the miniatures included within it are essentially priceless. As I noted, pieces of furniture are made from jewelry (with diamonds, emeralds, rubies, pearls) owned by Moore and her family members. Other items are made of gold, silver, rose quartz, jade, and like materials. Most of the books in the Library are first or unique editions; many are antiques. These latter items are so valuable, in fact, that Moore couldn't have them insured during the dollhouse's tour in the 1930s. Because of its extraordinary value, the miniature autograph book that belongs in the Library is no longer kept on display; instead, it is held in a safe at the Chicago Museum of Science and Industry.[31]

As noted, upon its completion Moore's castle traveled throughout the United States and Canada to raise money for charities. Typically, with Moore along for the visit, the dollhouse was exhibited in department stores; children and their parents paid a small admission fee to see the extravaganza, and the money went to charities usually chosen by Moore and local women's auxiliary groups. The tour raised over half a million dollars (in the throes of the economic Depression), most of which was geared to institutions such as children's hospitals. Moore's scrapbooks chronicle some of the cities of this tour. The books contain both stories about the exhibitions and ads for the display at the local department stores. The ads draw on a variety of facts about the dollhouse to bring in consumers to view it, much as one might be urged to see a film. Montreal's Henry Morgan & Co. produced a particularly elaborate series of ads: each appeared on a different day in the *Star* and *Gazette*, and each carried a different piece of information about the dollhouse and its tour. These ads functioned like literary or cinematic serials: although each could clearly stand on its own, to a certain extent they depended on prior knowledge of the story (Moore's identity, information about the tour in general, and so forth), and they also revealed additional information daily, building narrative tension for the readers. For instance, over four papers, the following announcements were made:

> IT TOOK 700 SKILLED CRAFTSMEN NINE YEARS TO BUILD COLLEEN MOORE'S DOLL HOUSE!
>
> IT COST $435,000 TO BUILD COLLEEN MOORE'S DOLL HOUSE!
>
> IT TOOK NINE YEARS TO BUILD COLLEEN MOORE'S DOLL HOUSE. IT IS ONLY 9 FT SQ BY 12 FT HIGH AND CONTAINS MANY MINIATURE WONDERS.
>
> THE WORLD'S SMALLEST BIBLE IS IN THE COLLEEN MOORE DOLL HOUSE—NO LARGER THAN A BABY'S THUMB NAIL.[32]

In addition to this information, sometimes photos of Colleen Moore in the Great Hall of the dollhouse would appear, giving a sense of the relative size of the place and also highlighting the star's attachment to it in name and person. As both this image and these serialized figures attest, one of the most alluring, as well as the most ironic, aspects of the castle is the relation between the vast expenditure of the undertaking and its diminutive size.

As a signifier of stardom and wealth, Moore's own body attests to

*the collector*

3 Colleen Moore in the Great Hall. *Photo courtesy of Joseph Yranski.*

this discrepancy as she literally sits inside the castle. If we see the castle itself as a part of her collection, this image thus literalizes Benjamin's suggestion that the collector "lives in" the objects she or he accumulates: "For a collector—and I mean a real collector, a collector as he ought to be—ownership is the most intimate relationship that one can have with objects. Not that they come alive in him; it is he who lives in them."[33] Furthermore, Moore simultaneously appears in these photos as a relatively down-to-earth person with a somewhat eccentric but common hobby and as a figure who is larger than life. The image is also an obvious and uncanny representation of her stardom and her own image on film. It is obvious as a publicity shot, a lure to interest fans to visit the dollhouse because they might also have the chance to view the star in person. And it is uncanny in that the hugeness of the star's size in relation to the house neatly recalls the size of her image on-screen in relation to our physical size as viewers. This image is, effectively, like a close-up of Moore on-screen, as her face or body would be blown up to be potentially two stories tall. Moore suggests that we play the role of inhabitants in the castle when we "tour" it; doing so reiterates our own diminutive size in relation to Moore's vast star image and physical body. Finally, the image of Moore in the castle is uncanny in a literal sense. Though the image might pretend to offer a representation of Moore at home with her dollhouse, it is extraordinarily "un-home-like" as she is too big for even this extravagant space.

But of course, this is the fantasy of the miniature. A miniature is modeled after objects that exist in real physical space (and are thus of a normal size), but it demands a fantasy on the viewer's part to imagine oneself in some parallel relation to it. This is in part what Gaston Bachelard means when he writes, "Miniature, to me, is solely a visual image."[34] The miniature invokes an act of the imagination, the work of the dreamer. Given the extraordinary cost of Moore's diminutive objects, for instance, they cannot truly exist in average human size. Our experience of them must be purely visual; our consumerist relation to them can exist only on this visual plane or via a purchase of a different sort of commodity fetish, one that can only symbolize the original object itself and never actually *be* it.

The initial, and in part the continued, context of the viewing of the dollhouse was undeniably related to issues of consumerism and commodification—and a consumerism with material, experiential, and fantastic dimensions. Thus, the early narratives of its attractions in-

*the collector* 43

evitably concern issues of consumerism, whether via the department store, the cinema, or Moore's star image. Indeed, part of Moore's star image (though usually that which circulated outside of her films) was directly related to money. For instance, she was known to be one of the highest paid stars of her day, and she also represented herself as an investor rather than a squanderer of her earnings, even long before her positive association with the stock market. Some Hollywood gossip did criticize Moore for squandering her cash on her hobby, yet the dollhouse itself came to be seen as an investment in charitable donations. More directly related to issues of consumerism is the simple fact that during its tour to raise money for charities the dollhouse was exhibited in department stores in each city. Children normally paid ten cents and adults paid twenty cents (twenty-five in Canada) just to see it. Money was then spent on a number of levels: people "bought" charity and a chance to see the dollhouse, and, while they were at the department store, they spent money on other consumer goods or at least consumed them visually. As Moore recounts of her New York tour:

> When we arrived in New York the doll house was set up in a corner of Macy's luggage department, scheduled to go on display on Monday morning. On Sunday Macy's advertised the doll house in four pages of pictures in the local papers. By Monday afternoon the crowds were so great, the entire floor had been put out of business. Before the store opened the next morning the crowds were already a block long, with ramps set up to contain them. Before the week was out, every department store in America was begging for the doll house.[35]

These queues anticipated those for the movies or for a museum today. Surely the expenditure is similar. The price to see the dollhouse in the 1930s was similar to that paid to see a film in Moore's heyday (though slightly less than to see a film in the 1930s). Moreover, although the dollhouse is no longer exhibited in department stores, one can, of course, still buy products associated with it at the museum gift store: a paper dollhouse and sticker book based on the original; magnets and picture frames of the dollhouse; a dollhouse mouse pad; Neff's book based on Moore's original one; and other typical fare, such as postcards.

These kinds of merchandising tie-ins are similar to others of paracinematic culture and are especially appropriate to consider in

4  Colleen Moore's miniatures. *Photo courtesy of Joseph Yranski.*

Moore's case, which I discuss later, by way of conclusion. For instance, Moore herself was reproduced in multiple fanciful forms: as a paper doll, a miniature porcelain doll as a tie-in for the dollhouse, a child's toy, and as a doll and compact in one. Turning Moore into a literal, material doll places her squarely in the role of a child (and also places her, presumably, in the hands of a child). This position is one inevitably invoked by some of her film roles but, more decidedly, by the dollhouse itself. Indeed, the association with children is present throughout the dollhouse, not only because the structure is based (loosely) on a child's toy, but also in its association with fairy tales. The fairy tales and dollhouse together therefore produce a very complicated relationship between age and history. The dollhouse is intrinsically recollective; as Susan Stewart argues, this is emphasized in its nostalgic function. Her description of dollhouses, in fact, sounds like a fairly accurate account of Moore's Fairy Castle: "The dollhouse

*the collector*  45

has two dominant motifs: wealth and nostalgia. It presents a myriad of perfect objects that are, as signifiers, often affordable, whereas the signified is not.... Use value is transformed into display value here. Even the most basic use of the toy object—to be 'played with'—is not often found in the world of the dollhouse. The dollhouse is consumed by the eye."[36]

In the case of Moore's Fairy Castle, this nostalgia is hardly a singular one. First of all, the making of the dollhouse originated out of a nostalgia for her childhood adventures and a happier time in the star's life.[37] Part of the intention of the display of the dollhouse is also to produce this nostalgia in its viewers. The inherent association of the dollhouse with children is also linked to nostalgia. Even now it appears in a museum that is especially targeted at children and their families.

Thus, via the nostalgic experience it presents, one mark of its complex temporal and historical structure is the dollhouse's relation to age. In its diminutive stature, the Fairy Castle looks like a child's toy. But Moore's dollhouse is hardly that: made of jewels and other valuable materials, it is meant to be looked at rather than played with. (In this way, even the "perfect objects" of the castle are not affordable.) In line with this seeming contradiction that defines the dollhouse, Moore simultaneously represents the perfect viewer of the castle as ageless and childlike; its viewers, she says, are children of all ages (and, presumably, all genders). This ageless universality is not unlike the targeted audience for the fairy tales that adorn the castle. Literary critic Jack Zipes argues against the "agelessness" that is attributed to fairy tales. Many critics before him, he argues, "[favor] the structuralist approach to explain the essence of the magic folk tale." He cautions his readers against this approach and argues instead for a historical approach that takes into account the specific social, cultural, and economic conditions of the particular authors of fairy tales. He writes that "formalist approaches to folk and fairy tales account in great part for the reason why we see the tales as universal, ageless, and eternal. The tendency here is to homogenize creative efforts so that the differences of human and social acts become blurred."[38] Certainly the Fairy Castle is hardly as "ageless" as Moore herself would profess; its opulence, use of rather adult themes (even if through fairy tales), and design for viewing rather than play all suggest that the castle is even more geared to adults than one might at first assume. Made in

Moore's own adulthood, too, it seems a provocative—and contradictory—response to her early assertion that when she is "too old to act" she will turn to writing. (Is it not strange that, by Hollywood standards, as Moore was becoming "too old to act," she began work on a dollhouse?) The construction of her dollhouse (and, later, the book about it) in middle and older age points both to Moore's continued embodiment of youth as well as the fact that acting and aging are not so incompatible. One might indeed wonder: In constructing her dollhouse, what age *is* Moore acting?

A possible answer to this question is that the age she is acting is not a biological one at all, but a historical one. Her turn to childhood at the same moment she is creating a text that embodies history in a material form is itself significant; as Carolyn Steedman writes, "Childhood . . . was brought into being in Western culture, as ideation, as an idea, as memory, as image, at the same time as history was brought into being."[39] Through the dollhouse and the time of childhood to which it points, the age of Hollywood in the 1920s is also acted out. Thus, through its connection to childhood, the dollhouse evokes a mythic representation of this fantastic-historical time and place. In his *Arcades Project*, Walter Benjamin draws important links between fairy tales and history. In fact, an early title of his project was "A Dialectical Fairy Scene." This work contains a utopian, if somewhat ambivalent, picture of childhood and child fantasy, especially as it is connected to fairy tales. Susan Buck-Morss describes these ideas as follows: "The 'trick' in Benjamin's fairy tale is to interpret out of the discarded dream images of mass culture a politically empowering knowledge of the collective's own unconscious past. He believes he can do this because it is through such objects that the collective unconscious communicates across generations. New inventions, conceived out of the fantasy of one generation, are received within the childhood experience of another." This fantasy across generations is especially possible because the child can "discover the new anew." Thus, the new generation, represented symbolically by the child, can awaken the utopian wish slumbering within historical objects and "reactivate the original promise of industrialism, now slumbering in the lap of capitalism, to deliver a humane society of material abundance."[40]

As this language foretells, the fairy tale most directly associated with the *Arcades Project* is that of Sleeping Beauty. But as this story would direct, the child does not awaken Sleeping Beauty; the child functions instead as merely a symbolic listener to this history. It is, rather, the historian who tells the fairy tales. As Buck-Morss underscores, "Of course, it is not to children that the fairy tale of the Arcades is to be told, but to those whose childhood is itself only a dream memory." And Benjamin sketches not only a complicated version of age but also of gender. That is, the child who is invoked by this dream memory is gendered male, "lost in the folds of his mother's skirt." But, again, while the historian and the listener (who becomes the agent of a new history) are presumably male, the story that is told is that of a (imaginary) woman: Sleeping Beauty. As Buck-Morss puts it, "The Arcades project was originally conceived as a 'dialectical fairy scene' . . . so that the *Passagen-Werk* becomes a Marxian retelling of the story of Sleeping Beauty, which was concerned with 'waking up' (as the 'best example of a dialectical overturning') from the collective dream of the commodity phantasmagoria."[41] In the case of Moore's dollhouse and its relation to the history, or age, of the 1920s and Moore's life, it would seem that Moore herself doubles as both historian and Sleeping Beauty. As she tells the story of Hollywood via fairy tales, her own image is awakened. But this is, of course, hardly the same as Benjamin's Marxist fantasy. In other words, because her historical age is known through opulence, consumerism, and fantasy, we don't wake up from a "dream of commodity phantasmagoria." But neither do we need to reawaken this particular dream. That is, the dollhouse also represents another facet of frozen time and a different kind of frozen wish. It is awakened by the childlike viewer and represented by the new generation who wish to see this woman at the center of the narration of her own history.

### NARRATIVE STRUCTURE

Certainly the association of a Hollywood star with the dollhouse makes clear its link to the cinema, which is, undoubtedly, often a consumerist venture. But the link is also made in its function as an object. As Stewart notes, a dollhouse is not a toy to be played with; rather, it "is consumed by the eye." Of course, this definition would not apply to most dollhouses—those owned by families and not housed in museums—for those toys have a real tactility, and their function is to be played with as well as to produce certain narratives about the home.

But in the case of Moore's dollhouse, which is not accessible for such play, Stewart's definition holds true. In fact, this mode of consumption (or consumerism) was also emphasized by Moore: "We decided not to put any figures in the doll house. When we tried, the dolls looked static and dead. With an empty castle and a full imagination, it's easy to people the rooms with running, laughing elves and fairies."[42] Its tie to Hollywood cinema is further emphasized, then, by its visual and narrative functions. This narrative function is evident in the way the castle retells classic fairy tales, in its telling of histories, and in the spectator's fantastic (or phantasmatic) relationship to the castle.

Thus, throughout the castle, and between the castle and other visual and written texts, spring multiple narratives, which are themselves fictional, autobiographical, historical. Like the dollhouse itself and the objects contained therein, these narratives are rich in structure, especially in the layers of connections formed among them. Indeed, Moore's Fairy Castle also comprises acts of collection and recollection in part by definition: it is, of course, a collection of miniatures; at the same time, the collection embodies recollection through storytelling. In "Telling Objects: A Narrative Perspective on Collecting," Mieke Bal asks, "Can things be, or tell stories?"[43] In the case of Moore's dollhouse, clearly the answer is yes. As a kind of narrative (or narrating) text itself, the dollhouse illustrates Moore's role as a storyteller, similar to that described by Walter Benjamin in his essay on Nikolai Leskov:

> Storytelling is always the art of repeating stories, and this art is lost when the stories are no longer retained. It is lost because there is no more weaving and spinning to go on while they are being listened to. The more self-forgetful the listener is, the more deeply is what he listens to impressed upon his memory. When the rhythm of work has seized him, he listens to the tales in such a way that the gift of retelling them comes to him all by itself. This, then, is the nature of the web in which the gift of storytelling is cradled. This is how today it is becoming unraveled at its ends after being woven thousands of years ago in the ambience of the oldest forms of craftsmanship.[44]

As this passage shows, Benjamin sees the storyteller as embedded in rhythms of the work of craft making. Storytelling takes place alongside other kinds of labor, he argues. By conjoining the art of making

*the collector* 49

narratives to other, more tactile arts, Benjamin himself utilizes language that merges these two art forms: stories themselves become woven fabrics that can become "unraveled" when those parallel crafts that formed them also become obsolete.

Moore herself retells many stories, and they, too, are embedded in the crafts and craftwork of the dollhouse and those related to it: in the structure of the castle itself, in the objects within it, in the books by Moore that accompany it, and in the other craft in whose creation Moore participated—the movies. Certainly this craft work is quite different from that which Benjamin describes, both because of its very different terms of labor and exchange and because the making of the dollhouse, at least, is defined by its unique qualities rather than the repetition that characterizes weaving and spinning. In this sense, storytelling does not (repeatedly) take place alongside the construction of the dollhouse; rather, storytelling becomes an actual part of its structure. And although the labor involved in its construction is over, the stories it (re)tells are retold again with viewings of the castle and through the reading of Moore's written works. Thus, Benjamin's definition of storytelling might be applied to Moore and the dollhouse first through its association with craft making (even though it also diverges from this aspect of the definition) and second through the essential *repetition*—rather than origination—of stories within and surrounding it.

The narrative fantasies that make up the house are obvious to any observer. First and foremost, perhaps, is the fantasy Moore demands on the part of her visitors to imagine themselves as actually entering the castle. The tour is therefore based on this imaginary experience, even though such positioning is, of course, impossible. Specifically, when one views the dollhouse at the Chicago museum, the tour begins in the back of the house, at the Kitchen (though Moore suggested that one "enter" through the Library). The dollhouse is encased in glass in the middle of the viewing room and set a couple of feet away from its visitors. As with many exhibits at this museum and others, telephones surround the display. What is especially striking about this aspect of the scene is that it is Moore's own voice we hear on the telephones. Through this museum technology, she is each visitor's personal storyteller: her voice guides us through our tour. So, as we "enter," she announces, "This is Colleen Moore, and this is my Fairy Castle. Come along with me on a trip to fairy land. In order to go on this trip, you have to pretend you are five inches tall so that you can walk through this room." Doubling the fantasy that we might become tiny inhabitants of the castle is the idea that the movie star is our actual host. Inviting us into her "home," Moore stresses her ownership of the castle; this position as owner-hostess, furthermore, underscores her role as a sort of director (one might say "author") of the structure. Her pronouncement and invitation clearly set the stage for the fantastic tour, for throughout the visit her narration frequently — and almost seamlessly — moves between fantasy and reality. The seamlessness is indeed underscored through the mechanical reproduction of her voice, giving her a virtual presence at the site.

In addition to the fantasies Moore weaves via the telephone, other stories the castle tells are painted, etched, carved, written, sewn into, and materialized by the castle and the objects it holds. For instance, the exterior of the small building is carved in many places with figures from various fairy tales. On the outside of the kitchen wall is a bas-relief from the novel *The Wizard of Oz*. High above the entrance to the Great Hall are the mounted and carved figures of Snow White, the Prince who saved her, and her evil stepmother, appearing as the Witch. Over the archway into the same room is a carving of Aladdin and his magic lamp. Fictional figures and the fairy tales they signify are similarly carved into structures in the interior of the castle. Some windows around the house are also etched with images from fairy tales; the large windows in the Great Hall, for instance, include representations from "Jack and the Beanstalk," "The Princess and the Seven Swans," "Prince Charming," and "The Princess and the Doe." Thus, the stories literally structure the house itself. And although the majority of the images are not explicitly based on film narratives, they prompt us to recollect films, especially those fairy tale–influenced films in which Moore starred, such as *Ella Cinders* (dir. Alfred E. Green, 1926), based, of course, on *Cinderella*, and the works that followed its success.

Fairy tales from all over the world are also a part of the castle's interior design. Most walls of the various rooms are painted with murals from such stories. Each story, or kind of story, helps to define the particular rooms they embellish, particularly in terms of gender and, of course, age. The Kitchen, the scene of so many fairy tales and nursery rhymes, is the only chamber that actually seems childlike. This is a result of the kinds of tales decorating the walls and the more playful

*the collector* 51

style used to depict them. The nursery rhyme characters and themes painted throughout the room also bear some association (either directly or tangentially) with food preparation or housekeeping, such as "Jack and Jill," "Little Jack Horner," "Humpty Dumpty," and "The Three Little Pigs." In contrast to the Kitchen, a sea adventure theme appears on the walls of the Library: images include Gulliver pulling Lilliputian boats to shore, Robinson Crusoe and Friday, and Neptune on a seashell throne. These images from boys' adventure books and Greco-Roman mythology alter the popular conception of a fairy tale.[45] At the same time, they work to gender the Library as a male's domain (in contradiction with the fact that the actual owner of its books is a woman).[46]

## LIFESTYLES OF THE RICH AND TINY

The Bedroom of the Prince also speaks to the gendered structure of the home and a further expansion of the definition of a fairy tale. Like the Dining Room and the Library, this room is full of tales about masculine adventure, not marital bliss. Whereas the Princess's realm is that of the home and the market, the Prince of the castle apparently ventures much further. His chambers are garnished with a certain international flair: the stories embedded in it stem from Russia, Japan, England, and elsewhere. Moreover, as Moore writes, "For no reason that I can offer, I began to think of the Prince's ancestry in terms of the Eastern world. Was he the great-great-grandson of a Sultan or a Czar? Was he descended from the figments of a Persian fairy tale?"[47] In spite of Moore's performed naïveté here, one needn't search far in film history to surmise her reason for this design. This image of the prince—as an Orientalist conglomeration of identities—could easily recall roles played by Douglas Fairbanks and, of course, Rudolph Valentino. Fairbanks was Ahmed in *The Thief of Baghdad* (1924), and Valentino, a contributor to the castle, was very popular on-screen in the title role of *The Sheik* (1921) and in many other films in which he was cast as an "ethnic type." Moreover, as both Miriam Hansen and Gaylyn Studlar write, Valentino's erotic appeal was largely based on his ethnic identity. Writes Hansen, "The dual scandal of his ethnicity and ambiguous sexuality was a function of the overruling, enabling stigma of Valentino's career: his enormous popularity with women."⁴⁸ One might imagine, therefore, that Valentino's popularity transferred to that of the Prince and appealed to the female "inhabitants" of and visitors to the castle.⁴⁹ It was in part Valentino's popularity, moreover, that influenced the Orientalist design of many motion picture palaces of his, and Moore's, day. Hence, in the design of Moore's palace, the furniture in the Prince's room is carved with motifs from the Russian fairy tale of "The Little Czar Saltar," a large chest shows scenes from Japanese fairy tales, and the sword by the Prince's bedside is, suggests Moore, Excalibur. Such a hybrid identity defines the Prince—and his room—more than other imaginary inhabitants or the real chambers of the place, and it also appears throughout the castle. Indeed, Moore hardly depended on just one national form of fairy tale or, as her inclusion of the legends of King Arthur and Swift's Gulliver attest, one definition of a fairy tale to bedeck and structure the castle, attesting to the pastiche nature of the castle as a whole.

Yet the dollhouse remains the Princess's domicile. Perhaps the fairy tale represented most often, and in a variety of ways, is "Cinderella." In the Drawing Room is a large mural depicting two scenes from the story: Cinderella's entry into her coach and her escape from the ball, as well as another image painted on the inside of a truly baby grand piano.⁵⁰ Given Moore's role in the 1926 film *Ella Cinders*, a modern reworking of the fable, her attention to this particular tale is not surprising. In this film, Moore plays a modern Cinderella whose ticket out of her wretched home life is not a glass slipper and a handsome prince but a train ticket and the promise of a contract with a Hollywood studio. Throughout, she is repeatedly rewarded for being herself: first she wins the ticket with an inadvertently comic (rather than glamorous) photograph, and when she arrives in Hollywood she eventually lands a part in a film by acting naturally, unwittingly performing before a camera. Even her eventual marriage (to hometown boy Waite Lifter) comes after he mistakes her for a pauper when she is actually playing a role for a film. Thus, realistic play—that is, a conflation between Hollywood representation and real life—characterizes the entire film. A number of Moore's other films were described as Cinderella fables, so this was a role that partly defined her work as a whole.⁵¹ Thus, in these objects that represent the fable is also embedded Moore herself. The role of Ella—or Cinderella—and its attendant fantasies reverberate throughout Moore's films in myriad ways, and also reverberate throughout the castle, as her own life is so directly linked to fantasy.

Moore "lives" in the Great Hall as well, the site where the photograph of her in the castle was shot. For, with its amalgam of tokens from a variety of fairy tales, it's like a miniature version of the castle itself: a museum within a museum, a collection within a collection. As Moore writes, "The Great Hall serves as the picture gallery and museum of the castle, and it contains a variegated assortment of articles on display. It is here that the little people could be presumed to show *their* tiny treasures."[52] The imaginary inhabitants, like Moore, are shown to be collectors—even pillagers, in that their objects come from a range of sources. On show here are, of course, Cinderella's glass slippers; very tiny reproductions of the Three Bears' chairs (suggesting that the castle's "inhabitants" also like miniatures); the Goose that Lays the Golden Eggs, along with some golden eggs in a nearby basket; Hans Brinkers's ice skates; and a large variety of framed portraits on the walls. The function of these objects certainly goes beyond a decorative one; like the paintings, etchings, and carvings throughout the house, the objects also work to tell stories. Their purpose, then, is like that of the toy, which Susan Stewart describes as follows: "The toy is the physical embodiment of the fiction: it is a device for fantasy, a point of beginning for narrative."[53] Through the glass slippers or the miniature chairs of the Three Bears, we can recollect traditional fables. The physicality of the objects, too, suggests an authenticity that the fairy tales alone would not. As a tangible residue from the stories, collected for display, these objects give the tales they represent a renewed life through their very materiality.

Moreover, such objects stand side by side with ones that Moore describes in a different way, rendering them with a different sort of authenticity—or perhaps another sort of fantasy. For instance, Moore describes a variety of objects in the Great Hall: "The Battersea table in the Great Hall holds the Goose that Lays the Golden Eggs, along with a basket of the golden eggs already laid. Two silver-and-gold knights in full armor who guard the entrance to the Great Hall came from the collection of the great romantic film star of the twenties, Rudolph Valentino."[54] Even in this brief narration, Moore seamlessly moves between the fantasy of the golden eggs to the real figure of Valentino. The association between the two at once lends a kind of credibility to the golden eggs yet also suggests that Valentino himself, like the Goose that Lays the Golden Eggs, was just another fiction.

Such movement between fact and fiction is evident in the paintings in the Great Hall and the narratives they entangle. Some of the paintings are of popular animated characters by their originators, and others are copies of masterpieces from various eras. In this way, works of both the real world and the world of fantasy (created in the real world) come together. In *Within the Fairy Castle*, Neff writes, "Perhaps no object in the Great Hall so exemplifies the mixture of real life and fantasy as the dollar-size miniature of Red Riding Hood, painted on ivory by Lisbeth Stone Barrett, a well-known miniaturist."[55] I agree that this painting, like many other objects in the Great Hall, does exhibit a certain fluidity between real and fantastic worlds, but other objects mark this juncture even more clearly. For instance, one painting is a tiny replica of one Leon Gordon made of Moore in the film *Irene* (dir. Alfred E. Green, 1926), and another is a portrait of her daughter Judy as a water sprite done by Alex Grig. Although this sort of posing as fictional figures for commissioned portraits is not uncommon, it still functions to show a merging between real and fantasy worlds, especially as the portrait of Moore here is actually of her as a fictional character she played. And perhaps even more real than the image of either Moore or her daughter in the pictures we see is the inherent labor that went into these and other objects.[56]

Like these objects, the one-inch books collected in the Library also exhibit Moore's strange, yet easy, mobility between fantasy and reality projected throughout the castle. Penned by real authors, some are works of fiction, others are simply souvenirs of sorts: a remembrance of Moore's friendship, or a ditty about the castle.[57] A great number of them bear some relation to film production: some are by screenwriters of Moore's era (such as Edna Ferber, Anita Loos, Clare Booth Luce, and Frances Marion), some are by authors whose work was adapted for the screen (Edgar Rice Burroughs, James M. Cain, Daphne Du Maurier, Warner Fabian, and John Steinbeck), and others are simply by friends of Moore who were part of the Hollywood community in some way (the designer Harold Grieve, William Randolph Hearst, and writer Adela Rogers St. Johns). Among these various volumes, many contain segments of the works for which the authors were famous, at least in regard to film: Du Maurier reproduced the first paragraph of *Rebecca*, Burroughs created a mini-version of *Tarzan* with illustrations, and Anita Loos offers the first line of *Gentlemen Prefer Blondes*. Thus reads the entry by Fabian, author of *Flaming Youth*: "To Miss Moore who is the author's idea of 'Flaming Youth.'" Harold Grieve penned the following, apparently in the form of a prose poem, with photographs to illustrate the written text:

> California homes decorated by H. W. Grieve A.I.D.
> Colleen Moore Boudoir, Bel Air.
> Day bed upholstered in peach satin stripe taffeta
>
> It is most important that the house should be
> a perfect background for the occupant both in
> color and type of decoration.[58]

Like the objects collected from fairy tales, these books appear as a residue of narrative, as well as of history. Indeed, these authors composed a history of sorts through their miniature souvenirs. So, through these books by actual historical figures, reality intrudes on the fantasy world of the castle.

Of course, this aspect of the castle existed from its beginnings. That is, although the imaginative origins of the castle were in fantasy, its material origins solidly tie it to the physical world. For instance, the architect Horace Jackson suggested that the "architecture be unreal, making the castle look as if it had come from the pages of a storybook."[59] At the same time, Moore recalls that her father was also concerned with other, real details: "'I want the water to run and the lights to burn,' he stated. 'I have to think of function!'"[60] Thus, the castle does have real running water and electricity; many of the objects are made to scale and can function (though in the case of the size of the rooms, Moore admits that "one has to go overscale in height to give the appearance of reality").[61] A tiny gun shoots, scissors cut, various objects can move, and, of course, the books can be read. The functionality of these objects might, then, act as a metonym for the functionality of history in the castle.

This particular function is also evident in Moore's writings. Her book about the castle provides an important memorializing function, parallel to that of the dollhouse. Essentially structured after the dollhouse itself, Moore's volume initially tells the history of the castle and then describes its particulars through a room-by-room tour. In her

5  Colleen Moore's miniature library. *Photo courtesy of Joseph Yranski.*

descriptions we can see how each room, and even each object within it, begets Moore's memories. For instance, when she describes "The Magic Garden" she recalls that the cradle of "Rockabye Baby" is set with pearls given to her by her Irish grandmother: "She had it made from a necklace, a pair of earrings, and a brooch she had inherited and worn from childhood. 'It'll be my tombstone,' she said with fey prophecy. 'More will visit it than my grave.' Annually more than a million people view the castle in the Museum of Science and Industry."[62] In her discussion of "The Catalogue of Authors" found in her Library and in her autograph book, Moore recollects many stories about her hunts for signatures from many famous figures all over the world. These stories not only offer a history of the accumulation of signatures, but they also neatly reiterate Moore's own place in the world of celebrity.

Her narration of "The Chapel" similarly includes other personal tales, which clearly tie her history of the castle to other celebrities and to her own religious background (Catholicism). For instance, she notes that the vigil light in this room includes a large diamond from her mother's engagement ring: "She left it to me with instructions to use it in the castle. I like to think that my mother's inspiration goes on in this vigil light."[63] Another item in this room that might be tied to fantasy as well as personal recollection and history (and celebrity) is a sliver of wood said to come from the "true cross."[64] Moore tells the story of this item: "This was a gift to me from Clare Booth Luce, who came to Chicago to look at the castle and was deeply moved by it. While we were regarding the chapel, Clare turned to me with tears in her eyes and said: 'I am going to give you something for the chapel, in memory of my own daughter, Anne Brokaw, who was killed in an automobile accident when she was a young girl.'"[65]

Stories such as this one illustrate the castle's function in relation to memory. Not only do the house and the objects inside it generate a range of recollections, but recollections themselves exemplify that many of the objects are memorials to Moore's family members and friends.[66] Like the objects that signify the residue and evocation of fairy tales and film narratives, many pieces also spark a memory of a real time and place. In these objects and in the collection as a whole, Moore sets up her viewers to thus remember both her career in Hollywood and its relation to her private life. Throughout the castle, then, she provides clues for the recollection of her own place in history.

Thus, the Fairy Castle's tie to the real world is even more concrete than it might at first appear. As a whole, in fact, the collection is itself a souvenir of a particular time and place. Benjamin writes, "Every passion borders on the chaotic, but the collector's passion borders on the chaos of memories."[67] The notions of chaos and memory structure Benjamin's ruminations on collecting in the *Arcades Project* as well. There he notes, "One must understand: To the collector, in every one of his objects, the world is present, and indeed, ordered—but according to a surprising relationship, incomprehensible in profane terms."[68] Such is true of Moore's collection: each object within it has its own history (both real and fanciful), in part imbued with Moore's personal recollections and in part more indirectly tied to the historical context of both the castle's and the star's production. In this way, the Fairy Castle is also what Frances Yates might deem a "theatre of memory." Early "memory theatres" were often structured in relation to Greek mythology or the Zodiac; they were based on the notion that an edifice can be constructed mnemonically, so that different chambers or portions of the structure are associated with different ideas, images, and objects.

The dollhouse itself does not bear such a direct relationship to these sixteenth-century modes of thinking about memory, yet its various rooms and the objects therein do reveal the mnemonic traces of Moore's life within and outside of Hollywood film culture. Indeed, both the objects and the rooms are ordered in fantastic ways, creating an almost endless proliferation of relationships. I would like now to expand these associations, to go from the rooms of the castle to the world outside that is present within them. Just as the rooms and objects are directly tied to Moore's personal reminiscences, the collection as a whole—like Moore's own life—is also connected to a broader history. In her written work on the dollhouse, Moore emphasizes these historical origins: "Perhaps only in that place and time—Hollywood in the twenties—could such a fantasy have been achieved. . . . It was a time of splendid extravagance and carefree self-indulgence, which seem inevitable to spur creativity."[69] Indeed, such displays of "extravagance" and "self-indulgence" were apparent in other aspects of film production, exhibition, and discourse.[70]

The castle's connections to film production are perhaps the most self-evident, yet still fascinating. Indeed, many of the miniatures and the castle itself are intimately tied to the extravagant and intricate design of the sets of 1920s feature films. In a sense, it was designed *as* a movie set; as Moore notes, many of its early builders "were miniature experts from the motion picture studio of First National—men who produced the scaled-down scenes for the photographing of hurricanes, earthquakes, volcanic eruptions, fires, or any catastrophe too costly to film in full scale."[71] The light bulbs for the castle were made by the Chicago Miniature Light Works, and the lighting effects were designed by Henry Freulich, Moore's own cameraman (she names him Sidney Hickox in *Silent Star*).[72] One might even say that the castle was designed as the perfect set on which to screen both fantasy and history. And given that the lighting was produced by Moore's own cameraman, we can see how the castle was more specifically designed to screen her own image of and in history.

Considering the function of the castle as a set of sorts, it obviously also shares a special correspondence with designs of homes in films of the period. In *Designing Dreams: Modern Architecture in the Movies*, Donald Albrecht sees an inevitable tension at work between progressive and conservative ways of thinking in such designs. Thus, whereas architecture of the time, exemplified by the work of Le Corbusier, essentially built on the philosophies of nineteenth-century domestic reformers like Catharine Beecher to make the home more efficient and thus more "humane" for its domestic laborers, the homes visualized in Hollywood films of the same era often refused such reform. For instance, writes Albrecht, "Modern design came to be associated with forces that were threatening domestic security: The technologically advanced kitchen which might free women to pursue activities outside the home was lampooned, while the bedroom and the bathroom became natural backdrops for loose-living women who had turned their backs on homemaking and indulged themselves in a life of pleasure."[73] Albrecht discusses these images of the home as constructed through Hollywood films made during the Depression; Moore's dollhouse suggests these same sorts of anxieties, perhaps in response to the very films in which she starred in the 1920s. We can see the tension Albrecht describes, for instance, in the greatly differing designs of the Kitchen and the Princess's Bathroom of Moore's Fairy Castle.

The Kitchen indeed evokes traditional children's fairy tales and includes the least extravagant furnishings; the Princess's Bathroom is more reminiscent of like chambers in a variety of the De Mille films, and those works that drew on his films' designs, that Albrecht describes. Albrecht quotes William De Mille on his brother's sets: "He made of the bathroom a delightful resort... a mystic shrine dedicated to Venus or sometimes to Apollo, and the art of bathing was shown as a lovely ceremony rather than merely a sanitary duty."[74] Moore's own description of the Princess's Bathroom suggests it was almost an exact replica of such cinematic designs: "The crystal-and-silver Bathroom of the Princess interprets the story of Undine, the sea nymph, who is etched on the wall at the back of the room."[75] The bathtub is made of silver, and the water flows from the mouths of fish on both sides of it. Although the design of the Kitchen and the Bathroom (and, really, almost all of the other chambers of the house) might seem antithetical to one another, they suggest another fantasy inherent in the castle: one can live a life of total luxury and simplicity at once.

The castle's rooms might represent movie sets, but the castle as a whole might also be connected to those structures that screened the films of Moore's era: the motion picture palace popular in its time and popularized also by historical account. These theaters have themselves become part history, part fantasy: Richard Koszarski notes that "although the 'picture palace' occupies an important position in the lore of the era, relatively few such theatres existed."[76] Those theaters that did exist presented films in extremely lavish settings, often outdoing the films themselves. Thus, the motion picture palace is wed to Moore's dollhouse structurally and discursively.[77] It is an edifice built for consumption by the eye and imagination; as such, it appears to let us intimately witness if not the real lives of stars, then the real wealth that defines the industry of moviemaking as a whole. Moreover, like Moore's dollhouse, the theaters often boasted an eclectic style of architecture and design and drew from a range of cultural forms, from Italian Renaissance to Eastern to even Aztec and Navajo styles. Further describing such theaters and their designers, Koszarski writes, "More fantastic still was John Eberson, whose 'imitations of exotic environments' were the most fanciful and individualistic of picture palaces. These 'atmospheric' theatres were not simply developments of some historical style but witty concoctions of fantasy and reality that borrowed freely from any and all traditions."[78] In delineating Harold Grieve's plans for the dollhouse, Moore suggests, "This may have been the moment when the popular eclectic movement in interior design was born," but considering the motion picture palaces before it, we might see a more direct influence on the castle's design.[79] Even the waiting areas were fantastically arranged; "decorated with imported antiques, or the reconstructed interiors of millionaires' mansions," some imitated opulent homes.[80]

Many millionaires in Hollywood—that is, well-known movie stars like Moore—had theaters in their homes, which nicely joins those private structures to the picture palaces. Indeed, given its position as a home marked by fantasy, it's only logical to connect the dollhouse to other cinematic structures of the time. That is, just as its details exhibit the castle's affinity with film sets and theaters, its design and display might be compared to the homes of well-known stars of the time. Prior to and during Moore's rise to stardom, this interest was developed through extratextual discourse on Hollywood. Richard deCordova discusses the evident fascination with stars' homes during this period. He argues that the unveiling of these homes typically produced a twofold effect: images of stars and their homes offered a view of "conventionality, stability, and normalcy" and luxury and excess at once. These portraits together worked "not so much to uphold traditional values of family and home as . . . to promote the values of consumerism that began to dominate American life in the teens and twenties." Moreover, deCordova claims, certain discourses on stars' homes were "obviously geared toward engaging the spectator vicariously in a spectacle of consumption."[81] The act of looking in on stars' home lives via magazines like *Photoplay* and *Architectural Digest* is not unlike looking in on the fantasy lives of the inhabitants of Colleen Moore's Fairy Castle. Indeed, the castle functions rather like a miniature version of the Hollywood star's opulent home, both figuratively and literally. And Moore had previously commissioned a dollhouse model of the home where she first lived with her husband, John McCormick.

In all its opulent glory, the dollhouse would also be compared to what is probably the most famous of the homes constructed during the same era: William Randolph Hearst's San Simeon estate. Unsurprisingly, Moore herself makes this connection in her memoirs, forging a link between her own life and the Hearst legend. She describes Hearst's estate in a chapter entitled "From a Fairy Castle in Fairy Land," recalling visits in the 1920s with other Hollywood stars and later in life with her daughter. Concerning a conversation with

Hearst's mistress, Marion Davies, during this last visit, Moore concludes, "She and Mr. Hearst were alone together in their fairy castle on the mountaintop." In the paragraph immediately following, she turns to a discussion of experiences more pertinent to her own history: "The idea for my own fairy castle—a miniature fairy castle—came not from Mr. Hearst but from my father, though my doll house has the same feeling about it as San Simeon."[82] Hence, in the memoirs, we initially get to know the dollhouse through San Simeon, and we do so from a figure who knew San Simeon personally. Such experience lends Moore the authenticity and authority essential for a credible historian, and it "credibly" links her to other celebrities and sites of her day.

This role as historian and the links between other celebrity historians is further marked by the San Simeon oral histories project, in which Moore and many of her contemporaries participated.[83] As was the dollhouse in relation to Moore, Hearst's home functioned as an outward extension of the media baron. In this way, telling the history of his home adds to the history, as well as the mythology, of Hearst himself. The oral histories project both functions as a roll call of who visited the castle (however incomplete, given the limits of the project) and narrates the life of the house by revealing details of its permanent and temporary inhabitants. Hearst's home, especially as depicted in these and other histories, shares a number of features with Moore's dollhouse. It is a place where real-life fantasies were projected. It is also a domestic space under threat—of things being stolen, of the disintegration of family, of the loss of history. Finally, of course, it is a site for collecting, in this case, celebrity visitors as well as priceless objects. Read in relation to her other textual productions, Moore's participation in the oral histories project marks these similarities, however tacitly, and signifies her association with extraordinary domestic spaces, as well as the various roles she plays as collector and recorder of histories.

The comparison of Moore's castle and Hearst's also sparks an important distinction in terms of gender and scale. Both structures are evidence of the fact that Hearst and Moore were collectors of exorbitant objects. For his "ranch," as he preferred to call it, Hearst plundered from and mined other cultures and national spaces. For her dollhouse, Moore plunders from her own belongings (in that, for instance, she turned her jewelry into furniture) and collects gifts from friends, but she also mines cultural history: fairy tales, Hollywood lore, and the like. Each case represents an amassing of great wealth (as well as an accumulation of friends and visitors), but of course on very different scales—literally and figuratively. We might read this distinction in terms of scale through gender: the enormous size of the Hearst Castle versus the diminutive size of Moore's Fairy Castle. The size of each, along with other historical occurrences, has, moreover, surely enabled Hearst's greater visibility historically (and touristically). Finally, and perhaps most important, at least for my purposes here, is the way each structure is in turn recollected in relation to the movies. Along with the oral histories project, Hearst's castle is, of course, memorialized—if also fictionalized—in Orson Welles's *Citizen Kane*. In his statement to the press on whether his film was based on Hearst, Welles himself writes:

> It was necessary that my character be a collector—the kind of man who never throws anything away. I wished to use as a symbol—at the conclusion of the picture—a great expanse of objects—thousands and thousands of things—one of which is "Rosebud." This field of inanimate theatrical properties I wished to represent the very dust heap of a man's life. I wished the camera to show beautiful things, ugly things and useless things, too—indeed, everything which could stand for a public career and a private life.[84]

Laura Mulvey links this design of the film to the role of the critic. She notes that, armed with psychoanalytic theory, the feminist critic has assumed the role of "investigator." It is through this role that one might "decode" a film such as *Kane*. As Mulvey writes, "*Citizen Kane* is built around the pleasures and problems of decipherment not only, explicitly, in the main subject of the film (the journalist's investigation of the Kane enigma), but also in the fact that it builds in a deciphering spectator by means of its visual language and address."[85]

In her reading of the film, she also likens the fiction to Hearst's public life. In this way, Welles's film, like Hearst's castle, offers a collection of clues to be read in terms of fiction and fact: "*Citizen Kane* is concerned with creating a way of seeing based on a pleasure of curiosity, to be satisfied by seeing with the mind, and this can only be achieved by offering the audience their own, autonomous entry into the film text."[86] Whereas Hearst's collection is fictionalized and memorialized through Kane, Moore's castle's relation to film is projected in the reverse. That is, rather than being the fodder for a fictionalized account of a life, it uses fictions as the fodder for its own production. This fodder is, like Welles's film, "concerned with a way of seeing based on a pleasure of curiosity." And surely this mode of seeing occurs through Moore's direct invitation to the audience to enter into her own fictionalized text. In so doing, we can also recognize, by seeing with the mind, how these fictions are invariably bound to Moore's real life as well.

This relation is underscored in the connection not between the castle and Hearst's domicile, but in that between the castle and Moore's own home. Over time, the dollhouse has come to stand in as Moore's home, but it is also connected to her actual home of this period in significant ways. Most overtly, Moore designed the interior of the castle with Harold Grieve, the same interior designer who was currently designing the interior of a new home for her in Bel-Air. Recent writings on Moore's Fairy Castle inevitably bring these two homes together, especially as they heavily draw on Moore's own writings for their information. For instance, in her 1996 piece, entitled "Colleen Moore: The Original Flapper in Bel-Air" and published in *Architectural Digest*, Annette Tapert writes, "Moore's ultimate dream house was not the Bel-Air mansion but a considerably smaller structure she commissioned to distract her from the breakup of her marriage. This was a miniature castle built one inch to the foot in scale.... It took the studio artisans that Moore hired seven years to construct it, and it cost her $435,000—nearly twice as much as her Bel-Air house."[87] Certainly she lived with, if not within, the dollhouse for far longer than she did the Bel-Air mansion. With the house completed barely over a year before the breakup of her marriage, Moore ended up becoming an absentee landlord, renting the mansion to a range of Hollywood players, such as Dietrich. In this way, her Fairy Castle, like Hearst's "ranch," acted as a refuge for Moore from her other home life. Since then, the dollhouse, like Hearst's ranch, has become a refuge for the star's history.

## DWELLING IN THE DOLLHOUSE

Just as Moore's dollhouse might appear as a miniature version of the celebrity Moore's home, it also lodges the celebrities of fairy tales, such as Cinderella and Sleeping Beauty, who are themselves not completely unlike Moore. Cinderella appears throughout the castle, marking Moore's film history; the Princess's Bedroom is defined by the tale of Sleeping Beauty in both the murals on the wall and the general decor. This room also houses, Moore declares, "Sleeping Beauty's bed." In fact, she discusses how she and designer Grieve conceived of the Princess's role as a consumer in the outfitting of the house: "He said the name of the period for the furniture should be Early Fairie. He went on to say that the Princess who lived in the castle must like antiques. She would go to the antique shops of fairyland to find her furniture—King Arthur's round table for the Dining Room, Sleeping Beauty's bed for her Bedroom. This was the premise on which we furnished the house."[88] Thus, part of the attraction of this room in particular is this insistence on the fantasy that we are looking in on a celebrity's—Sleeping Beauty's—personal belongings. But this commentary also represents the princess herself as a fan of sorts, collecting objects that allow her a closer relation to the world of celebrity.

This was the role that Moore also saw for herself: as fan and star at once. Indeed, she even penned a little newspaper story that sketched this amalgamation of identities. Under the headline "Reaction of Colleen Moore to Herself on Screen is 'Fan-Like': First National Star Declares She Has Same Emotions as Her Audience When She Watches Herself Perform on Screen," the story included the following passage: "A mirror shows one as he is at the moment of looking into it. The screen shows one as another character, as a person assumed at a time long previous to that at which one watches oneself on the silver sheet. . . . Every time I preview one of my pictures, I attend not as the girl on the screen, but as Colleen Moore, a film fan. I am another person from the one capering about in a projection of light onto a gilded smooth surface, otherwise known as cinema."[89] This remarkable little sketch illuminates Moore's very complicated understanding of her stardom and the multiple identities it necessarily produces for her: character, star, fan. It is, indeed, through a role parallel to that of a fan that she constructs a necessary distance to become also a historian of her own life.

The design of the Bedroom is also suggestive of the kind of historical project Walter Benjamin attempted to construct in his own collection of sorts, the *Arcades Project*. As I remarked earlier, we might see Moore both as Sleeping Beauty and as the historian who allows us to awaken her. In this way, my own dwelling in the dollhouse is itself authorized by Moore. I therefore see the design of my own essay as a *re*construction of Moore's work. "Collecting," writes Benjamin, "is an ur-phenomenon of studying: the student collects knowledge."[90] In this work I am not merely a student or scholar of film history, but also a student of Moore. In the complex structure of the dollhouse and in its intertextual relationship to her writings as well as her films, Moore has left clues for my own act of re-collecting. Her dollhouse thus illustrates an elaborate temporal design: through the clues she has left behind in this fanciful castle, Moore anticipates both the loss of her history and the eventual retrieval of it. In so doing, she invites the historian to reawaken and re-present the various relations that are preserved and made possible in this collection.

BEHOLD, THE STAR!

An important part of Moore's publicity machine was the marketing of inexpensive products connected to her identity as a movie star and a regular person. Thus, during the 1920s, at the behest of Moore's producer-husband, John McCormick, the Owl Drug chain sold an array of cosmetic products manufactured by Darnee with the Colleen Moore imprint and designed with a shamrock to signify her Irish heritage—the first tie-ins of their kind. These products included lipstick, talcum powder, bath astringent, toilet water, perfume, and compacts. They were also linked to other publicity ventures—such as a poll Owl Drug ran in a 1924 *Photoplay* concerning the relative success of Moore's new bob (final count: 10,255 for, 4,371 against)—which further circulated Moore's literal image throughout a wide consumerist culture. Through such commodities, Moore could be seen and known inside and outside the cinema; at the same time, the products themselves promised fans the potential to be closer to her by becoming more like her. Through other tie-ins, one could also have the chance to "have" Moore, as well as to become like her. Of course, given the ephemeral nature of beauty products (not to say beauty itself), these tie-ins allow only a temporary relationship with the star if they are to exist as mere novelties.[91]

At the same time, these products are clearly related to the visual realm in that beauty products encourage women to look their best and to become more attractive visual objects. Other tie-in gimmicks were similarly linked to the act of looking, thus drawing on Moore's image

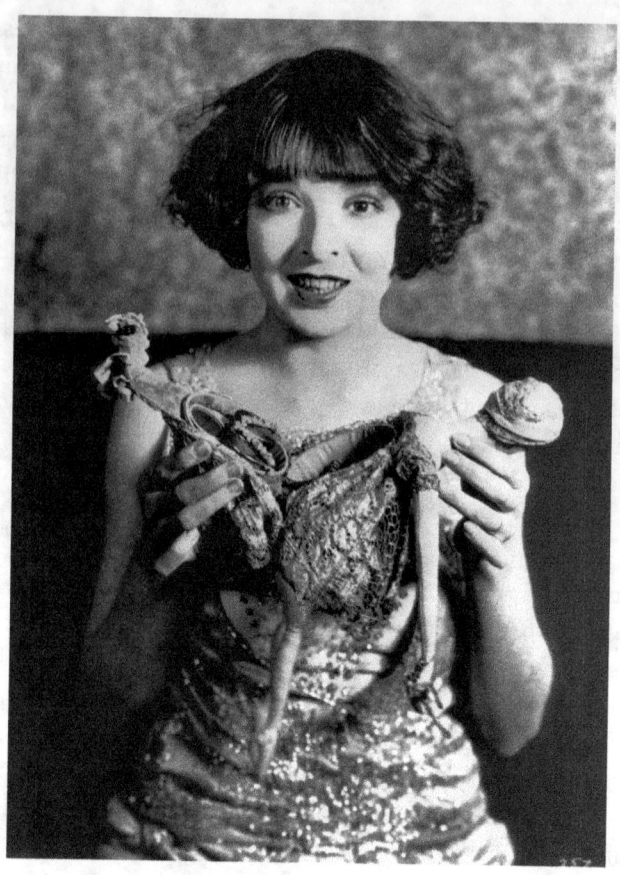

**6** Colleen Moore's doll and compact in one. *Photo courtesy of the Academy of Motion Picture Arts and Sciences.*

of and labor as a film star. For instance, a movie house in Tampa, Florida (one of Moore's hometowns), ran an exploitation contest in concert with her film *Naughty but Nice*. A peephole was housed in the lobby of the theater; spectators were invited to look in and see stills from the film. In tandem with this particular curiosity were tie-ups with other local businesses. For instance, a men's haberdashery included photos of Moore wearing garters; the local Kinney Shoe Store featured three pairs of her shoes; and another store featured her lingerie in the window.[92] These exhibits were far more racy than was customary with Moore, but they nicely underscore how the relationship engendered by the cinema between viewer and star is linked to other experiences of consumerism. In this case, the viewer gets to peep in at Moore and then choose which parts of her to buy. The intangible cinematic image becomes the material item that one can actually hold (and wear).

Even more visually representational than clothing and perhaps even more satisfying to hold were the manufactured dolls designed in the likeness of Moore.[93] The first followed her film *Ella Cinders*; known as the "Ella Cinders" doll rather than the "Colleen Moore," it explicitly embodied and, in effect, materialized the fantasy that Moore wove first in her films and later in her dollhouse.[94] Indeed, a second doll was manufactured to function as a tie-in for the dollhouse's 1935–1940 tour.[95] A miniature porcelain model, it was based on a popular doll first manufactured in 1929 called "Patsy." With her bobbed hair and round face, the doll resembled Moore already and thus was easy to adapt as Moore with her castle; moreover, the popularity of the Patsy doll also helped sales of the newly manufactured miniature version. In this way, it was based on two known figures, both real and fanciful: "Patsy" and "Colleen Moore."[96] These dolls, like the paper dolls of Moore that were also produced, allowed consumers the chance to have a material representation of the cinematic Moore. Makeup and clothing allowed one to be like Moore, and the dolls allowed one to have her. Although these items invite the viewer or owner to project a range of fantasies onto Moore, I am most interested in how they project a kind of preservation of the star's image in time. Drawing on the work of Gaston Bachelard, Carolyn Steedman writes, "In the practice of History (in academic history and in history as a component of everyday imaginings) something has happened to time: it has been slowed down, and compressed. When the work of Memory is done, it is with the *things* into which this time has been preserved."[97] In the case of Moore, her history is in part compressed into and preserved in these various things—but this history is also renewed or understood through the practice of collecting and, inevitably, of recollecting.

Finally, I would add to the image of Moore and her candies with which I began this chapter a concluding one, in which Moore is holding a reproduction of herself; here she herself becomes a literal doll. In this way, she can actually behold herself, echoing her fascination with her own stardom. Looking at such an image allows us to reflect on Moore's role in history and relatedly as a sort of historian through her own initial fandom of herself. She becomes a reproducible figure, an object to behold. But she is also a collectible—then and now. Meta-

*the collector* 69

**7** Remaking herself: Colleen Moore tennis doll.
*Photo courtesy of the Academy of Motion Picture Arts and Sciences.*

phorically speaking, this doll could be seen as the tangible figure of Moore in history for the historian. Of particular importance, all of these collectibles with which Moore was involved embody a temporal and historical function similar to that of her scrapbooks, the stack of photos found in her former home, or even her dollhouse. That is, they secure her place in time. Initially acting as promotions of her star image, the novelty of her present time (that is, the moment of their production: her stardom in the 1920s), they become the souvenirs of her past. These objects, as collectibles, look forward to a future when they will attain more value—a recollective value for the owner or the star and a monetary one for the collector. Therefore, like Moore's other collections, these objects also anticipate a future loss (the star will have aged, these works will no longer be reproduced) and a future rediscovery (of the object's monetary value and of the star's historical value).

This recollective value is embedded in the concrete objects themselves, but it is also neatly signified by the photographic. The photograph, too, has a certain kind of materiality: like a doll, we can hold it in our hands. This material nature, I'll show in the concluding chapter, is also true of writings by Moore and other women—in the form of books that we own, read, and write in. Similar to the book, then, the materiality of the photograph lies mainly in its objective of preservation. As we all know, reproduced frames from films are called stills; the movement of the film (or of the living star) is stilled by the photograph: its movement is arrested. In the photograph, as André Bazin notes, time itself is "embalmed." These photographs of Moore playing with concrete signifiers of her own stardom therefore host a double recollective function, displaying layers of representation in mechanically reproducible forms that will preserve and reawaken her presence for the fan, the collector, the scholar in the future.

# 2

## THE HISTORIAN

### *autobiography, memory, and film form*

> A desire for change can only come about by drawing on fantasy.
> —CLAIRE JOHNSTON, "Women's Cinema as Counter Cinema"

As the collector imagines the future, the historian must imagine the past. This is the goal of the memoir author: to bring the past forward into the present. A strange if also quite logical genre, the memoir is a work in which the writer is at once the subject of a history and the historian. Details of an avowedly private life are made public. Marlene Dietrich claims, "Diaries of famous writers surely have been written with some part of the brain contemplating publication."[1] In the case of the memoir, the writer consciously imagines how to merge private and public ways of seeing.[2] And in the case of women who worked in the film industry and went on to write their memoirs—the history of their lives that included this work—they seem ever aware of how their lives on-screen might represent, or be represented by, the stories they tell in writing. This new form of authorship, as writers of histories, transcribes and illuminates the multiple roles as authors women have played in the film industry and in film culture more broadly. A number of tropes, often intersecting, are common to autobiographies authored by female film stars and directors. First, of course, is the stated goal to set the record straight: these works, which spring from memory, are counterhistories, works that mean to correct institutionalized histories about their subjects. Second, some writers act as self-conscious producers of the genre; that is, like the critics to follow them, they comment on the complex production of a life history, recognizing the emergence of both patterns and digressions at once. Third is the reproduction of a teleological narrative common to much fictional film: most actresses trace a directional path that led them to become stars. In the various memoirs I consider in this chapter, their writers each had something at stake regarding the politics of history: they sought to reposition themselves in institutional memory, they attempted to reflect on the familiar representations of them and their work, and they hoped to adjust these images. The common tropes across their work, which often hail from the very context of the production of the memoirs, allow us to read the written works cinematically and to see their authors as potential models for our own historical production.

## GENDER AND THE POLITICS OF MEMORY

In general, both the rediscovery and the production of alternative histories have been an important part of feminist scholarship, as this work seeks to bring to light new knowledge about women's lives that have been forgotten or made invisible. In her landmark work, *Gender and the Politics of History*, Joan Wallach Scott examines how the discipline of history has developed to include an understanding of women as historical agents and to include women as historians. Reviewing over a century of historical studies in the United States and Western Europe, Scott shows that much of feminist rewritings of history has "revolved around the issue of woman as a subject, that is as an active agent of history." She ultimately argues that women's histories need to be integrated into broader fields of history, rather than "isolat[ing] women as a special and separate topic of history."[3] Mine is also a study of how women make history in a double sense. The difference—what I hope to add to, as I glean from, studies like Scott's—is that in the case of most of the women I discuss here, they were simultaneously the agents of history and the historians. Women such as Alice Guy-Blaché and Nell Shipman had to write their own histories because no one else was doing it; therefore, they produced histories through their memoirs for both present and future use. These histories, moreover, were not simply records of their achievements as individuals. Rather, their writings incorporate their work and presence into the wider field of film history.[4] Linda Arvidson's work *When the Movies Were Young* (published under "Mrs. D. W. Griffith") is perhaps the best example of this phenomenon, as she explicitly seeks to write a history of the silent era through her own experience, but all the women who have produced memoirs about their work in film industries inherently link their careers to the history as a whole. Still, explicitly elevating Guy-Blaché and her contemporaries to the status of historians might seem to be risky work, considering—as I shall discuss—the "fallibility" or fictionalizing function of memory. But in doing so, our knowledge of history, historiographical processes, and film culture can be valuably transformed. Not only can we again recognize the fallibility of institutionalized histories (and at this point in time, this seems common knowledge), but we can also consider how active such women have always been in the production of histories.[5]

Attempting to set the record straight, writers like Gloria Swanson, Leni Riefenstahl, and Alice Guy-Blaché emphatically counter public histories and representations of their lives. Interestingly, revealing herself to be a tireless researcher, Swanson admits to incorporating news accounts into her work. But she also notes, "In going through thousands of clippings and news releases, I have been consistently appalled at how inaccurate reports in the press often are," implying, of course, that her work will correct these inaccuracies.[6] Riefenstahl arguably has the most to gain from a "corrected" account of her own history; her book opens with a pointed epigraph from Albert Einstein: "So many things have been written about me, masses of insolent lies and inventions, that I would have perished long ago, had I paid any attention. One must take comfort in the fact that time has a sieve, through which most trivia run off into the sea of oblivion."[7] Attempting to suggest a parallel between Einstein and herself is a strategic rhetorical move, but the implication that the "distortions" of Riefenstahl's own life are "trivia" undermines her credibility from the outset. Still, predictably, throughout her 656-page tome she repeatedly distinguishes herself from the architects and leaders of the Nazi Party and the Holocaust. This distinction, too, is strategic: Riefenstahl doesn't suggest she was unfamiliar with Hitler and Goebbels, for instance, but instead suggests that she had autonomy from them in her film production. (She has Hitler himself declare this autonomy concerning *Olympia*: "Who else but you should make an Olympic film? And this time you won't have any problems with Dr Goebbels if the IOC [International Olympic Committee] organizes the games and we are merely hosts.")[8] Although Riefenstahl had perhaps the most pressing—and perhaps the most invidious—political incentives for countering popular representations of her life and work, in many ways Guy-Blaché had an even stronger case to make, considering her relative loss to history. Other memoirs therefore inform my reading and analysis, but Guy-Blaché's work forms the cornerstone of this chapter.

These women writers are not only active participants in the production of histories, but they are also *self-conscious* producers of their histories. That is, many of the authors reflect on the complex process of composing a life story. This sort of rumination commonly forms the opening of the memoir, thus framing our reading of it as a whole. Nell Shipman, Rose Hobart, and Gloria Swanson each describe the structure their memories and their written histories take, suggesting the natural emergence of patterns in their lives. Describing the "agonizing" experience of writing her autobiography, Swanson explains, "Forced to look intensely at the eighty years behind me, I have been amazed again and again to see patterns emerge and issues crystallize and relationships yield their significance in ways that were never quite clear while the events of those years were occurring."[9] Hobart, initially almost channeling Walter Benjamin or Gaston Bachelard, ends her preface as follows: "In writing this account, I became fascinated with the way each incident that surfaced was a cluster of occurrences with very little relationship to time. My husband, Bart, used to accuse me of talking with a 'steady digression to a fixed point,' and I became enthralled with watching this process of thinking jell as I wrote and how the results of each choice I made, no matter how casually, had an almost fatalistic inevitability about it. I can only hope that those who read it will be equally fascinated."[10] Both women understand that, on reflection, their memories, and therefore their lives, cohere into an almost causal narrative. But surely it's the process of writing that charts this narrative out of events that were otherwise a "cluster of occurrences," a series of unrelated or unfixed moments and relationships. And of course, such events will always be related through the subject who writes, who can therefore unify the events through her very presence as subject and historian at once.

Nell Shipman allows for the lack of resolution of these patterns: rather than seeing her life story as a "steady digression to a fixed point," Shipman sees "digressions" and themes as coexistent. Early in her memoir she writes, "An attempt to story one life has no single theme. If I wish for a leitmotiv in this patchwork of past happenings I'd symbolize it as a magic mantel, a covering into which was woven the warp and the woof of dreams, a garment of many broken threads which botch its dimly discernible pattern. Many broken threads going, seemingly, nowhere; but some running straight, so that their ends are traceable to their beginnings—'result' clearly linked to 'causal event.' Here we have, then, this life: good, bad, never indifferent, nothing to boast about; but lived."[11] In a sense, she, like Guy-Blaché, Ethel Waters, and, to some extent, Swanson and Hobart, sees the tensions and contradictions inherent in women's lives as well as in the historical accounts of their lives.[12] Some broken threads can't be resolved or matched but still appear in the same space of a life.

Most memoirs, however, especially those by stars, do follow a fairly direct line, suggesting a causal narrative chain that leads to their stardom or at least that signals the drive from childhood to be an actress. This is certainly the case with Colleen Moore, who describes her childhood as a movie fan and would-be actress, indicating, perhaps, her fandom for herself. Hobart's narration, which truly does follow digressions, also reveals a line to her future as an actress. Describing the summers she spent in Woodstock, New York, surrounded by artists, she, too, knew at an early age what she wanted to become. Talking with poet Edna St. Vincent Millay ("at least she would talk and I would sit entranced and listen"), Hobart makes up her mind: "It was sitting in a field of daisies, listening to her, that I decided to become an actress."[13] Other women mark this chain as less an independent decision and more a matter of economic necessity; such is the case for both Lillian Gish and Mary Pickford. But even in those less romantic beginnings is housed a romantic, or at least classic, narrative of success out of poverty (interestingly, often to make up for the loss of the father). And here the narratives of the actresses' lives suggest another sort of causal link: between their real lives and their work on-screen. So, as the writers work against the story of a happy childhood (or any childhood at all), they point to their fate as actresses and imply the links already inscribed between their public and private, imagined and real lives.

Pickford, for instance, notes that she is charged early on with caring for her family: "I don't believe I was more than five years old when I become Mother's deputy, a kind of little mother." Thus "cheated out of any real childhood," Pickford sets the stage for the roles she will play most of her life: a youngster, as in *Sparrows*, entrusted with the care of those barely younger than she.[14] In her roles on screen, she is both trapped in childhood and represented—perhaps because of her actual age when she played the roles—as older than her years, "a kind of little mother." Ethel Waters begins her memoirs, and hence the story of her life, even more emphatically:

> I never was a child.
> I never was coddled, or liked, or understood by my family.
> I never felt I belonged.
> I was always an outsider.[15]

Without fathers and without childhoods (Waters was put to work at eight—not as an actress, but as a bread maker and babysitter), Gish, Pickford, and Waters tell stories about overcoming unhappy and/or impoverished beginnings to become successful actresses. Yet, of course, success and the roles each played were relative to race. Their differences are marked on their bodies and in their roles: Pickford's diminutive whiteness helped make her "America's Sweetheart," and Waters's blackness, first and foremost, and then her roundness, set her trajectory toward the role of a mammy in film and television. Yet in each case, this is the fictional response to their real lives, the intersections of which are also ultimately met in their memoirs.

Thus, these written works invite us to read them cinematically in a number of ways. The narrative structure of the works allows us to see them cinematically in the most literal (if also the most limited) sense; the structure of the autobiographies often follows the same teleological nature of classical narrative film, and the authors make direct and indirect links between their private lives and the fictional stories of the characters they played or directed. This admixture doesn't necessarily weaken the historicity of the women's stories. So, when these writings expand the women's images in written form by taking up tropes that were also prominent in their films or by drawing on popular knowledge about them, they point both to the ways these women's lives were literally influenced by work in fictional production and to the factuality of film production itself. Certainly these facts point to a certain fictionalizing function inherent in the mem-

*the historian*

oirs, so that we might see this aspect of them not merely as troubling (and therefore of no use to "real" historians). These works thus reveal, in sometimes unexpected and provocative ways, how narrative films—and histories of these films—always juggle and recombine fact and fiction, reality and fantasy. Indeed, we can recognize how a movement between reality and fantasy is perhaps unavoidable in histories of narrative filmmaking and thus opens up provocative links between these categories. As Rosa-Linda Fregoso tells us in her tracing of Lupe Velez's "fantasy heritage," "I am interested in the concept of fantasy because I too want to appropriate it for twenty-first century cultural analysis and use it as a pretext for exploring my own ambivalence toward the 'cultural opposition between illusion and reality.' "[16] Similarly, women's memoirs about their work in film production, along with film fantasies about their lives and work,[17] draw attention not only to the cinematic productions as mere fictions; they also point to the reality involved in such work, and the imagination necessary for the recollection of forgotten histories.

These categories thus conjoined and intersecting, we can imagine histories differently. To Gaston Bachelard, "We dream at the frontier between history and legend."[18] For Bachelard, dreaming—or, more accurately, waking reverie—is an important act of imagination, for it allows for the continued production of knowledge and ideas. Interestingly, he notes that the very word for this act in French is feminine (*la rêverie*), while the complete thing, the dream (*le songe*), is masculine. The gendering of such words has an evocative relation to Greek legends about the invention of history: Clio is the muse of history, born of Zeus and Mnemosyne, who was the personification of memory. In his work on the representation of history, including a rumination on literal images of Clio, Stephen Bann writes that "we should not ignore the fact that Clio offers a more immediate, maternal sustenance; this primary relationship is also, no doubt, part of what Henry James called 'The Sense of the Past.' "[19] These modes of thinking—Clio's lineage, her maternal qualities—are productive of further reflection or reverie for the feminist scholar today. If dreaming, remembering, and the making of history are already feminine (albeit from different angles of the historical and philosophical lens), then it seems appropriate that women have had to imagine their histories for themselves—and, in the cases I am looking at, drawing even on the legends of fictional film. This is the sort of imagining, dreaming, and "fantasizing" that, as Claire Johnston notes, can produce a "desire for change" — that is, a desire to change how history is written and how it is read.

### REPEATING, REMEMBERING: ALICE GUY-BLACHÉ

The majority of the work concerning the world's first woman filmmaker, Alice Guy-Blaché, has been produced under the rubric of remembering her: writings and films about her seek to recollect and retrieve her lost work and her "lost" place in history. For instance, one of the first essays to initiate some revived interest in Guy-Blaché, by the film historian Francis Lacassin, is even entitled "Out of Oblivion: Alice Guy Blaché." In this short piece, printed in *Sight and Sound* in 1971, Lacassin declares, "Inaugurated in the prehistoric period and over before the history of the cinema was born, Alice Guy's career on both sides of the Atlantic has been either forgotten or attributed to other people."[20] Gerald Peary's "Czarina of the Silent Screen: Solax's Alice Blaché," originally published in the *Velvet Light Trap* in 1974, opens similarly: "Look through Rotha or Jacobs or Knight or any of the standard histories of the cinema and you will not find any reference to the existence of Alice Guy Blaché, though she directed approximately 270 films in the early silent era."[21] In fact, she was responsible for the production of more than seven hundred films, most of which have also disappeared.

Moreover, as Peary's statement illustrates, the breadth of Guy-Blaché's cinematic output is often contrasted in those works that lament her disappearance from history. So, in an open statement concerning "Women and the Formal Film" issued in 1979, a group of feminist filmmakers and scholars make the following proclamation: "Alice Guy is not represented in 'Film as Film' [a British film journal] and has scarcely been recognised anywhere. She was actively involved in film-making at the turn of the century, experimenting with narrative structures and the use of sound with film, but has long been forgotten by historians. Why are her films forgotten while those of Lumière and Méliès are used as standard texts?"[22] They then offer a general summons to women to fill such gaps in film history.[23] Other works stress the fact that no obituary appeared on Guy-Blaché's death in 1968 in spite of her tremendous labor.[24] Finally, a 1996 documentary about the early filmmaker, *The Lost Garden: The Life and Cinema*

*the historian*

*of Alice Guy-Blaché* (dir. Marquise Lepage), comments on and corrects this lack of obituary. It ends with this printed coda, which appears over an image of her gravestone in New Jersey: "Although she had been decorated by the French government and inducted into the Legion of Honour for her pioneering work in silent pictures, and went on to write, direct and produce hundreds of films, becoming one of the most celebrated filmmakers in the early days of American cinema, Alice Guy-Blaché's contribution to the art of filmmaking was totally forgotten."

These concurrent losses—of films and position in history—are not necessarily coincidences. Indeed, they are the products of the gendered nature of history combined with the ephemeral nature of early film. Thus, women's histories have been like early film. In the case of Guy-Blaché, one reason her contribution was "forgotten" is because the great majority of the films she made were not preserved or centrally archived at the time of their production.[25] Those histories that do exist usually note this lack of availability of her films. At the same time, in their repeated emphases that Guy-Blaché's work and life have been "forgotten," each of the above works attempts to correct this resultant historical amnesia: each attempts now to remember Guy-Blaché. They do so especially through her writings and the writings of others. I also consider the peculiarities of the construction of Guy-Blaché's history by bringing together written and cinematic forms. What, I ask, might we glean about film history and cinematic form through an analysis of words? Conversely, how might we read these words through film histories and theories of film form? These questions are particularly relevant in a study of a figure like Guy-Blaché, whose cinematic works were largely lost and whose written words sought to recollect them.

As Guy-Blaché has begun to appear in "standard histories of the cinema" since 1990, and as her films are now being found throughout the world, acts of remembering, recollecting, and retrieval remain significant on a number of levels.[26] By definition, they imply a certain repetition: to remember is to bring to mind again; to recollect is to gather together again or to remember; and to retrieve is to get back, to restore, to remember. We can thus deduce two important, if somewhat obvious, points concerning this work of remembrance and Alice Guy-Blaché. If we are remembering her and recollecting her work, then, first, her work (and our memory of her) has been lost, but second, at one point her work (and she herself) were "in mind," or known. In other words, she had to have been in mind once to be brought to mind *again*. Indeed, this is the assertion repeatedly made by those who have attempted to restore Guy-Blaché's history.

In their works on autobiographical forms, Leigh Gilmore, bell hooks, and Paul Freeman recognize that repetition, as well as the loss—or erasure—that necessitates it, are inherent in definitions of "remember" and "recollect" (respectively).[27] In *Autobiographics: A Feminist Theory of Women's Self-Representation*, Gilmore emphasizes the repetition inherent in remembering as she scribes the word "re-member"; she then defines it as "both the act of memory and the restoration of erased persons and texts as bodies of evidence."[28] hooks also notes the form of this word; she concludes "In Our Glory: Photography and Black Life" as follows: "The word *remember* (*re-member*) evokes the coming together of severed parts, fragments becoming whole."[29] In *Rewriting the Self: History, Memory, Narrative*, Freeman similarly focuses on the inherent repetition and loss inscribed in the word "recollection": "While the 're' makes reference to the past, 'collection' makes reference to a present act, an act . . . of gathering together what might have been dispersed or lost." He then considers the relationship between recollection and writing: "Framed another way, the word recollection holds within it reference to the two distinct ways we often speak about history: as the trail of past events or 'past presents' that have culminated in now and as the act of writing, the act of gathering them together, selectively and imaginatively, into a followable story."[30] For Freeman, then, the process of remembering is essential to writing histories. These notions about memory, autobiography, and writing have much to bear on the history of Guy-Blaché, because at the fore of all of the acts of remembering her are her writings and her spoken words.

Recognizing that her work and name had been practically erased from film history and thus endeavoring to re-place herself in this history, Guy-Blaché took on the task of writing her memoirs. These memoirs (and spoken interviews with her) have now become the dominant history of Guy-Blaché; the majority of works that treat her heavily depend on them for facts and for the story of her life. So, as the generic name "memoirs" suggests, the history of Guy-Blaché is mostly known through her work of remembrance and recollection.[31] This juxtaposition between memory and history is just one of many mergings between apparent oppositions in common representations of Guy-Blaché. Another such union exists between the private and public spaces of her life. Indeed, considering the fact that the process of remembering is normally a personal one, we also might recognize how the private history of Guy-Blaché (necessarily) became a public one with the publication of her memoirs and their subsequent circulation in writings about her.[32]

The very title of Lepage's documentary, *The Lost Garden: The Life and Cinema of Alice Guy-Blaché*, for instance, exemplifies the common tropes in works on the filmmaker. As it rediscovers her lost work, it both separates and conjoins Guy-Blaché's life and cinema, posing an intermingling between a private and a public history, as well as the filmmaker's personal and professional status (in other words, her life and her work).[33] Such contrasts and connections are not uncommon in representations of women in particular, and they are certainly consistent in almost all texts on Guy-Blaché. In fact, as constructed via discursive forms ranging from her memoirs to *The Lost Garden* to her own filmic works (especially those produced with her production company Solax), our understanding of Alice Guy-Blaché signifies a persistent merging of what might appear to be oppositional practices or spaces: public/private, professional/personal, institutional/familial,[34] history/memory, fact/fiction, and even image/word. These are the concurrent if unresolved threads that Shipman describes as she remembers her own life.

Given the life that bears them together, the separate components of each of these sets might also be linked: history is often understood as providing a seemingly objective, institutionalized view that then circulates in public and professional realms, whereas memory is more often understood as springing from a subjective and private position, one linked to personal and familial arenas. Tracing recent changes in the conception of these phenomena, Pierre Nora argues, "Memory and history, far from being synonymous, appear now to be in fundamental opposition." He then details what positions them oppositionally: "Memory is by nature multiple and yet specific; collective, plural and yet individual. History, on the other hand, belongs to everyone and to no one, whence its claim to universal authority."[35] History thus appears to have the status of fact, whereas memory—due to its subjective and hence fallible nature—appears potentially aligned with fiction.[36] Considering, however, the claim that history itself "guards" memory, the movement between these oppositional domains becomes evident and even inevitable. At the same time, the fallibility of history, which often springs from its very institutionalization, suggests a further kinship with memory, as I sketch later. I would add, finally, that it might be her very consistent movement between these seeming oppositions that, for decades, displaced Guy-Blaché from broader accounts of film history. As she moves between public and private, professional and personal, factual and fictional realms, we haven't known quite where or how to place her.

As the image/word dichotomy might appear to be the most puzzling pair I have laid out here, I would like to turn to it now, as it does suggest a way to place her in film history and film historiography. Indeed, it forces us to ask what happens when we seek to recreate a history of a filmmaker, the majority of whose films have been lost. One way to begin this work, as this chapter shows, is through the recollection of images in and from written forms.[37] That is, with the loss and relative inaccessibility of her cinematic texts, I suggest that we read certain written works, such as memoirs, not only as historical texts, but also as cinematic ones. In part, we can see the written work as an extension of the author's cinematic production. To this end, I read the memoirs as "histories" but also through particular theories of film form. In producing this sort of reading I do not mean to argue that the two forms (written and cinematic) are interchangeable, nor that Guy-Blaché's memoirs in particular are unreliable; rather, I suggest that seeing a provocative convergence of these forms can not only reveal insights into the history of the figures but can also suggest a renewed interest in the relation between writing and filmmaking. Finally, as these issues relate to the loss of images and the production of words, we can also see Guy-Blaché's memoir writing as one authorial mode that seeks to recover another form of authorship.

## SETTING MEMORY IN MOTION

Marcel Proust famously describes the recollection of memory and history, here imagining the nobility and circulation of memory:

> But for all that I now knew that I was not in any of the houses of which the ignorance of the waking moment had, in a flash, if not presented me with a distinct picture, at least persuaded me of the possible presence, my

memory had been set in motion; as a rule I did not attempt to go to sleep again at once, but used to spend the greater part of the night recalling our life in the old days at Combray with my great-aunt, at Balbec, Paris, Doncières, Venice, and the rest; remembering again all the places and people I had known, what I had actually seen of them, and what others had told me.[38]

Because it is the source that inaugurated the re-collection of Guy-Blaché's history, I focus my subsequent examination on her memoirs, which are clearly an attempt to reconstruct her history through the author's own recollective processes. The text generally follows a chronological line, if an incomplete, or at least interrupted, one. As the memoirs narrate, she was born in France in 1873, raised briefly in Chile, and returned to France as a young girl for schooling. When her father lost his publishing business in Chile, he moved with the rest of his family back to France and died soon after. With the death of her brother and the marriages of her sisters, Alice became the primary support for herself and her mother. She took stenography lessons (unusual for a woman at that time) and found a job with Léon Gaumont. When Gaumont began producing films to market with his burgeoning camera production, Guy asked permission to try to make some films as well; soon she became the sole director for the House of Gaumont. There she experimented with a variety of genres and techniques, including the chronophone (an early mechanism to produce sound films).

In 1907 she married Herbert Blaché, an agent for Gaumont, and moved to the United States. Blaché helped to set up Gaumont's American business; Guy-Blaché initially assisted him with his work, gave birth to their first child (Simone), and then began a studio of her own, the Solax Company. She had her second child around the same time that she moved Solax from Long Island to Fort Lee, New Jersey. She supervised hundreds of films for Solax, but the company was dissolved in early 1914. She then went on to work for her husband's new company, Blaché Features, as a director and his assistant. Not long after Blaché ran off to Hollywood with one of his stars, Guy-Blaché followed him in an attempt to repair their marriage. Although she made a number of films for other companies, she suffered great financial loss during this period. After the clear failure of her marriage, she returned to France with her children, where she unsuccessfully sought work in the film industry. She toiled to restore her reputation in film history; she could not retrieve any of her lost films during her lifetime, but she was awarded the Legion of Honor in 1955. Having traveled with her daughter throughout the latter's diplomatic career, mother and daughter retired to the United States, where Guy-Blaché was also reunited with her son's family. She died in 1968.

Even though we see this image of Guy-Blaché's life, the memoirs seem incomplete; moreover, the often tangential stories the author tells create interruptions in the chronological detailing of her life. In this sense, the text seems to exemplify Walter Benjamin's definition of an (anti-)autobiography; that is, the memoirs are not an autobiography but a series of reminiscences. In relation to his brief memoirs, "A Berlin Chronicle," Benjamin writes, "Reminiscences, even extensive ones, do not always amount to an autobiography. . . . For autobiography has to do with time, with sequence and what makes up the continuous flow of life. Here, I am talking of a space, of moments and discontinuities. For even if months and years appear here, it is in the form they have at the moment of recollection. This strange form—it may be called fleeting or eternal—is in neither case the stuff that life is made of."[39]

Roughly ordered in a chronological sequence, Guy-Blaché's *Memoirs* are in fact made up of such "moments and discontinuities": throughout the work, one brief story or image begets another, often with seemingly little connection between them. A short text, it includes a series of sketches whose individual length, in a sense, resembles many of her early short films. The sketches tell stories about her life: her upbringing, her entry into film production, her marriage, her move to the United States, and, finally, her relative disappearance from historical records.

The stories Guy-Blaché tells are, obviously, narratives of her own *history* and the larger history that shaped her. Although many historians did not have access to the actual volume, *The Memoirs* managed to set the scene for much of the historical work on Guy-Blaché done in the 1970s and 1980s, as those works draw from Guy-Blaché's words (whether in the form of her memoirs, extracts from that text, or interviews with her).[40] On the other hand, the filmmaker's memoirs set a rather different scene for texts like Lepage's *The Lost Garden*: whereas the memoirs *utilize* memory to produce a history, the film's structure—and the history it produces—greatly *resembles* processes of memory.⁴¹ Decrying what he sees as the newly emerging distinction between history and memory and the subsumption of one into the other, Pierra Nora proclaims, "History is perpetually suspicious of memory, and its true mission is to suppress and destroy it."⁴² In the case of Guy-Blaché's memoirs (as well as many texts about her), it seems that memory is instead suspicious of history.

Because they did not include her, Guy-Blaché did not recognize the histories of the period in which she worked as completely true; hence, she attempted to reconstruct, or transform, those histories through her memories. Nora sees this sort of activity as a necessary process. Further examining phenomenological trends in the transformation of both history and memory, he claims, "The passage from memory to history has required every social group to redefine its identity through the revitalization of its own history. The task of remembering makes everyone his own historian."⁴³ This suggestion might seem a bit hyperbolic, but Nora nicely stages the relationship between history and memory that is made (and indeed reconnected) in memoirs like those of Guy-Blaché. The primary task of memoirs is often precisely to connect (or reconnect) history and memory via personal narrative. As Mark Freeman points out in consideration of the truth that autobiographies can tell, "The reality of living in time requires narrative reflection and that narrative reflection, in turn, opens the way toward a more comprehensive and expansive conception of truth itself."⁴⁴ Although "truth" is often the purview of history rather than the more commonly fallible memory, we might see how changing notions of what constitutes history, or histories, changes our notions of the truth as well. Indeed, the inevitable narrativization of memory in turn forms narratives of history. So, considering memoirs—those narrativizations of memory and memories—as *histories* allows us to understand, or know, history, and the truths and nontruths that it produces, through a different lens.

The memoir and the autobiography thus constitute a sort of pivot between memory, history, and truth. Through the narrative process, they reveal the workings of the author's memory and tell an important history. Arguing against a conflation of memory and history (as I likewise would), Jacques LeGoff acknowledges, "Memory is the raw material of history. Whether mental, oral, or written, it is the living source from which historians draw. . . . Moreover, the discipline of history nourishes memory in turn, and enters into the great dialectical process of memory and forgetting experienced by individuals and societies. The historian must be there to render an account of these memories and of what is forgotten, to transform them into something that can be conceived, to make them knowable."[45]

Although LeGoff cautions against privileging memory over history, his remarks comment usefully on Guy-Blaché's project. Guy-Blaché would not entirely appear to be the objective historian that LeGoff insists on, yet she also acts as the historian he describes. Indeed, we must recognize her role as a remembering historian: her memoirs are an account of (her own) memories, which had otherwise been forgotten, and she attempts to render them into a history that might be known. As "the raw material" of her own history—and that of early cinematic production—her memories are turned into a narrative that clearly displays the dialectical relationship between history and memory in the production of knowledge.

In her memoirs, Lillian Gish directly remarks on this relationship among history, memory, and truth. In a sense, her claims offer both a commentary on and counter to Guy-Blaché's circumstances: "[D. W. Griffith's] claim that history books falsified actual happenings struck me as most peculiar. At that time I was too naive to think that history books would attempt to falsify anything. I've lived long enough now to know that the whole truth is never told in history texts. Only the people who lived through an era, who are the real participants in the drama as it occurs, know the truth. The people of each generation, it seems to me, are the most accurate historians of their time."[46] Certainly I do not wholeheartedly agree with her assessment; though a very strategic point to make in an autobiography, her privileging of *autobiographical* history belies, as Shari Benstock, Paul Eakin, and others would point out, the also synchronous fictional nature of autobiographies. Yet the *relationship* between history, memory, and even autobiography that she proposes here—that is, that autobiographical accounts sown from memory might correct historical ones—is an important one to make, especially in the case of those autobiographical subjects who have been silenced, marginalized, or otherwise misrepresented in official histories. Indeed, LeGoff insists that we be careful in how we privilege memories and histories: "Memory, on which history draws and which it nourishes in return, seeks to save the past in order to serve the present and the future. Let us act in such a way that collective memory may serve the liberation and not the enslavement of human beings."[47]

The context of Gish's statement directs us to the inherent problems with granting certain memories and not others the status of historical truth. Quite simply, she is making a case for historical truth in regard to early film pioneer D. W. Griffith. As is well documented, Griffith utilized his familial "memories' to produce an extremely racist depiction of "history" in *Birth of a Nation*.[48] The narration of his familial memories, and then American history as the logical offshoot of these memories, attempts to erase or legitimate the injustices produced by the American institutions of racism and slavery (not to mention cinema). Guy-Blaché, on the other hand, depends on her memories to illustrate (albeit, often indirectly) how institutionalized sexism has erased, or marginalized, her position in history; the writing of a new history through her memories is an attempt to make herself and her labor as a filmmaker visible and known.

These two very different cases thus point to the fact that arguments about truth are always political, ideological, and historical; because of the embedded and very complicated nature of these arguments, it is difficult to make a general case about the truth-value of memoirs overall in the writing, or rewriting, of histories. Although we must consider the potential veracity (or lack thereof) of these historical or remembered truths, I investigate *how* a history is constructed through memories and what various truths its facets of construction tell. Benjamin explains, "I am not concerned with what is installed in the chamber [of memory] at its enigmatic center . . . but all the more with the many entrances leading into the interior."[49] Furthermore, I am interested in the way the many entrances of memory shape the enigmatic center of history.

## TECHNOLOGIES OF MEMORY AND FILM

For Guy-Blaché, one of those entrances unsurprisingly lies at the entrance to the memoir itself. Indeed, in spite (or possibly because) of the evident recognition of being silenced or marginalized in history, Guy-Blaché's memoirs possess a rather humble beginning: "In an era in which 'retrospectives' are fashionable, perhaps the souvenirs of the eldest of women film directors may find some favor with the public. I have no pretense to making a work of literature, but simply to amuse, to interest the reader by anecdotes and personal memories concerning their great friend the cinema, at whose birth I assisted."[50]

This statement is significantly modest on a number of levels, and as such it opens up a number of important questions. First, the metaphor that Guy-Blaché invokes asserts that she did not labor as the mother of the cinema but rather as an assistant: a doctor, perhaps, or a nurse or midwife.[51] Interestingly, these same metaphors—concerning the "birth" of the cinema as well as the "assistant" to its birth—circulate in other important writings on film, but perhaps most peculiarly in Christian Metz's *Imaginary Signifier*.[52] His particular invocation of the metaphors of birth and midwife have a provocative bearing on both Guy-Blaché's wielding of the terms and her position in film studies.

In "Story/Discourse: A Note on Two Kinds of Voyeurism," Metz writes: "I'm at the cinema. I am present at the screening of the film. *I am present*. Like the midwife attending a birth who, simply by her presence, assists the woman in labour, I am present for the film in a double capacity (though they are really one and the same) as witness and as assistant: I watch, and I help. By watching the film I help it to be born, I help it to live, since only in me will it live, and since it is made for that purpose: to be watched, in other words to be brought into being by nothing other than the look."[53]

His misunderstanding of the labor of a midwife notwithstanding, the "double capacity" Metz describes here—which goes beyond the singular one Guy-Blaché takes for herself—is important to note, especially because he genders both the originator of film and the subsequent spectators of film as female. In so doing, he also takes up the position of "woman" himself.[54] While Guy-Blaché refuses the position of birth mother of film itself and takes only the position as assistant and witness, the double capacity Metz describes might instead characterize Guy-Blaché's role as historian. Telling the story of her labor as a filmmaker, Guy-Blaché is at once a creator of and a witness to history. Taking a cue from Metz, we might see subsequent historians and theorists—a special brand of film spectators—also as witnesses. Most, though, as Guy-Blaché suggests, and as film history has until recently borne out, have *mis*recognized her work in the history of film production. In her memoirs, however modestly, she thus produces a new image, or story, that readers themselves can also bring into being.

Oddly, though, in so doing, she also denies her labor as a writer, for she refuses the position of a "great" author; rather, she will "simply... amuse" her readers ("if I have any," she even notes later). As she claims in the prologue, the memoirs are only an "anecdotal history."[55] Designating the memoirs as souvenirs, moreover, also trivializes the work, for souvenirs are often considered to be mere trinkets. But more specifically, as its French origins tell us, a souvenir is an object to help one remember. Often, a souvenir is a reminder of travel through time and space—a tiny reproduction of the Eiffel Tower, a foreign coin, a sand dollar found on the beach, a movie ticket stub. Souvenirs take us on a path of remembering also made possible by film. Such travel is like that plotted for Guy-Blaché in *The Lost Garden*, but it also characterizes, of course, the movement and form of cinema in general. Hence, even as Guy-Blaché attempts to humbly trivialize her work, her language inevitably connects—and makes visible—her authorship as a writer (an autobiographer, a historian) and a filmmaker.

Both this modest posture and a tension around the author's visibility are fairly typical in nineteenth-century traditions of women's writings, from which Guy-Blaché's work in part springs.[56] In *Private Woman, Public Stage: Literary Domesticity in Nineteenth-Century America*, Mary Kelley sketches how attempts to separate the private from the public sphere created a complicated situation for nineteenth-century women writers. Describing the scene that necessitated female authors' humble poses, Kelley writes, "Unlike a male, a female's person was to be shielded from public scrutiny. Neither her ego nor her intellect was cultivated for future public vocation. After all, her proper sphere was the home. She was to stand in the background, out of the way. Even her exercise of moral, social, or personal influence was to be indirect, subtle, and symbolic. Her voice was to be soft, subdued, and soothing. In essence, hers was to remain an invisible presence."[57] One way to remain invisible, even as they were becoming published writers, Kelley documents, was for women to remain "secret writers," anonymous authors. Though not so invisible (at least in the sense Kelley invokes), the voice that opens Guy-Blaché's memoirs is just such a "soft, subdued, and soothing" one, unlikely to insist on her importance in the public field of history.

Continuing to draw on metaphors of visibility and the visual, Kelley acknowledges that even attempts at secrecy or anonymity could not hide women's entrance into the public sphere. As she notes, entering the public realm "suggested a new assertion of a woman's being, for, simply stated, to be a published writer was to have a visible influence, a public role beyond the home. It was to leave woman's private domestic sphere for man's, to meddle in the public affairs of men." Clearly, such women were in a paradoxical position: they resisted the denial of their activity in the public sphere by entering the literary marketplace, but they often did so in secret, via anonymity or even in disguise as men. In fact, these acts of secrecy, paradoxically, unveiled the women's complicated and contradictory social positions: "And it was ironic that to be a secret writer was also to announce that resistance, to call attention to it. To screen themselves, their being, in public, was inadvertently to dramatize in public the private subjugation of their lives."[58] Judith Fetterley also recognizes these inherent contradictions. In fact, she underscores how women writers themselves directly played with these contradictions. Contrary to Ann Douglas's claims that the tone adapted by nineteenth-century writers was one of "authorial innocence," Fetterley asserts that many women writers were "in conscious tension with the posture of 'innocence.'"[59] Surely aware of the complexities involved in being the first *woman* filmmaker, Guy-Blaché displays in her memoirs a similar "conscious tension" with "authorial innocence." Thus, as the memoirs move forward, Guy-Blaché subverts the image she paints early on, that the memoirs are purely "anecdotal," written only for her readers' amusement.

Kelley's metaphors might direct us to the complex layers of Guy-Blaché's (visible) authorship. First, as I noted earlier, we can see Guy-Blaché as an author in a dual sense: she is both a filmmaker and a writer. The issues of visibility and invisibility that Kelley raises certainly have bearing on both roles. As a director, Guy-Blaché was in some ways an "invisible" presence, for she almost always worked behind the scenes. At the same time, because she directed and produced these constructions of images, she was clearly not invisible in the sense Kelley describes. (As the trade journals of the day document, she was a fairly well-known personage in the filmmaking community.) In fact, Guy-Blaché's rather prominent position in an evolving technological industry producing the newly emerging visual culture might influence and alter the ways we know, or *see*, her in film history. Furthermore, the history she authored in her older age was precisely that of her authorship as a filmmaker. In other words, her literary authorship was an attempt by her to return to visibility after her film authorship had been made invisible. Her work in film production thus highlights the very particular and complex tension between visibility and invisibility that she experienced and that she describes, in part, through a guise of innocent modesty.

Indeed, after their humble beginning, her memoirs attempt to illuminate not only her visible influence on and in film history but, more specifically, her influence on the visible: the world of cinematic production. We might thus consider another definition of "screening" oneself than that which Kelley offers. Surely a screen does not just hide what is behind it; it also acts, as does a movie screen, to unveil images before it. Whereas nineteenth-century women writers had to screen themselves *from* the public, after her initial modesty (which is only a screen anyway — and an ephemeral one at that), Guy-Blaché tries to screen her history *in* public. That is, she tries to make it visible rather than hide it. Given her work as a filmmaker, this attempt to make her history visible is even more significant. In his discussion of the relations between images and language in the reconstruction of histories, Stephen Bann sees how the forms meet through narrative. "Even if [images] succeed in representing ('placing before us') what 'language is deficient in describing,'" he writes, "they are still dependent on the narrative effect which language, and language alone, is qualified to achieve." The images he considers, therefore, "can be rescued from Time only by being inserted into a discourse which mimes the process of chronological sequence. They can be rescued by Time only by narration."[60]

Without recourse to her films, Guy-Blaché must depend on narration. This is a narration that is at once dependent on the form of her films as well as on countering the telling of the history in which she worked. Thus, her modesty is indeed undermined throughout the book by her repeated insistence on her presence in film history: many of the "anecdotes and personal memories" she offers illustrate her important role in history making. Even as she later claims, "I make no pretense to undertake the history of cinema in the United States. I confine myself to reporting what I have seen and heard," what she did see and hear was highly significant, especially because what she "saw" defined precisely her role as film author. Moreover, she was not only an onlooker or eavesdropper to cinematic inventions in the United States and France. She tells of her participation in the discovery of filmic "tricks" such as double exposures, fade-outs, the turning of films in reverse, and of her use of "science" to produce effects of realism.[61] She also asserts that she imported this same sort of technical and cinematic invention to her films made in the United States, where, she claims, she received "critical praise" for such ingenuity.[62] The most significant study of Guy-Blaché to date follows a similar line of historical reasoning. In *Alice Guy Blaché: Lost Visionary of the Cinema*, Alison McMahan sets the history of Guy-Blaché in a triple context: her film production, the legends about the filmmaker, and pivotal moments and achievements in film history. She thus binds Guy-Blaché to the very history from which she was displaced, in effect telling the history of film through this filmmaker.

Along with these declarations concerning the specifics of her technical work, Guy-Blaché records how she fought for her position at Gaumont: "I had been left to work out alone the difficulties at the beginning, to break new ground, but when the affair became interesting, *doubtless lucrative*, my directorship was bitterly disputed. However, I was combative and thanks to president [Gustave] Eiffel, who always encouraged me with kindness, the whole Board of Directors, recognizing my efforts, decided to leave me at the head of the service."[63]

Guy-Blaché's "combative" battle for her position at Gaumont in one sense parallels her battle for recognition in film history. In fact, she refers directly to her attempts to retrieve her position in film history throughout the volume. For instance, she notes her contact with French historian Georges Sadoul over her relative absence in his work on French film history: "Sadoul . . . who, misled, and doubtless in all good faith (he says himself that he is ignorant of that epoch and speaks only from hearsay), has attributed my first films to people who probably worked for the Gaumont studios only as actors, whose names I don't even know." She emphasizes that, after meeting with her and seeing documents to prove that "the films in question" were her work, Sadoul agreed to make some changes to his text, though "his numbering still contains errors."[64] In the final chapter of her memoirs, Guy-Blaché points out that for many decades her work was not even

*the historian* 93

recorded in Gaumont's own company history. From what she says, she attempted to rectify this mistake early on, but Léon Gaumont died before he made the proper corrections to the history.

Thus, Guy-Blaché's initial modesty, and her tone throughout the book (which seems to derive from a refusal to assign culpability to particular persons), camouflages her attempt to intervene in a history which had, at the time, excluded her. But of course, this intervention is still apparent, clearly countering her initial claims that the memoirs are meant "simply to amuse."[65] We see the seriousness of her venture not only in the passages in which she explicitly takes credit for discovering or utilizing certain cinematic inventions or in those in which she engages with the histories that excluded her. In fact, we see the sincerity of her critical project even in the "anecdotes" she tells. Many of these anecdotes, which one would hardly call "amusing," might serve to comment both on the recording of Guy-Blaché's history and on the impact of reading memoirs themselves as a form of history. In part, they do so by revealing themselves as "screen memories."

In Freud's essay "Screen Memories"—a work that the editor James Strachey notes is thinly disguised autobiographical material—Freud maps out the workings of memory through his own self-analysis. That is, he includes a dialogue between patient and doctor, yet he is really in each role himself. He creates this discussion between his two divided selves to discover what is fictional and what is real about a particular remembered experience. His divided selves in effect enact the process of understanding a screen memory: because a screen memory is an "amalgamation" of two different phantasies (or, possibly, one "real" memory and one fictional one), it must be divided to be fully understood. In initially describing the memory in question, he thus tells himself, "You projected the two phantasies on to one another and made a childhood memory of them. . . . I can assure you that people often construct such things unconsciously—almost like works of fiction."[66] Attempting to explain what is nonetheless "genuine" about those fantasies, he goes on to define "screen memory":

> There is in general no guarantee of the data produced by our memory. But I am ready to agree with you that the scene is genuine. If so, you selected it from innumerable others of a similar or another kind because, on account of its content (which in itself was indifferent) it was well adapted to represent the two phantasies, which were important enough

to you. A recollection of this kind, whose value lies in the fact that it represents in the memory impression and thoughts of a later date whose content is connected with its own by symbolic or similar links, may appropriately be called a *"screen memory."*[67]

Thus, as he says later, the screen memory is "one which owes its value as a memory not to its own content but to the relation existing between that content and some other, that has been suppressed."[68] As he implies in these definitions and states directly elsewhere in this essay (as well as in other works, including "A Disturbance of Memory on the Acropolis," a somewhat similar autobiographical sketch), Freud understands the workings of memory to be inherently transformative. In remembering, we may construct a "remembered" experience that is in part fictional, but memories also reveal — if not an actual experience — our ideas of an experience.[69]

Considering the concept of the screen memory, like those visual metaphors that Kelley uses, can again highlight the fact that Guy-Blaché's memories were, of course, of her work around the movie screen. Many of the stories in the volume are thus screen memories in this double sense: they both hide and reveal an aspect of her history, and they narrate stories of the cinema. Yet the concept of the screen memory is not merely useful for its metaphorical possibilities for film historians and theorists. It also allows us to ponder how we might utilize memoirs in the production of history, for it at once admits to the fallibility of memory and asserts memory's *reliability*, often through its very complicated form. As a project of historical recovery, or what Gilmore might term "re-membering," many of Guy-Blaché's anecdotes and claims function as possible "screen memories"; that is, the director's genuine assertion that her place in film history was revoked seems to be projected on to stories of her film work throughout the text. It is impossible to prove the veracity of some of these claims or stories, but their inclusion is telling. For instance, at the end of the volume, when Guy-Blaché describes the final straw that led her to leave the United States and return to France, she comments, "America, they say, always takes back everything she gives you." And she ends the work with a recollection of a remark by Roosevelt: "It is hard to have failed, it is worse to have never tried."[70] These remarks serve to grant the autobiography a certain tone, both melancholic and angry, that we can see projected onto recollections of earlier times.

This melancholic and angry tone is even more prominently projected in an apocalyptic story of the cinema—that is, an apocalyptic screen memory—that she tells early in the memoirs. At the end of chapter 2, which precedes the chapter in which she recalls her entrance into filmmaking and the "birth" of her first film, she recounts an early "disaster begun by the cinema" in which many people, including most members of an acquaintance's family (the Dillayes), were killed in a fire presumably started in a projection booth. She ends this chapter thus: "Seventeen persons in this family which had never known sorrow perished in that terrible catastrophe.... Also, a year later, the eldest daughter of Dillaye, who had been separated from her mother, died of a kind of consumption. Dillaye had to wait long before he could return to his usual occupations."[71]

Aside from the memory of this family's tragedy, what other narratives does this story tell? For one, it seems possible that in recounting a catastrophic story of the cinema, Guy-Blaché foreshadows the way her image will be extinguished from the cinematic record. To borrow a cliché, for Guy-Blaché, work in the film industry was both a blessing and a curse: she loved the labor but rightfully despised the fact that her work and her memory seemed lost to film history. As a literal and figurative screen memory, this recollection appears to foretell Guy-Blaché's (metaphorical) death in the discourse of film history. Moreover, it tells of two kinds of separations: the separation, or loss, that family members endured (and that the daughter in part died from) and the father's separation from his family and his career. This sort of story—devastating in its vision of work, family, history, and the loss thereof—seems to play out in various histories of Guy-Blaché.

Other seemingly disparate stories that Guy-Blaché tells might bear even clearer associations in their close proximity to each other. That is, the "moments and discontinuities" that make up the memoirs might be woven together in suggestive ways. For, in *The Memoirs*, Guy-Blaché offers a series of reminiscences that, read in relation to one another, offer enlightening angles from which to view certain connections between her work, her personal life, and her place in film history. Such connections are precisely what define screen memories, whose value lies not in their own content but, as Freud states, in "the relations existing between that content and some other, that has been suppressed." Other theorists also suggest that memory both is structured and creates meaning through links between images or ideas.

An especially provocative series of linked images and ideas appears in chapter 7 of the memoirs, where Guy-Blaché tells a number of stories about her research into various social institutions to provide effects of realism in her films. She follows these sketches with information about changes in the control of Solax, a brief mention of actress and director Lois Weber, a short story about the discovery of the North Pole, and other tales of early film production. The content of each of these stories is interesting in itself, but the meaning becomes even more interesting when we read the stories in terms of one another.

Guy-Blaché declares at the end of chapter 6, "The trade of the cinematographer is not always a happy one. Concern for the truth obliges one to see and document sources which are sometimes tragic." Chapter 7 bears out this observation, beginning with the detailing of a number of visits Guy-Blaché took for film research: to an orphans' asylum, a "hospital for the incurable," a "madhouse," a Night Court session, and a prison. Most of the stories expose broken and divided families, and some imply culpability on the part of men. For instance, at the Night Court session, Guy-Blaché witnessed a fourteen-year-old girl, with no family or friends, found guilty of prostitution. After the girl was sentenced to a reformatory, Guy-Blaché reports, "A jailer came to take her; she followed quietly. Someone beside me murmured, 'What about the men?'" Next she recounts the case of a young mother sentenced to six months of detention because she was "afflicted with an acute case of venereal disease": "When her baby was taken from her arms, she cried out piercingly 'Leave me my baby, I beg you. Leave me my baby.'"[72] The next brief tale concerns a "poor idiot," a man incarcerated in Sing Sing for attempting to "kiss a woman against her will." Although Guy-Blaché does not seem unsympathetic to this man's plight, her sympathies, as registered in part by comments she attributes to others, primarily lie with the women's experiences. These short narratives clearly reflect her recognition of women's disadvantaged social position in public and private spaces. And all of the (unamusing) anecdotes document and bemoan the plights of broken families; such a point of view is consistent with the rest of the memoirs, though it remains relatively tacit in relation to her own family and marriage.

However, the next two sketches are quite telling. The first concerns Guy-Blaché's visit to a prison, culminating in her stop at the electric chair: "The director was so kind as to invite me to sit in it. I did so.

They put the manacles on me and the director said 'now, there is nothing to do but make contact. . . .' I asked if death were instantaneous. 'Around eleven seconds,' he answered, 'some resist longer.' He even invited me to attend an execution which would take place the next day. I refused. I have kept a photograph which I never see without a shudder."[73]

Immediately following this story is Guy-Blaché's recounting of significant changes at Solax and then her mention of Lois Weber's work. I reproduce both short passages in full here:

> My husband, having finished his contract with Gaumont, had taken the presidency of Solax. I abandoned the reins to him with pleasure. I never attended any of the conferences where the Sales Co. composed the programs; I would have embarrassed the men, said Herbert, who wanted to smoke their cigars and to spit at their ease while discussing business.[74]

> Herbert Blaché had directed, in the little Gaumont studio at Fort Lee, a singer named Lois Weber who recorded several songs for the chronophone. She had watched me direct the first little films and doubtless thought it was not difficult. She got a directing job and certain Americans pretend that she was the first woman director. My first film, of which I speak in the first part of these memoirs, dated from 1896.[75]

Next she describes an "imposter" who attempted to take credit for the discovery of the North Pole. After he filmed a recreation of the adventure, "America swallowed it," she contends, until "Peary arrived in his turn and took the crown" (79). The sequence of these tales, and the relations inevitably intimated between them, is really rather astounding.

We might better understand these relations through philosophies of memory and film, particularly as the two phenomena structure Guy-Blaché's history in many ways. Indeed, as Sigmund Freud, Walter Benjamin, Frances Yates, Henri Bergson, and others have shown, memory flows through associations between images and ideas. For Benjamin, for instance, memory might be imagined as the streets of Berlin, so that one path leads to another; to Yates, the "art" of memory also has a spatial quality, for in remembering we might move from one image to the next as from one room of a house to another.[76] Bergson offers a different sort of spatial metaphor to explain the workings of memory, as he imagines it operating as a series of electrical currents. Offering an image of embedded circles to illustrate the relation between memory and perception, Bergson writes:

> We maintain, on the contrary, that reflective perception is a *circuit*, in which all the elements, including the perceived object itself, hold each other in a mutual state of tension as in an electrical circuit. . . . It is the whole of memory, as we shall see, that passes over into each of these circuits, since memory is always present; but that memory, capable, by reason of its elasticity, of expanding more and more, reflects upon the object a growing number of suggested images—sometimes the details of the object itself, sometimes concomitant details which may throw light upon it.[77]

Focusing on the embedded relationship between these circles and hence the way memory "expands," Bergson's description here is quite like Benjamin's contention that acts of memory produce "endless interpolations into what has been." Moreover, understanding memory as a kind of electrical current, Bergson illustrates how memory itself might forge connections between images and ideas.

Film form inevitably shapes such links as well. Indeed, connected by Guy-Blaché's acts of remembering, each story has the effect of an afterimage on that which follows it, so that it is difficult to read the recollections in isolation from one another. Stressing that the mind itself creates an afterimage, Hugo Münsterberg discusses how precinematic games and devices help to provoke visually and mentally the semblance of depth and movement. The "positive afterimage," he says, is "a real continuation of the first impression" in the second. Such continuity is produced, for instance, by the thaumatrope, a nineteenth-century optical device that rapidly spins a two-sided card to merge the images on each side. Notes Münsterberg, "As soon as the card is quickly revolved about a central axis, the two pictures fuse into one. If a horse is on one side and a rider on the other, or a cage is on one and a bird on the other, we see the rider on the horse and the bird in the cage."[78] In part, what allows us to fuse the images is the "circuitry" of memory itself.

Certainly such contraptions as the thaumatrope and the later zootrope presaged the invention of film. A more complex fusion takes place through cinematic montage, the welding together of images on film. For theorists like Sergei Eisenstein, montage defines the

*the historian* 99

aesthetic, intellectual, and even political possibilities of film form: "Montage is an idea that arises from the collision of independent shots—shots even opposite to one another."[79] The collision of two shots (or, in some cases, two images within a shot) creates a new idea. According to Eisenstein, montage can have a physiological, emotional, or intellectual aim. (Of the three, he privileges the intellectual, for he believes it can lead to political change.) Through montage—and through the intellectual response of the spectator to the montage—film form can stimulate relations and associations between images and ideas.

Laid out next to each other on the page, Guy-Blaché's reminiscences suggest such a spatial and cinematic, as well as an intellectual or associative, relation to one another, so that one echoes in the next, and the next after that. Hence, we might see how the description of sitting in the electric chair resonates—as an electrical current, like memory itself—in the filmmaker's comment that she "abandoned the reins" of Solax to her husband "with pleasure."[80] Indeed, through the collision of these two notions is born the suggestion that not only did Guy-Blaché lose control of her company, but she also lost control of her place in history. The image of the electric chair, along with her husband's insistence that she would "embarrass the men" at business meetings, also resounds in her mention of Lois Weber, who, as she claims here, received her start through Herbert Blaché. She thus emphasizes how the recognition of another woman's work has displaced the recognition of her role as the first woman filmmaker in history. Moreover, following the mention of Weber with the story of the imposter who tried to credit himself with the discovery of the North Pole (through a cinematic reenactment of the event!) is also a significant rhetorical gesture. For Guy-Blaché, Weber is like an "imposter" who attempted to take her own rightful position. At least, history has been reconstructed, much like many early actualities that merely "reenacted" historical events, to put Weber in Guy-Blaché's place. These memoirs, then, represent Guy-Blaché's attempt, not unlike that of Peary, to "take the crown" for her achievements.

Similar to her early modest proclamation that her memoirs are merely an attempt to amuse her readers, Guy-Blaché here performs a certain humility: at least, she does not directly make claims of culpability regarding the end of her career. But also like the early proclamation, the modesty inherent in this indirect approach is belied in the connections that readers themselves might make between colliding anecdotes, this montage of memories. Like an afterimage produced by optical devices or the more complicated process of cinematic form, the flow of memory, narrative, and even of thought demands forging at least some links between the stories she tells. It seems, too, that although the above passages are not cited in any historical works on Guy-Blaché, their tenor resounds in works that emphasize her loss (one might even say "death") from history and that also blame her husband, directly or indirectly, for the end of her career.[81] Thus, the memoirs, undoubtedly and inevitably structured in great part as memory itself is structured, influence subsequent written and filmic histories of Guy-Blaché in myriad ways: in their form, their tenor, and their recollection of her history.

### STRANGE FICTIONS

Both memory and autobiography, a genre essentially based on the telling of memories, manifest rather precarious relations between fact and fiction. One defining characteristic of screen memories, for Freud, is that they are constructed "almost like works of fiction." In more general parlance, memory is frequently defined as elusive; part of its elusive nature is the often impossible task of determining its truth. Yet critics of autobiography also focus on the genre's association with fact, or truth, as well as fiction. As Leigh Gilmore suggests, "Authority in autobiography springs from its proximity to the truth claim of the confession, a discourse that insists upon the possibility of telling the whole truth while paradoxically frustrating that goal through the structural demands placed on how one confesses."[82] A complex relationship between fact and fiction thus defines memory and autobiography; because of this condition, it is nearly impossible to unravel the intertwining of these elements. Surely the examples from Guy-Blaché's memoirs illustrate a very complicated knot of such discursive parts, and they are especially provocative in light of the field they illuminate: the history of the production of visual images. I would, then, like to conclude with a final example that is indeed a "fictional" one, but that also comments on the inextricability of seemingly opposing categories—whether public and private, history and memory, or fact and fiction—in regard to Guy-Blaché's life and history.

In an early 1912 issue of the *Moving Picture World*, fictional film narrative and the story of Guy-Blaché's life and work literally come together. In a section entitled "Manufacturer's Advance Notes" is a parody of a film summary.[83] Called "A Solax Celebration," this parody tells the tale of a New Year's party at Solax. Listed as featured players in this drama are Madame Alice Blaché as "The Cause" and Herbert Blaché as "A Relative—but an outsider." The "Synopsis" is as follows:

> The good people living in the Solax community, realizing that they have cause to make merry and celebrate before the advent of a New Year, because the Almighty had been so fortunate as to guide their bread-winning footsteps in the direction of the happy atmosphere of the Solax Studio, banked together, like the big happy family which they are, and gave expression to their happiness in the form of a gift to the immediate cause of their good fortune and sunshine.... The plot is not a thick one, but the execution progresses smoothly and with "spirit." The events took the leading figure entirely by surprise, and her emotion and her gratitude brought forth a lump in her throat.[84]

The first two scenes describe the party, but the third, entitled "Jealousy," does indicate a certain "thickness" of the plot. It is narrated as follows: "A near relative to The Cause [Herbert Blaché] and a neighbor to us all was jealous of the aforesaid tribute paid to his kin, so, in order that he may not be outshone in hospitality, invited the mob to invade the sanctified quarters of the Gaumont Company, where he showed some wonderful Gaumont productions."[85] Though this parody hints at the way Herbert Blaché attempted to displace his wife within the production of film narratives and film history, parceling out what is historically accurate and what is fabricated about this story is an impossible task.

This example offers a movement between fact and fiction that enables us to read each in a different light: the plot summary reveals both the sometimes fictional character of history and truthful nature of fiction.[86] This sort of intertwining is similar to what Lee Grieveson deems a "hybridity of textual logics" activated in other early cinematic narratives, particularly fiction films which include shots that recall earlier actualities. Concerning moments in *Traffic in Souls* (IMP/Universal, 1913) in which immigrants arrive at Ellis Island, Grieveson explains, "Here the fictional and the real stand momentarily side by side in a literal enactment of the more general enmeshing of fact and fiction in early cinema."[87] Though set somewhat differently—particularly by incorporating trade journal discourse as perhaps innately between fact and fiction—the narrative about "A Solax Celebration" clearly exhibits a hybridity of textual logics already in place in American cinema. In the case of "A Solax Celebration," a seemingly factual event masquerades as fiction; at least, one narrative masquerades as another. This type of guise, which seems consistent with the narratives of many of Guy-Blaché's Solax films, brings together a number of elements concerning histories of Guy-Blaché (including, of course, her own). First of all, the very opposition between fact and fiction is one that often informs thinking about the relationship between history and memory; the line between the former two is here blurred much like that between the latter coupling. As well, although "A Solax Celebration" entwines fact and fiction, it also clearly intermixes Guy-Blaché's public and private spheres. It indicates her independence from her husband and at the same time suggests tension, or at least competition, between the two. More important, the narrative points to Guy-Blaché's abilities to manage a business—yet a business in the form of a family. As such, it attests to her skills at moving between public and private spheres, professional and personal life.

Finally, because "A Solax Celebration" is a fiction of a fictional film in written—rather than purely visual—form, this example brings us back to yet another set of distinct categories, or media, that also form our understanding of Guy-Blaché. She was indeed a filmmaker and a writer. As a dual author, she produced both cinematic narratives and a written history. But, of course, these textual forms are forever conjoined. Most obviously, the memoirs link these media because, in written form, they tell the history of her authorship as a filmmaker. Additionally, the filmmaker's writings have provoked historians to seek out her films so that her place in history is further secured. Finally, the memoirs, with her films, have helped in the construction of a (cinematic) documentary about her life and work. In this sense, Guy-Blaché's work has come full circle, a route whose nonlinearity is inevitable when one's history is structured through acts of remembering.

## THE CRITIC

### *Louise Brooks, star witness*

The tragedy of film history is that it is fabricated, falsified, by the very people who make film history. It is understandable that in the early years of film production, when nobody believed there was going to be any film history, most film magazines and books printed trash, aimed only at fulfilling the public's wish to share a fairy-tale existence with its movie idols. But since about 1950 film has been established as an art, and its history recognized as a serious matter. Yet film celebrities continue to cast themselves as stock types—nice or naughty girls, good or bad boys—whom their chroniclers spray with a shower of anecdotes.—LOUISE BROOKS, *Lulu in Hollywood*

The myth of Pandora is about feminine curiosity but it can only be decoded by feminist curiosity, transforming and translating her iconography and attributes into the segments of a puzzle, riddle or enigma.—LAURA MULVEY, *Fetishism and Curiosity*

In "Star Treatment," episode twelve of Kevin Brownlow's and David Gill's thirteen-part *Hollywood* documentary series, silent screen star Louise Brooks is on hand (and on-screen) as an expert to testify about Clara Bow's life and work. Yet, unlike the other talking heads—such as Adela Rogers St. Johns, Cedric Belfrage, and Charles Buddy Rogers

—Brooks neither worked with Bow nor did she appear to know her well personally; in fact, from the film we learn that she only met her at a voice test for talking pictures. Still, she seems to be an expert on the subject, because, as James Mason narrates, she "experienced similar star treatment" to Bow's. Even so, Brooks is not merely a sympathetic fellow traveler when she discusses Bow, and in fact she does not mention her own experience at great length. What Brooks appears to be in this short segment—indeed, this is how she represents herself— is an astute critic of Bow's career and the very industry in which she worked. Such a role helps sketch her seemingly paradoxical position in film history: she is known both as an image, an object of the camera, and as a viewer of images, a critic and historian.

Brooks appears on-screen as an expert more often than any of the other interviewees in this segment. Her commentary not only adds to an understanding of Bow; it also offers some insight into Brooks's position in Hollywood and in film history. For instance, whereas the other interviewees offer mainly personal anecdotes about Bow, Brooks occasionally offers mini-lectures on Bow's work, including what made and unmade Bow's stardom. Over two clips from *It* (1927), for example, Brooks describes and comments on the scenes. In each case, she concentrates on Bow's own creative control: "Everything she did was completely original, and [Clarence Badger, director of *It*] said when you started to direct her, you got mad." The fact that "all those things were hers," says Brooks, "was what made her so marvelous." Brooks's interest in the star's creative control over her performance most likely stems from Brooks's own avowed origination of her image. Hence, she makes a fine witness to Bow's history because she herself experienced and, even more important, keenly observed her own making and unmaking as a star.

When Brooks does offer anecdotes herself, each of these tales situates her significantly and typically. For instance, she claims that when she asked her then-husband Eddie Sutherland to invite Bow to a party, he refused. This story serves as a simple piece of evidence concerning Bow's lack of acceptance in Hollywood, but it also allows Brooks to enjoy a position above the rest of the Hollywood set that wouldn't accept Bow. Similarly, when she describes meeting Bow at a voice test ("She knew all about me," swears Brooks), she claims that Bow's Brooklyn accent was not so bad after all. Certainly the documentary grants Brooks this position of expert; in part, it does so through showing the similarities between Brooks and Bow. Hence, Brooks's story about the voice test is introduced by narrator James Mason as follows: "Louise Brooks, also having problems at Paramount, was ordered to join her for a voice test." These facts, and Brooks's various comments about them, prove her to be an authority on Clara Bow's—and her own—"star treatment."

Near the end of the segment, Brooks neatly analyzes Bow's eventual downfall: "She was the biggest star. She was the biggest money-maker in Hollywood, above Garbo, above them all. But as soon as Schulberg lost interest in her, that of course was when she began to slip inside her own head. Because Clara really didn't exist. She didn't exist off the screen. She manufactured this whole person." This analysis is both persuasive and telling. It is even consistent with certain claims in star studies that to be successful, stars had to enjoy a similarity with their on-screen personas. Given the morality codes (and contractual clauses) of her day, Bow could not fully maintain her film persona off-screen; or, when she did, she was shunned socially and in the press. Brooks's interest in the "manufacture" of "this whole person" is revealing on another level as well, for her own cinematic success— and her own eventual failure—rested on the manufacture of herself as "Lulu" in G. W. Pabst's *Pandora's Box*. More important, while Brooks was fascinated by the demise of various actors of her era, especially in the culpability of Hollywood culture in this demise, she was also quite interested in how star images and personas were produced in the first place. (Actually, for her, the two couldn't be divorced, as she saw her own downfall linked to her need to control her behavior and, resultantly, her representation on and off camera.) Her focus on Bow's control, or even "authorship," of her film scenes is certainly illustrative of this interest, as Brooks's own authorship of and control over her image greatly defines her place in film history.

Thus, the role Brooks plays in the *Hollywood* segment is typical of many historical representations of her as witness, critic, and even author. Crossing rhetorical genres and media forms, these texts simultaneously reveal Brooks to be both an intellectual—a film historian and film critic—and a great screen presence. These histories include Roland Jaccard's anthology *Portrait of an Anti-Star*; Kenneth Tynan's *New Yorker* "Profile: The Girl in the Black Helmet"; Barry Paris's biography of Brooks; Brooks's own *Lulu in Hollywood*; notable theoretical pieces concerning Brooks and *Pandora's Box*; Richard Leacock's 1984 documentary *Lulu in Berlin*; the more recent documentary *Looking for Lulu* produced for Turner Classic Movies; and other short essays and interviews. Perhaps because the role of the intellectual seems an odd one for a film star to play, Brooks also labored to play a highly sexualized being both on-screen and off. She sometimes even labors intellectually to represent herself as an anti-intellectual woman interested only in sex. These two roles, or selves, finally, merge in her writings about and as "Lulu." Through her rhetorical and cinematic construction of her image, Brooks works to redefine not only the role of the star but also that of the critic, yet her insistent collapse of her own persona with that of the highly sexualized Lulu illustrates that she hasn't the control of her image—or her destiny— that she would like to profess.

WRITING THE HISTORIES OF A LIFE

In 1977, in an essay entitled "Why I Will Never Write My Memoirs" and published in the British journal *Focus on Film*, Louise Brooks announced, "In writing the history of a life I believe absolutely that the reader cannot understand the character and deeds of the subject unless he is given a basic understanding of that person's sexual loves and hates and conflicts. It is the only way the reader can make sense out of innumerable apparently senseless actions.... I ... am unwilling to write the sexual truth that would make my life worth reading. I cannot unbuckle the Bible Belt. That is why I will never write my memoirs."[1] Six years after this statement, Brooks's *Lulu in Hollywood*, a collection of seven autobiographical essays, was published. For a woman who defines herself as "an inhumane executioner of the bogus,"[2] the relation between her original proclamation and the subsequent publication of her autobiographical essays seems to point to, at best, a contradiction and, at worst, a hypocrisy (or downright lie). For not only were most of the essays that were eventually collected in *Lulu* first published before her declaration, but the very title, *Lulu in Hollywood*, gives the collection the appearance of memoirs, Louise Brooks's most well-known role was that of Lulu, the central figure in G. W. Pabst's film *Pandora's Box* (1928), and the essays, for the most part, document her experiences in and out of Hollywood during the 1920s and 1930s. Because the title points to Brooks's infamous role and her life as an actress, *Lulu in Hollywood* looks like Louise Brooks's memoirs, thus making Brooks appear less truthful than she would like us to believe.³

But it's also more complicated than this, for *Lulu in Hollywood* is admittedly difficult to categorize: not exactly a history of a life, it would appear that *Lulu in Hollywood* is *not*, according to her own definition, Louise Brooks's memoirs. Indeed, the collection does not offer a complete history of her life; much of her life, in fact, is not documented in the work. Of the seven essays gathered in *Lulu in Hollywood*, six, primarily dealing with her experiences between 1920 and 1935, were previously published; one, detailing her youth and her initial move from Wichita, Kansas, to New York City, was written expressly for the original publication of the collection. ("Why I Will Never Write My Memoirs" was not included in the original collection. In his biography of Brooks, Barry Paris says it was "eliminated" from *Lulu*.⁴ It was added to the 2000 volume, as was Tynan's essay.) The span of time the collection covers is thus relatively short, for it ignores the years following Brooks's work in the film industry. In other words, it ignores the period during which she was actually writing the essays rather than living the experiences the essays document. Although the work does, then, represent Brooks's memories of this time, it does not document a full history of her life. However, it does document her life as a critic of Hollywood culture, film, and stardom. She analyzes roles various figures played in film and film history, and in so doing she contemplates how histories of film have been narrated. This form of analysis—often acute, always based on personal experience and subjective observation—is present in all other written and visual work to which Brooks contributes. Alongside her iconic image as Lulu, this analytical role signifies the way she has been perceived historically and critically. Thus, these two sides of Brooks—sometimes seemingly incompatible—are registered in works as diverse as her own essays, the variety of biographical and theoretical work concerning her, interviews, documentaries, and even the relatively private space of her own personal library.

Illustrating Brooks's production of a critical discourse, several essays in *Lulu in Hollywood* focus on other figures in film history; these essays are less autobiographical per se, though in each Brooks offers a biography of other actors and players in Hollywood through a critical autobiographical lens. In its limited history, however, *Lulu* manages also to employ the complicated critical lens that characterizes all of her work. Her critical discourse is in fact wedded to the limitations of the history she reveals, in that her role in history is defined as both timeless and ephemeral, much like the iconic portraits that represent her. For instance, as I alluded to earlier, the title of the collection also points to a contradiction in terms, a false chronology of Brooks's (and certainly Lulu's) life. First of all, of course, Pabst's film *Pandora's Box* was produced in Germany, not in Hollywood.[5] But, more important, Lulu never quite made it in Hollywood. The bulk of Brooks's time in Hollywood[6]—and the bulk about which she writes explicitly in *Lulu in Hollywood*—occurred before her role as Lulu in Pabst's film. Thus, to assume Brooks was in Hollywood as Lulu before she actually *was* Lulu implies that Brooks was *always* Lulu (a position that is not exactly refuted by Brooks). Moreover, after her roles in Pabst's films *Pandora's Box* and *Diary of a Lost Girl*, Brooks was more resistant than ever to working in Hollywood, as she would tell it, or was no longer as desired in Hollywood, as the industry would have it.[7]

Contradiction, or rather paradox, as well as the conflation between actor and character, are what Hollywood stars are often made of. And these star images, as many scholars have noted, are constructed in the conjunction between films and the publicity materials, often written discourse, surrounding them. As John Ellis notes, "Stars are incomplete images outside the cinema: the performance of the film is the moment of completion of images in subsidiary circulation, in newspapers, fanzines, etc. Further, a paradox is present in these subsidiary forms. The star is at once ordinary and extraordinary, available for desire and unattainable."[8] Recognizing and marketing this phenomenon was an early boost to the film industry. The very concept of the star, Richard deCordova contends, was born of the production and promulgation of knowledge about film actors by studio publicity departments, films, and fan magazines. Yet, in early cinema the knowledge that was circulated about both the star's public and private lives was "redundant": "The real hero behaves just like the reel hero. The knowledge which emerged concerning the star was restricted to the parameters of this analogy. The private life of the star was not to be in contradiction with his/her film image—at least not in terms of its moral tenor. The two would rather support each other. The power of the cinema was thus augmented by the extension of its textual and ideological functioning into the discourse on the star."[9] The circulation of discourse on stars therefore supported the industrial economy either through the convergence between the star's public and private images or, as we see in later cases, through the disjunction between these images. Star studies usually focuses on stars within this industrial economy and the discourses surrounding and constructing it.

As the passage from "Why I Will Never Write My Memoirs" shows, Brooks seems to fit the bill of a typical star: her "real life" did seem redundant to her "reel life," and this redundancy was most apparent in writings about her.[10] However, other factors point to how Brooks is not such a typical case. Most important, she doesn't fit neatly into Hollywood's industrial economy. She was not well-known for her pictures in Hollywood (though she made twenty-one of them); instead, her most infamous role was in a German film that essentially assisted in withdrawing her from the limelight in Hollywood. Moreover, many of the predominant writings that constructed Brooks's image appeared well after her film career was over.[11] Hence, her image, though now fairly well-known, circulates through relatively marginal (and at times cultish) fields. I am interested in focusing not so much on the industrial economy in which Brooks's image circulates as on the economy of discourse that encircles and historicizes her.[12] Similar to the processes of the industrial economy in which stars themselves are clearly commodities, this discourse is also circulated, exchanged, even reproduced. Indeed, it circulates through journalistic, historical, and theoretical works alike concerning Brooks.

This discourse is peculiarly economical in yet another sense, as it can almost always be traced back to Brooks herself. In fact, almost everything written about Brooks is (sparingly) managed through her own writings. What is most significant, and perhaps ironic, about this fact is that Brooks, often viewed as pure image and even an allegory of the cinema, constructs her own image through her own voice, particularly through her own written discourse. So, perhaps what I term an economy of discourse, or an economical discourse, is not in and of itself a paradox, but rather an important turn by film historians and film theorists; through emphasizing Brooks's voice by drawing on her own written works, these writers implicitly see her as a witness of cinema instead of as a pure image in cinema. She looks rather than is simply looked at. The paradox surrounding this discourse appears when even Brooks's own writings (and certainly those that follow her own) continue to paint her as an image, an allegory of the cinema, "an impulse," Sabine Hake claims, "that turns women into embodiments of abstract ideas."[13] Much about this image, moreover, remains elusive, which might stem from the paradoxical project of constructing a filmic image through writings.

Perhaps for this reason, the anthology *Louise Brooks: Portrait of an Anti-Star* brings together an amalgam of genres and a variety of authors to document and represent its subject. In general, the writings and photographs contained in the biographical collection extend and reiterate Brooks's image as an "anti-star" (an actress who bucked Hollywood conventions), especially her cinematic and extratextual image as Lulu. The volume includes several essays by the editor, other contributors, and Brooks herself. It also contains two poems; a letter from Brooks, entitled in the collection as "An Answer to an Admirer"; ninety photographs (fifty-three of which are stills from *Pandora's Box* and *Diary of a Lost Girl*); and panels from two different comic strips inspired by Brooks.

The flow of the poem "Touch of a Glance" by Tahar Ben Jelloun, which essentially opens the collection, displays the interchangeability of Louise and Lulu in the narrator's fantasy, an interchangeability typical of the collection as a whole.[14] In its focus on Lulu, and Pabst's films, the volume is greatly like *Lulu in Hollywood*, as it primarily defines the actress through the role she played in *Pandora's Box*. Indeed, even Roland Jaccard's short biography of Brooks and introduction to the collection, " 'Thank God I'm Alone,' " initially limits the facts of her life to the time from when she was born to her work with Pabst; such linearity implies that Brooks was born to play Lulu. Though Jaccard ends up mentioning events from the later part of Brooks's life, he concludes by insisting, "If it hadn't been for the one chance meeting with this extraordinary character, 'Lulu,' and with one director, Pabst, it is more than likely that Louise Brooks would be totally forgotten today."[15] Considering the fact that the majority of the photographs in the volume are stills from Pabst's films, the narrative that they tell is also largely Lulu's story.[16] The photographs, like the brief biography, predominantly fix Brooks in time as a younger woman and especially as Lulu. This collection of writings and images follows the logic of Frank Wedekind's original design of Lulu:

> Sweet creature, now keep in your proper place,
> Not foolish nor affected nor eccentric,
> Even when you fail to please the critic.

> You have no right with miaows and spits inhuman
> To distort for us the primal form of woman,
> With clowning and with pulling stupid faces
> To ape for us the childlike simple vices.
> You should—I discuss this today lengthily—
> Speak naturally and not unnaturally.
> For since the earliest time the basic element
> Of every art is that it be self-evident.[17]

Significantly, many of these photographs were supplied by Brooks from her private collection. She also provided the information contained in the biography. As Jaccard notes, "Above all, we must thank Louise Brooks herself, who was good enough to give us all the personal and unedited photographs that appear in this book, as well as an enormous amount of incredibly detailed and invaluable information (we owe her all the information that makes up the biography, the filmography, and the bibliography of this book.)"[18] Such contributions display the collaborative nature of this particular collection. Such collaboration, and even collusion, in the construction of her image and history is common in studies of her. Along with supplying photographs and texts like the bibliography of her writings, Brooks's primary contributions to the work are her own essays. Considering this fact, we can see her image as a dual one: as the timeless beauty Lulu and as a writer. Moreover, as a writer, Brooks is also like Lulu: she is seemingly straightforward and deceptive at the same time, and despite her demurral in "Why I Will Never Write My Memoirs," certainly she is often concerned with issues of sexuality.

This dual image reveals the fundamental imbrication of visual and written texts that forms our understanding of Brooks. Fully aware of the tangled relation between word and image in Brooks's case, Jean-Michel Palmier opens his essay in the collection with the following epigraph from Frank Wedekind: "In describing Lulu, I got the idea of depicting the body of a woman by the words she spoke. Each time she would express something, I asked myself whether that looked young and pretty." Considering the fact that Brooks's own essays are included in the volume, here she is, at least in part, "depicted by the words she spoke"—or, at least, by those she wrote. Indeed, as the collection pays tribute to Brooks as Lulu and the eponymous anti-star, it also clearly pays tribute to her as a writer in its collaboration with her. This tribute rests in large part on fixing Brooks in time as Lulu.[19]

Such complicated and often contradictory impulses are not atypical in the construction of almost any star (or, apparently, "anti-star") image, and they are definitively characteristic in representations of Brooks. They are, for instance, in line with certain aspects of *Lulu in Hollywood* concerning the conditions surrounding its publication as well as its very title. Moreover, noting these kinds of contradictions lays a foundation for a further examination of Brooks's own insistence on her "cruel pursuit of truth and excellence," or her "obsession with veracity," as James Card deems it.[20] Throughout her writings, Brooks poses as a teller of truths: like Wedekind's original Lulu, her art is self-evident. At the same time, however, the truths she tells are often either ambiguous or simply contradictory. The questionable truths of *Lulu* circulate around what she reveals and what she keeps secret (she writes about some aspects of her life and ignores others) as well as the repeated conflation between Brooks and Lulu.

This subjective truth and evidently carefully constructed self-representation in the collection point to a further supposition: *Lulu in Hollywood*, like Lulu in *Pandora's Box*, is a performance by Brooks. Indeed, a glance at the excerpts from reviews of the book that were used as blurbs on the Limelight edition show this to be the case; while the publishers meant to market *Lulu* as a history of sorts, John Lahr of the *New York Times* is quoted as saying, "These terse, raffish, authoritative essays are among the best discussions of American film I have ever read.... She is terrific on actors and acting because her language is free from critical cant or hyperbole.... At 22, she made film history as Lulu. At 75, her *Lulu in Hollywood* is another poised, extraordinary performance."[21] (Considering the title, the cover illustration of *Lulu in Hollywood*, which is based on an original German poster for *Pandora's Box*, and Brooks's repeated insistence that she *was* Lulu, these two performances are not so dissimilar.) Indeed, she performs in the written work as she does in the cinematic work: in both, she is Lulu.

Lulu's performance (and the performance of Lulu) is, moreover, based in great part on Brooks's often evasive testimony concerning her sexuality, that is, the performative production of herself as sexual subject.[22] This sort of performative production has been the subject of much recent debate. As Judith Butler notes, such performance of

*the critic* 113

gender and, in turn, sexuality, reveals how sexuality itself can be at once truthful and ambiguous: "If the inner truth of gender is a fabrication and if a true gender is a fantasy instituted and inscribed on the surface of bodies, then it seems that genders can be neither true nor false, but are only produced as the truth effect of a discourse of primary and stable identity."[23] In the case of Brooks, the oscillation between sexual identities is produced by a complex body of discourse surely influenced by her movement between national spaces. Indeed, Lulu's performance of sexuality, or the witnessing of it—of at once a truth and an ambiguous sexuality—is generated and repeated by critics, film historians, film theorists, and, of course, by Brooks herself.

This obsession with not only veracity but sexuality is similar to that which Richard Dyer finds through his work on Marilyn Monroe. As he observes, "Foucault has discussed [the interest in sexuality] in *The History of Sexuality* as emerging in the seventeenth century, whereby sexuality is designated as the aspect of human existence where we may learn the truth about ourselves. This often takes the form of digging below the surface, on the assumption that what is below must necessarily be more true and must also be what causes the surface to take the form it does."[24] Certainly this assumption seems also evident in the case of Brooks and the writings that circulate about her. At least according to the statement from "Why I Will Never Write My Memoirs," Brooks's refusal is dependent not merely on her inability to write a history of her life, but on her inability to compose a history based on truth, particularly on a "sexual truth that would make [her] life worth reading." In Kenneth Tynan's interview with Brooks for his *New Yorker* "Profile," she claims that in the late 1940s, when she was strapped for cash after falling out of favor with the film industry, she actually did begin to write her memoirs: "To earn a little money, I sat down and wrote the usual autobiography. I called it 'Naked on My Goat,' which is a quote from Goethe's 'Faust.' In one of the *Walpurgisnacht* scenes, a young witch is bragging about her looks to an old one. 'I sit here naked on my goat,' she says, 'and show my fine young body.' But the old one advises her to wait awhile: 'Though young and tender now, you'll rot, we know, you'll rot.' Then, when I read what I'd written, I threw the whole thing down the incinerator."[25] Thus, her "cruel pursuit of the truth" seems to have a dual, and even self-canceling, function in and for the essays in *Lulu in Hollywood*. Her need to tell the truth prevents her from writing her memoirs because, when she first began writing, she could not "tell the truth" about "sexual loves and hates and conflicts." She is saying she is honest, then, about what she cannot reveal.

At the same time, truth figures prominently in what Brooks *has* written. Throughout the essays in *Lulu*, she repeatedly emphasizes her dedication to writing, or telling, the truth. Indeed, it is in the essay written expressly for the collection in which she claims to be "in cruel pursuit of truth and excellence, an inhumane executioner of the bogus." Shortly thereafter she continues, "Never having experienced the necessity for lying at home, I went into the world with an established habit of truthfulness, which has automatically eliminated from my life the boring sameness that must be experienced by liars." Including these details early in the collection is clearly an attempt to represent herself as a reliable narrator, and she reiterates this quality throughout the essays. For instance, in "Marion Davies' Niece," Brooks points to how others, such as George Marshall, also saw her as truthful: "According to George, it was my truthfulness that made him fond of me, because truthfulness is a form of courage." His testimony by proxy seems placed to lend credence to Brooks's own claims about her veracious character. And certainly the essay "Pabst and Lulu" (which is the most frequently reprinted of all the essays in *Lulu in Hollywood*) is a long exegesis on truth and nature in its focus on her "natural" ability to play the role of Lulu and her admiration of Pabst's "truthful picture" of Lulu's world.[26]

Hence, the truth detailed in the essays at times concerns Brooks herself and at other times concerns those whose lives she witnesses: Marion Davies, Lillian Gish, Greta Garbo, Buster Keaton, Charlie Chaplin, Pipi Lederer, W. C. Fields, and other Hollywood stars of this period. In fact, many of the essays collected in *Lulu* were originally billed as Brooks's reflections on her contemporaries in Hollywood; thus, what was autobiographical about them was less a writing of self-image than precisely Brooks's position as a witness. For instance, two essays, "The Other Face of W. C. Fields" and "Gish and Garbo," allow Brooks to probe the star treatment of other actors in Hollywood. About Fields she writes, "No, it wasn't fame that distorted Fields. It was sickness and the clutching fear of being discarded to die on the Hollywood rubbish heap. . . . He was an isolated person. As a young man, he stretched his hand to Beauty and Love and they thrust it away." Such remarks, like her discussion of

Lillian Gish in particular, parallel her contentions concerning her own demise in Hollywood. Offering an abbreviated history of the "destruction" of the star system in the 1920s, Brooks paints Gish as a powerful and assertive woman, much as she would represent herself: "Of all the detestable stars who stood between the movie moguls and the full realization of their greed and self-aggrandizement, it was Lillian Gish who most painfully imposed her picture knowledge and business acumen upon the producers." For this reason, she was the first star "marked for destruction" by Hollywood producers. And although Brooks pictures Gish as the opposite of herself sexually, her end is written as identical to Brooks's own: "Stigmatized at the age of thirty-one as a grasping, silly, sexless antique, the great Lillian Gish left Hollywood forever, but not a head turned to mark her departure."[27] The door was then open for new stars like Brooks, but Brooks here easily prophesies—that is, with hindsight—her own treatment in the American movie business.

Remarking on her role as critic, Kenneth Tynan notes, "Since 1956 she had written twenty vivid and perceptive articles, mainly for specialist film magazines, on . . . her colleagues and contemporaries."[28] These perceptions, corresponding to Brooks's definition of truth, often had to do with sex; even telling an anecdote about a bridge game with Humphrey Bogart leads Brooks to recount Bogart's "attitude about sex." And "Marion Davies' Niece" offers the occasion for Brooks not only to discuss details of Davies's infamous relationship with William Randolph Hearst but also to disclose tales of various lesbian love affairs. Part diatribe against the evils of Hollywood players, part confession of her own role in Pepi Lederer's suicide (and indeed her own role in the cruel Hollywood gossip mill), the essay in fact connects Lederer's suicide to her (lesbian) sexuality, or more accurately to the response of others to her sexuality. In such essays, Brooks writes about what she observed—in New York, Hollywood, Germany, and elsewhere—from the standpoint of Lulu.

## DRIFTING AROUND THE EDGES OF DISCOURSE

Often, seemingly in contradiction to what she elsewhere says about sexual truth, Brooks is a witness, or perhaps an informant, of sexual behavior, her own and that of her contemporaries.[29] This position of informant and of an often subversive sexual figure presents the clearest example of the economical Brooksian discourse, circulated throughout the discourse concerning her. Significantly, as a star figure, Brooks has appeared, only to disappear and subsequently reappear, in three major periods. First, of course, she was visible during the late 1920s and early 1930s through her work in New York, Hollywood, and Weimar Germany. She later resurfaced in the mid-1950s following Henri Langlois's retrospective in Paris in 1955 at which he featured a Brooks film (*A Girl in Every Port*) and an enormous photograph of Brooks from *Pandora's Box*. James Card helped initiate Langlois's own interest in Brooks, and the exhibition itself helped trigger Card's writings on her, Brooks's own writings in such journals as *Sight and Sound* and *Film Culture*, and the nascence of what many term the Louise Brooks cult. Another peak in interest in Brooks appeared in the late 1970s and 1980s with Tynan's *New Yorker* piece; *Louise Brooks: Portrait of an Anti-Star*; the publication of *Lulu in Hollywood*; Leacock's documentary; notable theoretical pieces concerning Brooks and *Pandora's Box*, particularly Mary Ann Doane's "The Erotic Barter" and Thomas Elsaesser's "Lulu and the Meter Man"; and Paris's biography (it is in these latter texts that I am primarily interested).[30] Consistent in each of the histories of Brooks, the actress is presented as one who is knowing yet not always knowable, as one who might be defined, or known, through her cinematic and erotic role as Lulu and through her own words. Recognizing not only the omnipresence of particular issues surrounding Brooks but also the omnipresence of Brooks's written and spoken words in such varied works suggests the inherent trouble with, as well as the value in, drawing on works, such as the writings of a star, which are otherwise marginal in theoretical discourse.

Kenneth Tynan's "Profile" of Louise Brooks, "the Ravishing Hermit of Rochester," is, in many ways, a profile of Brooks's early sexual exploits (as well as Tynan's response to them). Even when he isn't directly discussing her sexual behavior (which is usually based on Brooks's own words), Tynan occasionally describes her experiences in terms of sexuality anyway: "After her fling with Fox, Paramount cast its young star . . . in another downbeat triangle melodrama." He quotes an entry from his journal after viewing *Pandora's Box* some years past:

Infatuation with L. Brooks reinforced by second viewing of "Pandora." She has run through my life like a magnetic thread—this shameless urchin tomboy, this unbroken, unbreakable porcelain filly . . . a creature of impulse, a creator of impulses, a temptress with no pretensions, capable of dissolving into a giggling fit at a peak of erotic ecstasy; amoral but totally selfless, with that sleek jet *cloche* of hair that rings such a peal of bells in my subconscious. In short, the only star actress I can imagine either being enslaved by or wanting to enslave; a dark lady worthy of any poet's devotion.[31]

In all of its astonishing excess, Tynan's own shameless portrait of Brooks touches not only on her sexuality but also on her seemingly visible truthfulness: Louise Brooks is "a temptress with no pretensions." Indeed, sexuality and truth are here, as elsewhere, categorically bound. Later, for instance, Tynan says of Brooks's role in *A Girl in Every Port*, "There is no melodrama in her exercise of sexual power. No effort, either: she is simply following her nature."[32]

This focus on an unpretentious, honest, or "natural" sexuality is also evident in Barry Paris's 1989 biography of Brooks. He opens the book with a lengthier version of the excerpt from "Why I Will Never Write My Memoirs." Like Tynan (and like Brooks herself), Paris frequently details Brooks's sexual exploits, often seeing them as illustrations of her "cocky high spirits" and as important markers in her personal history. He titles the chapter detailing Brooks's early entry into New York glitterati "Scandals" after *George White's Scandals*, the first musical revue in which Brooks performed. Often relying on Brooks's own stories, the chapter marks her New York experiences through various scandals, particularly ones in which she was directly involved; her personal scandals here, too, mirror her professional performance in White's revue. Later, to mark the conspicuous shift in Brooks's life, Paris remarks, "Whatever else could be said about Louise's life now, it was safe to say she had obliterated her past. As far as she and her *amours* were concerned, there was no trace of the ex-movie queen about her, her surroundings, or her life."[33] Thus, the end of Brooks's work in film parallels the end of her love affairs.

Paris's heavy reliance on Brooks's own accounts of her life is not, perhaps, entirely surprising. And because he has been said to have written the definitive portrait of Brooks, Kenneth Tynan is also not a surprising source of information for Paris's work, particularly in one of Paris's later chapters of the biography entitled "The Cult." This chapter, in fact, begins with an epigraph by Tynan: "She was the most seductive, sexual image of Woman ever committed to celluloid. She's the only unrepentant hedonist, the only pure pleasure-seeker I have ever known." (Marked as a proper noun, "Woman" here seems to reflect the "primal form of woman" that Wedekind describes in his prologue to the Lulu cycle.) Paris follows this avowal with one of almost equal magnitude: "For Tynan, whose sexual adventures were legion, that was saying something." It takes one to know one, Paris seems to be saying. He goes on to remark, "Thus spake the man who, aside from [James] Card and [Henri] Langlois, contributed more than anyone to the growth of the Louise Brooks Cult."[34] The quote by Tynan that opens Paris's "Cult" chapter is not attributed to a source and does not come from his "Profile."[35] However, it does neatly point to the ongoing aspect of the work on and by Louise Brooks: much of what is said about Brooks circulates through what seems to be a small inner circle (a cult, as Paris would have it), in which Tynan maintains a leading role. Indeed, as is clear from Tynan's interview with Brooks, much of what is said about her can be traced back to a single, economical source: Louise Brooks herself. Utilizing Brooks as such a witness transforms her persona from pure image to active participant in the construction of her roles on- and off-screen.

Brooks's own performative testimony of an ambiguous sexuality is a particularly popular focal point for those writing on her.[36] In fact, what seems so attractive about her sexuality and sexual exploits is their apparent elusiveness, particularly as evidenced by her alleged lesbianism. Throughout *Lulu in Hollywood*, however, and despite what she says in "Why I Will Never Write My Memoirs," Brooks does, in Tynan's words (playing on Brooks's own), frequently "unbuckle the Bible Belt." To be sure, while she provides the reader with some juicy details, she also manages to leave other details out. The elusiveness of her sexual exploits and indeed her sexuality itself thus hinges on a subjective—and even elusive—truth.

As a critic of film history and film culture, Brooks vowed to tell the truth. Yet the truth she vows to share is more equivocal in some cases than in others: it is often a partial truth, either because she won't fully disclose certain details (especially pertaining to her own sexuality) or because it's a subjective truth, a belief of hers rather than a fact. Therefore, the rhetorical strategies she employs as a critic are themselves double-edged: emphatic in their frankness yet often simultaneously evasive. This strategy is often reproduced in writings about her, which testifies to her importance as a critical source for others but also to the complexity of her reliability. Sometimes lacking facts about Brooks's life, critics turned to her work in fiction to comment on what might be missing. Thus, Andrea Weiss observes in *Vampires and Violets*, her work on lesbians in film, "Brooks was not a lesbian but rather, like Lulu, drifted around the edges of various sexual definitions. Her reputation for sexual ambiguity and gender transgression was nurtured both by rumor and by the various roles she played."[37] Merging her two identities as actress and star highlights the performative nature of her sexual identity and questions the truth Brooks repeatedly insists she is telling. This conflation could also be understood as Brooks's refusal of a certain identity as one or the other, character or actress, that in turn grants her sexual identity ambiguity or, more precisely, mobility.

Her sexual mobility was itself enabled by her transnational mobility; like other contemporaries who moved between national spaces and were known or represented as "transgressive" heterosexuals (like Pola Negri), bisexuals (Marlene Dietrich, Delores Del Rio, Greta Garbo), or lesbians (Mercedes de Acosta, Alla Nazimova), Brooks moved between the United States and Europe. Her association with European culture and film—though in a reverse direction from that of Negri, Nazimova, Dietrich, and Garbo—seemingly allowed for a broadening of her sexual identity as well. She was able to thus court the image of a "European exotic" through association.[38] Moreover, she self-identified, either in a competitive or an awe-struck spirit, primarily with Dietrich and Garbo, whom Patricia White aptly describes as "European, arty, mysterious, androgynous."[39] Reading her sexual identity through her transnational movement, we can recognize Brooks's sexuality as mobile rather than ambiguous. This recognition accents her movement not simply in the space between sexual identities (which might claim she is neither straight nor lesbian) but *within* the space of these identities (over time she is both straight and lesbian), for merely claiming Brooks's sexuality as ambiguous threatens to erase the possibility of a lesbian identity at all.

Like much that is known and written about her, stories about Brooks's sexual identity also "drift[ed] around." Drawing on Paris's biography, Weiss notes, "Brooks proudly claimed that 'by the time I got to Hollywood, everybody thought I was a lesbian.' "[40] The popularity of this story seems to rest originally, as Weiss implies, on Brooks herself (partly on her refusal to deny rumors that she was a lesbian) and on some of her key film performances, especially *Pandora's Box*. But, as is also clear from Weiss's comment, this story was popularly *circulated*. Weiss's own telling of the story attests to its circulation: the statement by Brooks is taken from Paris's own quotation of a letter from Brooks to Kevin Brownlow in 1969.

In *Lulu in Hollywood*, Brooks details the circulation of the lesbian rumor through a story about her work in *Pandora's Box* (a story later retold by Paris in the biography). After describing the lengths to which Alice Roberts went to "preserve her reputation" as a heterosexual after playing the lesbian Countess Geschwitz who dances with Lulu at her wedding, Brooks says:

> At the time, her conduct struck me as silly. The fact that the public could believe an actress's private life to be like the one role in one film did not come home to me till 1964, when I was visited by a French boy. Explaining why the young people in Paris loved *Pandora's Box*, he put an uneasy thought in my mind.
> "You talk as if I were a lesbian in real life," I said.
> "But of course!" he answered, in a way that made me laugh to realize I had been living in cinematic perversion for thirty-four years.[41]

Feigning a disbelief that the "public could believe an actress's private life to be like the one role in one film," Brooks clearly performs a contradictory position in regard to the relation between cinematic images and the social world. Noting that she "had been living in cinematic perversion for thirty-four years," Brooks both separates and collapses the distinction between reel life and real life. By telling this story she is able at once to put a stop to the rumor (she was "uneasy" about it; to her it is "cinematic perversion") and continue its circulation as a story. Thus, the mobility of Brooks's sexual identity stems from the circulation of these stories, which "drift around the edges" of representation.

Of course, as is evident from the story in Weiss's *Vampires and Violets*, Brooks shouldn't have been surprised that the public believed she was a lesbian. In fact, she brags to Tynan about her own cultivation of such an image. When she was in the "Follies" she roomed briefly with Fritzi LaVerne, who was known to have "seduced more 'Follies' girls than Ziegfeld and William Randolph Hearst combined." She says, "That's how I got the reputation of being a lesbian. I had nothing against it in principle, and for years I thought it was fun to encourage the idea. I used to hold hands with Fritzi in public.... But I only loved men's bodies. What maddens me is that because of the lesbian scenes with Alice Roberts in 'Pandora' I shall probably go down in film history as one of the gloomy dikes. A friend of mine once said to me, 'Louise Brooks, you're not a lesbian, you're a pansy.' Would you care to decipher that?"[42]

She then quickly changes the subject. But, as in the earlier quote from *Lulu*, here Brooks appears simultaneously to acknowledge and dispel the rumor that she was a lesbian. She had "encourage[d] the idea," but, hoping to set history straight, she also declares that she "only loved men's bodies." Seeming to court a static heterosexual identity, Brooks flirts with a more ambiguous, or fluid, sexuality (certainly a nonheterosexuality) that can move her from "gloomy" dyke to indecipherable pansy. Brooks's sexual mobility emerges through her own attempts to control and promote the circulation of stories that she might be a lesbian. These stories are themselves founded on Brooks's—and Lulu's—circulation *among* lesbians: Fritzi, Peggy, Pipi, Countess Geschwitz.

Further indicating Brooks's tendency both to avow and disavow a lesbian identity, Barry Paris writes of a similar story the actress tells about "encouraging the idea" that she was a lesbian. Paris quotes a letter from Brooks to Herman Weinberg in 1977: "When I am dead, I believe that film writers will fasten on the story that I am a lesbian.... I have done lots to make it believable. Peggy Fears and I used to hold hands in public and make Blumie and George Marshall wild. All my women friends have been lesbians.... Out of curiosity I had two affairs with girls—they did nothing for me." As these (shifting) stories show, and as Paris aptly puts it, "She was always playfully inconsistent on the subject." Not only is she inconsistent about her likes and dislikes, however; it appears that she is also inconsistent regarding who were the key players in these performances of her likes and dislikes. Certainly Brooks's inconsistency regarding the lesbian from the *Follies*—was it Fritzi LaVerne or Peggy Fears?—might be chalked up to a simple mistake, a lapse of memory. But Paris claims that a general inconsistency in Brooks's stories is somewhat consistent. Attempting to explain such "liberties" in one case, Paris comments, "It was [gay men's] prose more than their sexual persuasion that annoyed her, but there was no denying that deep ambivalence—her lifelong appreciation-deprecation of homosexuals."[43] Clearly testifying to a lesbian identity, which might be mistaken as a more complete truth or history of her life, appears to be the particular notch on the Bible Belt that Brooks won't openly unbuckle.

## THEORETICAL PRACTICE

The fascination of all who write on Brooks centers, as I have noted, on questions of her sexuality and her veracity. Indeed, her reputation for candor submits her writings as a useful source for all who write about her, for the greatest similarity among these writers is a fondness for quoting her. This union of Brooks's words and image, though leaving us with questions, is produced and reproduced in all writings concerning the star—from popular to biographical to theoretical—indicating important links (some troubling, some enabling) among film history, biography, theory, and film itself. Certainly it's not uncommon for a biographer to draw on his or her subject's own words as a source for the biography. But such a turn is less common in film theory texts. Many important works in star studies scholarship do draw on the commentary of stars, but this commentary is most frequently extracted from interviews. (Of course, this strategy occurs largely because most stars are not published writers on film.) What's interesting to me about the appearance of Brooks's writings in film theory texts is that most of these works would not easily fall under the rubric of star studies; her writings also seem to fall under a different category in film studies: part autobiography, part commentary and history, part analysis.[44] Drawing on Brooks's writings to comment on her persona usefully rejoins her voice and image, but at times doing so also reiterates more distressing trends when looking at her, particularly when seeing her as an allegory of the cinema. Allowing her voice to authorize this emblematic position often effaces the part that men have played in constructing this role through projecting their desires onto her.

Heide Schlüpmann comments on this latter dilemma in her essay on Pabst's *Diary of a Lost Girl*, "The Brothel as an Arcadian Space?," in which she examines how the realism of Pabst's film is controlled through the apparatus of the film medium. The film, she claims, speaks to a male viewer through the female star. In line with much feminist film criticism on Hollywood texts, Schlüpmann argues that the male viewer identifies with the apparatus, whereas the female viewer is drawn to identify with Brooks's character. This is a troubling process, for "the heroine's masochism is indeed not a 'female' one, but rather the incarnation of repressed male energies," so the female viewer is left to "[deny] her person and her sex."[45] As an apparent punctuation to such points, Schlüpmann includes two photographs in her essay, both of which she captions with quotes from Brooks.

Both photographs are from the set of *Diary*, but neither are stills, and each caption is about Pabst. Next to the first photograph (Brooks standing outside, dressed in a fur, with her signature haircut) is included the following statement by Brooks: "[Pabst] was conducting an investigation into his relations with women, with the object of conquering any passion that interfered with his work." Next to the other (in which Brooks is seated outside on a canopied veranda, wearing a black dress with crepe sleeves, hair slicked back) is the following quote: "Pabst chose all my costumes with care . . . as much for their tactile as for their visual seductiveness."[46] The inclusion of these photographs and their adjoining captions serves a dual purpose. First, each illustrates how Pabst projected his own views about and desires for women onto Brooks, thus emphasizing Schlüpmann's supposition that the cinematic apparatus—and the women in it—is controlled by masculine desire. Second, by quoting Brooks on Pabst, Schlüpmann gives voice to the woman whose image is otherwise projected and seemingly controlled by a man. By conjoining her visual image and her own words, this move allows Brooks a sense of agency that is otherwise missing from the film—that which Schlüpmann, moreover, sees as a masculine apparatus.

In their respective essays "Lulu and the Meter Man" and "The Erotic Barter," Thomas Elsaesser and Mary Ann Doane also look closely at Pabst's work, focusing on *Pandora's Box*, and both take into account Brooks's writings. Both, too, pursue the omnipresent fascination with the sexuality and truth of Louise Brooks (though neither addresses questions concerning her ostensible lesbianism). These essays have an interesting history. In her first footnote to "The Erotic Barter," Doane writes that her essay "is a revised and expanded version of work I did on *Pandora's Box* in the context of a seminar on

Weimar cinema at the University of Iowa in the spring of 1978. The work was cited and rebutted by Thomas Elsaesser in his extremely provocative essay, 'Lulu and the Meter Man' . . . which I, in turn, cite and criticize here." Although this is where the history of the essays end, Doane goes on: "Since my ideas about the film and also about the process of film criticism have changed significantly in the last ten years, I have chosen not to respond directly to Elsaesser's critique (*which I believe is a misrepresentation of my earlier work in any event*). Instead, I concentrate on clarifying the distinctions between my current view of the film and his often compelling arguments in the *Screen* essay."[47] Like Brooks and those writing about her, Doane is persistent about recognizing that she has been misrepresented and thus now hopes to represent herself more truthfully.[48]

In "Lulu and the Meter Man: Louise Brooks, Pabst, and 'Pandora's Box,'" Elsaesser repeatedly touches on and examines questions concerning sexuality and truth. Throughout his essay, while he attempts to define modernism and its essential characteristics, Elsaesser also stresses the indeterminacy of Lulu's sexuality. Thus, whereas *Pandora's Box* signifies "sexuality of the cinema," Louise Brooks/Lulu signifies the sexuality of *Pandora's Box*. Says Elsaesser, "Pabst, one is tempted to say, wanted a *mise-en-scène* that would make Lulu a phantom, and the hyperreal magic of her sexual presence is the indeterminacy, at all these levels, of her sexual identity."[49] Like Brooks's descriptions of her sexuality (and those portraits that follow hers), Elsaesser wants to stress the visibility of Brooks's sexuality but wants also to claim it, at some level, as invisible, or at least unknowable: her "sexual presence" retains a "hyperreal magic" that is "indeterminate." And, as I mentioned earlier, because Elsaesser doesn't speak of Brooks's lesbianism, lesbianism itself remains invisible in his essay; indeed, it becomes the "phantom."[50] Thus, the sexuality that he wants to elucidate for modernist cinema is, although "indeterminate," apparently heterosexual and definitely female, recalling both Tynan's fantasy about Brooks and Wedekind's conception of "Woman."

In Elsaesser's essay, the figure of Louise Brooks often mediates this tension between an invisible and a visible sexuality. At times, this tension is depicted as a characteristic of cinema itself. Examining an early critique of *Pandora's Box*, Elsaesser writes, "There is an evident irritation that Louise Brooks is neither active ('she does nothing'), nor actively passive ('she does not suffer') which contrasts unfavourably one kind of body—that of the cinematic representation—with another, the expressive body of the theatre performance. Compare this of [Henri] Langlois' '(her) art is so pure that it becomes "invisible"': praise that implies a diametrically opposite visual (and literary) aesthetic."[51] Elsaesser here points to a shift in aesthetics from theater to cinema: describing theater as performance and cinema as representation (via the critique he is examining), he notes the common conception of cinema as providing a passive image and theater an active performance. The very fact that the film *Pandora's Box* was adapted from Wedekind's plays easily presents a juxtaposition between theater and cinema for early critics (a juxtaposition that can be further underscored by the fact that works presented in the German theater and cinema were competing for audiences).[52] Furthermore, this tension between theater and cinema is played out through Brooks's portrayal of Lulu as either "active" or "passive."[53] And as Elsaesser's own critique illustrates, these tensions between activity and passivity, visibility and invisibility are most apparent through Brooks's "sexual presence." Seeing Brooks's sexual presence as allegorical of the cinema, Elsaesser thus appears to repeat a strain evident in the "Louise Brooks Cult" (the purity that Langlois comments on and that Elsaesser quotes above). In Sabine Hake's words, he "confirms the allegorical impulse that turns women into embodiments of abstract ideas."[54]

As he explores this issue, Elsaesser draws on Wedekind's conception of Lulu.[55] Although he resists the conception of Lulu as "purely passive," he nevertheless continues this discourse, searching for the exact definition of Lulu and, in particular, Brooks's portrayal of Lulu. He later links the debate to the primacy of the "right to the look and the image" in the cinema. In a brief, dizzying section in which he moves from examining the film to looking at the "female spectator," to the "general position of women in our society," to the star system, Elsaesser claims that the possession of the look and the image appears at first to be ambiguous in Pabst's film. In an illustration of this notion, Elsaesser asserts that Lulu's husband, Dr. Schoen's, "undoing" is shown when he loses the right to look and becomes instead "the object of the gaze." Conventionally (and certainly problematically) understanding this condition as "feminised," Elsaesser continues:

> Such is the logic of the visible that underpins the general position of women in our society, encouraged to objectify their narcissistic self-image as that which regulates their lives: in order to be and to assure themselves of their existence, they seek a gaze in which to mirror themselves. . . . Lulu has no gaze, hence the fascination of her smile. . . . The few times she frowns or looks puzzled, Pabst neutralises her gaze by inserting a cut that disperses, disorients the direction, as in the deliberate mis-match of the opening scene. Some of the difficulties of finding the right actress, as well as Louise Brooks's detailed account of the shooting, confirm the importance that Pabst attached to the look that poses no threat. At one stage he considered Marlene Dietrich for the part, but is reported to have said: "Dietrich was too old and too obvious—one sexy look and the picture would have become a burlesque."[56]

I quote this passage at such length to illustrate some of the turns Elsaesser takes when he discusses the tension between the look and the image. Linking Lulu with "women in society," he emphasizes the translation of film to life: as Lulu loses the look and becomes the object of the gaze, "such is the logic of the visible that underpins the general position of women in our society." Thus, Pabst's "neutralising" of her gaze is representative not only of cinematic conventions but of societal conventions as well. Of particular importance, Elsaesser stresses that the casting of Louise Brooks was an essential step in the neutralization of Lulu's gaze. But most important, Elsaesser himself mimics a "cut that disperses, disorients the direction," interestingly proving his own point that the cinematic neutralization of a woman's look is indeed translated into (or from) real life, or at least into (or from) theory.

Elsaesser notes that Pabst "is reported to have said" that he preferred Brooks over Dietrich for the role of Lulu. What he doesn't say (but what is clear from his footnotes) is that the reporter of this comment is Louise Brooks herself. In fact, Brooks was also the unnamed reporter of Wedekind's comments regarding Lulu's passivity. In both cases, Brooks's gaze and observations as an active witness of *Pandora's Box* (and, at times, modernity) authorize Elsaesser to make many of his claims, but, with the exception of the necessary footnotes, her gaze and her reporting of her observations become "neutralised."[57] Like Pabst, Elsaesser inserts a "cut that disperses, disorients the direction" when he either uses the passive voice ("is reported to have said") or removes to the "original" source ("Wedekind himself writes"). His own writing, then, enacts the same "logic of the visible" that he otherwise critiques. Indeed, throughout "Lulu and the Meter Man," Elsaesser greatly depends on Brooks's *Lulu in Hollywood* as a key source for his arguments. At times she is a visible source, an authoritative witness, but at other key moments her own authority is lost in the body of Elsaesser's text.[58]

Coincident with Brooks's own obsession with truth and Elsaesser's seeming attempt to uncover the "logic of the visible," Mary Ann Doane frames "The Erotic Barter" with remarks concerning modern conceptions of truth and performance. Moreover, the image itself, the "exposure of the flesh," might also be illusory, another performance of deception. Says Doane, "She is pure image. . . . Lulu is *outside of* the mise-en-scène. There is a somewhat fantastic hallucinatory quality attached to her image." This possibility of illusion is clearest when Doane claims that Lulu is "outside of the mise-en-scène," existing in a "timeless and spaceless realm of the idea rather than the fact." Although it might appear to resist chronology or a specific period in history, this timelessness of Lulu becomes precisely what is modern about Pabst's film and its representation of Lulu. Claiming that Schoen's son Alwa's desire for Lulu in the film is a "desire to escape history . . . desire for a femininity which is outside of time," Doane examines the effects of Lulu's apparent timelessness: "Her temporality is that of the moment—the glance, the smile that signifies no lasting commitment. It is also a femininity which is despatialized, a hallucinatory image characterized by diegetic resistances. Its modernity, then, in a somewhat paradoxical manner, is constituted by its ahistoricity."[59]

The notion that Lulu's "temporality is that of the moment" is not unlike Henri Langlois's remarks which Doane earlier quotes (and which Elsaesser and Peter Wollen quote as well), claiming that Brooks is "outside of time."[60] This timelessness also allows Lulu's sexual identity to retain a sense of mobility; it is not fixed *in* time.

Yet, even though (or perhaps because) Lulu's ephemerality characterizes modern time, Doane attempts to fix Lulu in time and space. Earlier in her essay she asks where Lulu exists. This question (and her subsequent focus on Lulu's timelessness and despatialization) is part of an important corrective to many histories of Weimar Germany, such as Peter's Gay's *Weimar Culture*, in which women are virtually absent (Marlene Dietrich's legs are one obvious exception). Doane's solution to women's absence in Weimar histories and Lulu's despatialization and ephemerality in Pabst's film is to recover Lulu's voice and her own power of looking through Louise Brooks. Thus, Lulu exists *in* Brooks. For instance, Doane excerpts "typical critical responses" to *Pandora's Box* that focus on the film as a star vehicle for Brooks. These quotes lead to a conflation between Brooks and Lulu; the film—or at least the discourse surrounding it (certainly including Brooks's own)—appears to be simultaneously about both women.

By quoting Brooks's comments on both Weimar Germany and Lulu, Doane recovers another place for women outside the frame of the sexual cynicism of the film; as opposed to "giving looks," Brooks *looks at* Weimar culture. And in this way, Lulu and Brooks together are set within the national space of Weimar Germany—a position that might seem obvious, but one that also enables her sexual mobility. Characteristically, the venue that Brooks witnesses is that of multiple sexualities (many represented as inherently indeterminate). Doane notes, "Louise Brooks, describing the city in which she worked on the film, refers to 'girls in boots advertising flagellation,' a nightclub which displayed 'an enticing line of homosexuals dressed as women,' another with 'a choice of feminine or collar and tie lesbians,' and the 'collective lust' which 'roared unashamed at the theatre.'"[61] These images, which frame Doane's essay and precede her comments regarding Weimar's "confrontation with the facts," significantly intersect notions of the "real" and of an indeterminate, or unfixed, sexuality that is also a focus of Elsaesser's essay and other works by and about Brooks. Brooks's witnessing of the facts of Weimar is a witnessing of a similar "transgression of traditional boundaries" which "constitutes [Lulu's] eroticism . . . [and] desirability." Thus, the "real" witnessed by Brooks is one in which the performance of sexuality is central. Significantly, however, Brooks is here merely a witness to varying forms of sexual identities or transgressions: although events happen around her, she is not represented as an active participant.

So, although "Lulu's luck has run out" because "the modernist impulse to dehistoricize becomes coincident with the exclusion of women from the scene," Doane attempts to re-place a woman in the scene through the performer Louise Brooks.[62] Although she concludes that *Pandora's Box* remains the story of "modern anxieties of *male* consciousness," Doane consciously or unconsciously recovers a voice and the power of looking for women in the Weimar era. Of course, Brooks as the representative of this recovered voice is certainly not a "traditional protagonist" in the story of Weimar culture, thus emphasizing that women, for Doane, have remained either (like Lulu) catalysts for crisis in Weimar society or (like Brooks) in positions outside the center of the republic.[63] The effects of drawing from Brooks's own writings are thus clear, but knowing the outcome of doing so doesn't answer why one would draw from Brooks in the first place, particularly in the field of film theory. I would posit that the primary reason is that the other consistent characteristic linked to Brooks's image (besides a mobile, or elusive, sexuality) is her intelligence. Having a reputation as an intelligent woman validates Brooks as a reliable witness of Weimar and Hollywood. Her reputation for intelligence, moreover, is underscored by her reputation for honesty.

Describing Jack the Ripper in one of the final scenes of *Pandora's Box*, Doane writes, "The eye is not only the organ of desire, but that of performance and deception as well." Although Doane is referring to Jack the Ripper, she might as well be characterizing the eye of Louise Brooks. For Brooks, an "inhumane executioner of the bogus," the eye is also an organ of candor and veracity. As the actress-writer looks at Weimar Germany, G. W. Pabst, the role of Lulu, and even her own history, she assumes the position of an intelligent witness. But how might this position be a deceptive performance? For she is also, we know, a product of the modern period, which, as Doane notes, "cultivated a . . . sophistication wherein not to be deceived meant to know that everything is deception."[64] Considering the "playful inconsistencies" with which she peppers her reminiscences, Brooks's performance might be not one of truth but one of deception, or at least one that plays with the deceptiveness of the truth.

## SHOT/REVERSE SHOT

Certainly, then, Brooks shares some similarities with her critics, for they, too, necessarily each play the role of observer. Often beset with her visual image as Lulu, theorists, biographers, and fans alike describe her, project on to her, and even pay tribute to her. Of course, looking is fundamental to any film viewer, whatever role that viewer eventually plays, but for viewers of Brooks, as I have shown, the act of looking is extended. What becomes part of their fascination with the actress is Brooks's own ability (and even desire) to look at herself and at others. In fact, James Card encouraged Brooks to write in the first place because she appeared to possess such insight about films and her experiences in film. Screening films with her, he says, was "always supplemented with discussions marked by Brooksian analysis so penetrating and often so startling in its freshness of view that our curatorial dogma has been severely bruised."[65] This insistent trope of looking, observing, perceiving could very well be what attracted Richard Leacock, one of the originators of the direct cinema movement in the United States, to make a short film about Brooks with Susan Woll (*Lulu in Berlin*, 1984). With fellow filmmakers Robert Drew, Albert and David Maysles, D. A. Pennebaker, and, later, Frederick Wiseman, Leacock helped to found this documentary style, which was defined as observational filmmaking, guided by reporting rather than control.

Direct cinema has clear commonalities with Brooks. Because it was understood as observational filmmaking, the movement was greatly concerned with the filming of the "truth," though direct cinema's relationship with truth and deception, veracity and illusion was a tenuous one. As Jeanne Hall writes, the conventions utilized in films such as *Primary* (commonly proclaimed to be the first example of direct cinema) imply that direct cinema "offers viewers greater access to the truth."[66] Writes the film editor Patricia Jaffe, "Direct cinema . . . is based on *recording life as it exists at a particular moment before the camera*. The role of the film maker in this instance is never to intrude by directing the action—never to alter the events taking place (except insofar as his presence adds a factor to the environment). His job is simply to record what is there as he sees it."[67] This insistence on direct cinema filmmakers' access to the truth through their mode of production is not unlike Brooks's repeated avowals of her own veracity. Giving up a certain control over the situation and instead simply reporting what was there before them allowed filmmakers like Leacock, Pennebaker, the Maysles brothers, and Drew to make more "authentic" documentaries. As Leacock announced, "Many film-makers feel that the aim of the film-maker is to have complete control. Then the conception of what happens is limited by the conception of the film-maker. We don't want to put this limit on actuality. What's happening, the action, has no limitations, neither the significance of what's happening. The film-maker's problem is more a problem of how to convey it." Documentaries other than those by Leacock and his cohorts, claimed Drew, were "fake."[68]

Of course, since the peak of direct cinema filmmaking, many critics have examined the very *in*authenticity, or impossibility, of these claims to truth. Considering phases of documentary production following direct cinema, Bill Nichols contends that self-reflexive documentaries "[make] patently clear what had been implicit all along: documentaries always were forms of re-presentation, never clear windows onto 'reality'; the film-maker was always a participant-witness and an active fabricator of meaning, a producer of cinematic discourse, rather than a neutral or all-knowing reporter of the way things truly are."[69] More specifically, in "The Documentary Film as Scientific Inscription," Brian Winston skeptically examines the "simplistic" claims of direct cinema filmmakers and their champions, noting, "It is the experimental method and the place of the camera as scientific instrument that provides the context in which the filmmaker/observer emerges—heavily disguised as a fly on the wall."[70] In her examination of the rhetoric of the direct cinema movement and documentary film theory concerning it, Jeanne Hall notes, "One need not watch these films to know that they do not serve up the 'truth at twenty-four frames per second,' but one *does* need to watch them to understand cinema verite's special brand of realism."[71] And Paul Arthur plainly states, "Direct cinema's stipulation of transparency and noncontrol as a paradigm of authenticity is at once futile and disingenuous."[72]

One particular clue to this "disingenuous" nature might be found in a further allegation by Arthur: that direct cinema was necessarily drawn to the performative. Arthur claims, "Significantly, the existential locus of performance provides implicit justification for the camera's presence. Far from exhibiting the flux of spontaneous behavior, what occurs on direct cinema's makeshift stage is already mediated, learned, in greater or lesser degree intended for visual/auditory consumption." Certainly this sort of mediation exposes a kind of inauthentic rendering of the truth. Arthur continues: "A constant theme of direct cinema is the blurring and remapping of lines between mandated roles and autonomous expressions of personal identity. Designation of celebrity helps maintain the fiction that camera observation is part of a natural landscape of behavior. Whether the camera is addressed directly or buffered by a profilmic audience or interrogator, it is there because of an inherent complicity by which one's 'image' or personal identity is a mutual construct of performer and receiver."[73]

We can see a fascination with celebrity in many works of the direct cinema movement: the films about politicians John F. Kennedy and Hubert Humphrey, as well as Nehru; *Meet Marlon Brando* by Drew Associates; Pennebaker's films about musicians; and even Wiseman's works, such as *Salesman*. This draw toward celebrity and performance is also clearly apparent in Leacock and Woll's *Lulu in Berlin*. In general, another shared quality between Brooks and the direct cinema movement is the love of performance, no matter what either Brooks or the purveyors of the movement might contend about truthfulness.

These are very interesting and telling connections between Brooks and the direct cinema movement, but they are also, in a sense, generic ones. Made almost two decades after the revolutionary heyday of direct cinema, *Lulu in Berlin* is hardly a definitive example of this style of filmmaking. Less than an hour long, it is primarily made up of an interview Leacock conducted with Brooks at her home in Rochester, New York. Sometimes Brooks herself fills the frame; frequently Leacock is shown as well; indeed, the piece is largely a filmed conversation between the two, peppered with lengthy clips of the three European films starring Brooks: *Pandora's Box*, *Diary of a Lost Girl*, and *Prix de beauté*. Aside from its implicit claims of authenticity (Brooks's own, as well as the film's), its obvious fascination with performance, and the fact that it was made by Richard Leacock, *Lulu in Berlin* does not share much else with direct cinema works before it.

Indeed, the action filmed is rather passive, as it consists solely of Brooks and Leacock sitting at a table, chatting; it is not the filming of the kind of event or even experience that was typical of direct cinema. The interview itself is clearly staged; Leacock explicitly tries to direct the conversation and even appears rather uncomfortable throughout. (His years behind the camera, perhaps, did not prepare him for the position in front of one, as the costar of one of his films.)[74] The piece is shot in color stock rather than black and white, the latter often a signature of direct cinema. Moreover, the filmmakers did not utilize the look made possible by a moving hand-held camera in action; instead, the camera is generally static, focused only on its subjects, occasionally panning between them or moving in for a close-up of one of their faces. (At times, close-ups are edited in to create a seamless auditory transition; this sort of "invisible" editing is, of course, a standard of direct cinema, as well as Hollywood filmmaking.)

Finally, the film's very heavy reliance on the interview strategy is fairly inconsistent with the conventions of the direct cinema movement, which tended to shun the strategy. In an interview with G. Roy Levin published in 1971, Leacock discussed this resistance to interview filmed subjects: "The danger is that when you ask questions you in effect tell them what you want, because almost all questions are leading questions." Later he reiterates this point: "We started out in the whole tradition of the television guy asking the questions. We really tremendously wanted to get away from that. It's so easy to fall into the interview thing, such an easy way to get out of a hole."[75] Because the interview seems overly directive, filmmakers like Leacock claimed to avoid it in favor of unobtrusive observation. But Hall points out that "a close look at the first films of Drew Associates suggests that the filmmakers routinely conducted interviews—and routinely edited half of each exchange from the finished film."[76] Considering this quest to make the interviewer invisible and thus mask certain facets of the production of the film, one might argue that *Lulu in Berlin*—in showing what really happened—is a truer model of what the direct cinema filmmakers advocated. In any case, its use of a lengthy interview, or conversation, illustrates the fact that the film does share some conventions with direct cinema filmmaking, but it also diverges from the style in other ways.

Even though recognizing the movement from which a film springs might be useful in our understanding of the work, genre or style alone doesn't tell us everything (and sometimes an emphasis on predetermined formal structures creates even more confusion about a text). In this case, because *Lulu in Berlin* seems to deviate from as much as adhere to the prescriptives of direct cinema filmmaking, we learn even less about what it is. Indeed, like *Lulu in Hollywood*, it does not easily fit into a single generic category. Certainly it is a documentary film in a broad sense. No matter how much we might doubt or deconstruct a documentary's access to truth in general or question Louise Brooks's sincerity in particular, we can still recognize the *aim* of this film as an ontological one: it attempts, at least, to present a real person discussing real events of her life. It is, in part, then, a biographical documentary, as it offers "true" stories of Brooks's acting career, especially her work with Pabst. At the same time, because it is so highly dependent on Brooks herself—that is, because it relies on Brooks to tell her own stories—the film is also autobiographical in nature. Finally, one might also read the film as Brooks's biography of Pabst; its title draws attention to her work with the German director, and throughout the film Leacock presses her to tell stories that concern Pabst.

Perhaps the tension between genres produced by the film is inevitable. As Michael Renov argues in "History and/as Autobiography: The Essayistic in Film and Video," "Autobiographical writing has been characterized (much as the essay has been) as essentially heterotopic." Renov's project is to connect the already "hybrid" forms of the essay, autobiography, and documentary film and video. Hence, he examines a number of visual texts that he terms "essayistic": "These visual works, like the literary essay form, can be said to resist generic classification, straddling a series of all-too-confining antinomies: fiction/non-fiction, documentary/avant-garde, cinema/video. In ways that can be specified, these texts are notable for their negotiation of three terms or critical axes around and against which the essay effect can be said to form: history, subjectivity, language."[77] Although not really an avant-garde piece, *Lulu in Berlin*, too, fluctuates between generic categories as it negotiates "history, subjectivity, language." It performs this fluctuation and negotiation largely in relation to two other issues of importance to direct cinema in particular and documentary overall: direction and voice.

As I noted, direct cinema filmmakers maintain that they resist "direction" in their works. This claim of resistance interestingly resounds in *Lulu in Berlin*. In fact, the issue of whether the film is being directed or, more pointedly, who is actually directing it, speaks to both the generic definition of the film as well as its negotiation of "history, subjectivity, and language." The film's seamless editing does suggest a nonexplicit direction by Leacock. That is, on the surface, *Lulu in Berlin* appears to be a film of Brooks talking, sometimes in conversation with Leacock and often in monologue. It almost seems as if Brooks herself is directing the piece; at least, she appears to have control of the conversation. At the same time, there exists a tension between Brooks's own control or direction — or even authorship — and that of Leacock: it often seems that his direction is hardly replaced by hers. Indeed, throughout the film, minor interruptions — some so carefully edited as almost to be erased — raise certain questions concerning the lack of direction, authorship, or authority by Leacock. And the same interruptions certainly challenge Brooks's own authority over the work.

One lengthy sequence neatly illustrates this point. The first part of the sequence comprises, not surprisingly, a discussion about Brooks's relation to Lulu. Outlining how Pabst used to supervise all facets of the production of his films, Brooks repeats a story she tells in *Lulu in Hollywood* about how Pabst ruined her favorite suit in order to create a realistic display of emotion on her part for the final scene of *Pandora's Box*: "He wanted something that was mine and I loved so I would feel terrible in it, and I did. Here I was in my beautiful suit and it was ruined so it made me feel like this [she crosses her arms over her chest and grips her bathrobe], and that's how I was at the end of the picture." These comments are followed by the final scene of the film, over which Leacock and Brooks briefly discuss her attraction for the actor (Gustav Diessl) who played Jack the Ripper. After they talk, the scene continues with only its music audible, but near the end of the long clip, Leacock again cuts in: "I was reading from your article: 'It is in the worn and filthy garments of the streetwalker that she feels passion for the first time—comes to life so that she may die. When she picks up Jack the Ripper on the foggy London street and he tells her he has no money to pay her, she says, "Never mind, I like you." It is Christmas Eve and she is about to receive the gift which has been her dream since childhood. Death by a sexual maniac.'[78] I think you wrote that, not Wedekind." Brooks responds, "Yes, yes," and the clip continues to the end. This exchange underscores how Pabst essentially created an effect of reality: using Brooks's *real* dress, he was able to garner *real* emotion from her. The conversation, then, nicely leads into a further discussion about how Brooks was also like Lulu in real life.

But also significant in this scene is the fact that Leacock reads from Brooks's own prose to discuss *Pandora's Box* and even likens her to Wedekind: his comment "I think you wrote that, not Wedekind" plainly acknowledges her authorship of the passage, but it also suggests that her written representation of Lulu is so authentic that it could even be mistaken for Wedekind's work. (And, of course, his final comment is a somewhat superfluous performance, because he begins by announcing that he is reading from Brooks's essay.) Through this dual acknowledgment, Leacock appears to relinquish the direction of the discussion of Brooks/Lulu to the actress. But as the sequence continues, he begins again to vie for this control. After the clip from *Pandora's Box* ends, we see a medium close-up of

Leacock alone. He queries, "What intrigues me is the Lulu in real life. To what extent, having made the film not really knowing what Lulu was about, to what extent had your life been, in a sense, the life of Lulu?" The camera pans over to Brooks, who retorts, "Let me go on with the story, and then I'll get to that." Here she is discussing not the suit nor her role in *Pandora's Box*, as she was before the clip began; rather, she is telling the story of her return to New York (seemingly after *Diary of a Lost Girl*) and her subsequent call from Pabst to return to Europe to make *Prix de beauté* with René Clair.[79] A cut appears to have taken place between stories via the insertion of the close-up of Leacock, but it is imperceptible. As the two continue to converse, however, following cuts are more discernible, if still quite subtle.

The first cut comes after a fleeting interruption in the story. As Brooks tells Leacock about her meeting with Clair, he interrupts her to say that he never met the man. The camera remains focused on Brooks as she glares at him and moves on with her story. She tells of a dinner she had with Pabst after her rendezvous with Clair and then pauses in her own conversational flow to ask Leacock if he has ever heard of a London aristocrat she describes. The camera pans to include him in the frame as he responds that he hasn't; suddenly, then, a close-up of Leacock is edited into the picture. This edit seems to interrupt Brooks's monologue, though what has been cut is unclear: the scene quickly returns to the image of the two of them at the table, and Brooks continues to discuss an anecdote concerning the dinner with Pabst. After she appears to have completed the story, however, there is another cut, this time made possible by an insertion of a close-up only of Brooks. Over the close-up, we hear Leacock say, "I'd like to ask you, you in your article, you describe in relation to *Pandora's Box* where in a sense that Pabst, you felt, was also acting the role of Dr. Schoen in relation to you. And I think [you said] 'he was not aroused by sexual love.'" Irritated at his interruption of her, Brooks now interrupts Leacock, "Sexual love?!" Continuing to quote Brooks, Leacock goes on, "He was not aroused by sexual love, which he dismissed as an enervating myth. It was sexual hate that engrossed his whole being with its flaming reality." Though she appeared to be quite cross during the initial interruption, Brooks now perks up, murmuring, "Yes, yes, yes."

Ultimately, however, she refuses this line of discussion and instead asserts, "But I want to tell you about *Diary*." This comment, which we see her begin to make after her acquiescence to Leacock's statement, is audibly carried over to another close-up of Leacock edited into the sequence. This initial visual cut is followed with an audio one, which is in turn followed by another visual cut—an image, again, of Brooks and Leacock in the same frame—as Brooks begins another story about Pabst. Bridging the oral and visual elements of the film, such almost imperceptible cuts appear throughout the film in order to control the flow of Brooks's monologue. (In fact, two more cuts quickly follow these last few: one is made possible by the insertion of a still, and the other is an obvious jump-cut, one of the only such edits in the documentary.) For instance, even while Brooks attempts to control the drift of her story and, as a result, the film itself, she loses this control through the course of its editing.

Still, Louise Brooks's literal (and literary) voice helps to structure and challenge that of the film as a whole. In a sense, the enunciative voice of the film is guided by Brooks's diegetic voice. The film is, after all, largely a visual representation of her speaking, or even her writing. Her speaking, autobiographical voice guides the biography (or biographies: that of Brooks, as well as that of Pabst) that the film tells. As an autobiographical, biographical, and essayistic piece, *Lulu in Berlin* negotiates those terms that Renov highlights—"history, subjectivity, language"—largely through Brooks's own voice. In fact, the piece is further essayistic in that Brooks tells many of the same stories that she narrates in her written essays, especially "Pabst and Lulu"; the very title of the film seems to be a direct echo of Brooks's contemporaneously published *Lulu in Hollywood*. Even, then, taking into account Nichols's caution that a single voice of a film subject does not guide the (enunciative) voice of the work, it seems that Brooks does largely direct the work's point of view. Indeed, voice and point of view—the oral and the visual—are neatly combined in the image of Brooks speaking. She thus generally controls her own history—the history of her subjectivity, in fact—through her own linguistic performances. Even as Leacock and Woll at times redirect her words, her dialogue, her stories, they also clearly focus the film on, and thus through, Brooks. In fact, at times that redirection is made possible through Brooks's own words, as the earlier examples show: twice during the film Leacock quotes Brooks's essays to guide the conversation.

Ultimately, the film is a visual representation of Brooks, yet it visualizes her as a speaker and a writer rather than a pure image. We see her sitting at the table with Leacock, and we see her in clips from her European films. Moreover, we see her looking at herself and her history to verbalize what she has witnessed. Indeed, the documentary emphasizes her role as such an observer in the opening and closing sequence of the film: a scene from *Prix de beauté* shows Brooks's character in a projection room watching herself on-screen, singing. She is suddenly shot in the theater; we first see her still body in the theater before her moving image on-screen, and then we see her from the opposite angle, lit by the projection of the film behind her. She is literally trapped by this cinematic image, though she also, at least initially, has the power to see herself. Leacock and Woll's film, like Brooks's essays before it, gives voice to her silent image in Pabst's works; indeed, it reveals Brooks's image as a double one. She is the silent screen star and she is the woman who looks at the star in order to speak and write about her.

At one point during the interview, Brooks claims that she didn't have confidence in her beauty or in her talent as an actress: "To be a great actress you must know what you're doing. When I write my little pieces, I know exactly what I'm doing. When I acted I hadn't the slightest idea of what I was doing. I was simply playing myself, which is the hardest thing in the world to do." In *Lulu in Berlin*, Brooks again plays herself, though now as an observer and a writer: the film is thus a performance by both the star and the writer. In many ways, the documentary offers a definitive portrait of Brooks as it produces such a double image—or, rather, an image of a voice. Hence, it merges word and image, the written and the visual, for the images that we see (and the stories that we hear) are guided by Brooks's own words. This vision, in turn, might point us toward recognizing the value of allowing other women in film history to tell their own histories. At least, it might stress that we should hear their voices among others in the narration of their histories.

But is such a conclusion about Brooks truly conclusive? Or does the dual representation of image and witness that the film offers produce further doublings? For instance, her image as an observer and a thinker is itself complicated by the film: the documentary, via Brooks, paints the star as an intelligent observer and historian of herself and her contemporaries, but Brooks attempts to contradict even this portrait. Twice in the film she claims that she didn't fit the model of the intellectual that Pabst wanted. Early on she declares, "He knew instinctively that I was Lulu. . . . But off the set he wanted me to be an intelligent woman, a well-disciplined actress, but I wasn't!" Pabst approached his work "intellectually," Brooks says, "but he couldn't approach me intellectually because there was nothing to approach!" And later she describes a gathering with Pabst and Heinrich Mann as a "very intellectual tea, and very boring!" These delineations of herself as what Roland Jaccard might deem an anti-intellectual are consistent with other stories in *Lulu in Hollywood* and Barry Paris's biography. Paris, for instance, includes an excerpt from Brooks's reconstruction of part of *Naked on My Goat* (the autobiography that she claimed to destroy), which she produced at James Card's behest. As Paris points out, "'Mary' is Louise. 'Tony' remains a mystery": "It is Sunday, no *Scandals*, and Mary is sitting in her brass bed in the Algonquin trying to read Mencken's *Prejudices*. When the phone rings, she throws Mencken across the room and grabs the receiver. It's Tony cooing at her like a dove."[80] Here she represents herself both as an intellectual and not: she reads a literary critic's work, but she tosses the book aside with the promise of a lover taking its place.

The visual doubling in *Lulu in Berlin* offers clues to an understanding of these seeming contradictions. In the film we literally see two Louise Brookses. One is the young and glamorous Brooks of Pabst's films, her glossy hair in her signature bob, her body almost constantly moving, clothed in form-fitting fashions (even when trashed by her director); the other is the aging woman, her long gray hair pulled back from her head, her body seated, adorned only in what seems a white nightgown under a blue quilted bathrobe. The film thus tacitly counters her luminous image as a young star with this staid image of her as an older woman. Moreover, it silently points to the *real* story of her life that Brooks refuses to tell: that of the period that followed her stardom and that of her life in old age. This vision of Brooks is indeed in stark contrast to the image for which she is most known. Yet, it is also as an older woman that Brooks is able to look back and perceptively observe her old life as the star of Pabst's films. In other words, it is as an older, apparently intellectual woman that she is able to claim her younger self as an anti-intellectual (however disingenuous this claim might be). By filming Brooks as she was in her older age—and especially by shooting her via certain direct cinema conventions, without stylized lighting or sets—*Lulu in Berlin* "commits to celluloid" a new image of the star. So, even as the film focuses on the stories of her youth, it visually begins to round out her life story through this double representation of her.

Considering these various dualities and tensions, we might ask how much we can trust Brooks's claims. At what point do we believe—or disbelieve—her word? *Lulu in Berlin* certainly lends credence to Brooks's authority, as its own voice is that of the star herself. But its visual representations of Brooks, which are also a part of its voice, illuminate the difficulty there is in negotiating and balancing visual and written images. As a film of Brooks acting and talking, it mediates between the star's image made on-screen and her image constituted on paper. Moreover, it reveals consistencies between the two forms precisely in the inconsistencies and doublings we can see produced in each.

## CONCLUSION: LOUISE, L'AUTEUR

As I've elaborated, Brooks can be defined through the conjoining of written and visual texts. The merging of these forms has created and sustained her double image as the object of the camera and the subject who comments on what she sees. Moreover, it was through the meeting of cinematic and written texts that her champions, such as James Card and Henri Langlois, drew her out of her "intense isolation." And although the appearance of her written and filmic autobiographical texts crystallized her position as an author, she was surely authoring and directing her image long before either the publication of *Lulu in Hollywood* or the release of *Lulu in Berlin*. In part, her authorship was forged through her conduct as a reader. At least, the acts of reading and writing were invariably forged in her own work and in discussions of her.

As a sort of postscript to *Lulu in Hollywood*, Lotte Eisner's "A Witness Speaks" follows Brooks's autobiographical essays and reflects on these issues of authorship, intelligence, and Brooks's signature beauty. In her brief piece, Eisner recalls her first meeting with Brooks on the set of Pabst's *Diary of a Lost Girl*:

> Pabst introduced me to the actress playing the heroine of the film, a young American woman of fascinating beauty who was sitting there

**8** Reading stars: Colleen Moore re-poses. *Photo courtesy of the Academy of Motion Picture Arts and Sciences.*

reading. Incredibly, what this beautiful young woman was reading was a translation of Schopenhauer's *Essays*. Of course, I assumed that this was a publicity stunt of Pabst's; he knew perfectly well that I was a university graduate. However, I grew increasingly aware of an almost magical power emanating from this strange young woman, who spoke very little. . . . And this Louise Brooks, whom I scarcely heard speak, fascinated me constantly through a curious mixture of passivity and *presence* which she projected through the shooting.[81]

I quote this passage not to underscore the notion that a beautiful woman reading is "incredible" (here even to a female critic), but to highlight the possibility that Brooks's own witness questioned the authenticity of Brooks's performance for her audience off-camera. At the same time, Eisner began to trust Brooks *implicitly*, for, as she remarks, she scarcely heard Brooks speak; rather, she simply sensed a "magical power emanating" from the young actress. Brooks's truthfulness (Eisner implies that she was *really* reading, rather than posing for a publicity stunt) is here understood as innate.

Eisner focuses on Brooks's silent presence, but later in the piece she emphasizes her strength as a writer: "This fiercely independent woman has, in her solitude, become an authentic writer. She has provided us with essays on the cinema of her era and on the stars she happened to encounter and to observe . . . essays striking in their evenhandedness and insight."[82] Two rhetorical tropes particularly stand out in these remarks. First, Eisner continues to represent Brooks as honest: she is an "authentic" writer, and her essays are "evenhanded." Second, Brooks herself has the power not only of voice but also of vision: she has been able "to observe" her contemporaries with "insight." It might seem that this typical merging of sight and speech would bring a clarity to Brooks's own image and her history, but as I have shown throughout, even adding Brooks's voice to such an image as Eisner describes increases the star's ambiguity rather than her verity.

In fact, in *Lulu in Hollywood* Brooks tells a story similar to Eisner's that highlights the way her reputation for intelligence (as well as deception) also stems from her own work. The story is brief, and it accompanies a photograph in the volume. Hence, it is another example of a literal merging of photographic image and written word, not unlike *Lulu in Berlin* or that which Heide Schlüpmann includes in her essay. Under a photograph in which she is surrounded by books but is not reading any herself (though her companion is), Brooks declares, "This is my favorite publicity still because I posed it myself when I went to Hollywood in 1927. I found myself looked upon as a literary wonder because I read books. I'm posing with Keen Thompson, who wrote the screenplay for *Now We're in the Air*."[83] Finding herself "looked upon" in Hollywood, Brooks began to manufacture her own image; she thus began to direct the looking in Hollywood. Here she notes that she took advantage of the manner in which she was already perceived ("looked upon as a literary wonder") and redirected this perception from her own position. Part of this redirection entails posing with a man who is reading to her; thus, she also parodies the view that she couldn't actually be a "literary wonder" on her own. In this photo, surrounding herself with many books (rather than just posing with one) and sitting with a man who is reading *to* her, Brooks exaggerates the truth.

In all honesty, Brooks was a reader, and her sojourn in Rochester was largely defined by reading as well as writing. Paris recounts the story of her scribbling in the margins of library books, a practice for which she became infamous.[84] Her personal collection of books, donated to the George Eastman House, attests to her active reading. In fact, these books mark another melding of her roles as reader (or viewer) and author. Throughout them we find Brooks's penned comments, not surprisingly often focused on the veracity of the respective writer's claims. Her jottings refer invariably to sexual practices and mere physical appearances of various Hollywood players. In comments lodged in Herman Weinberg's biography of Josef von Sternberg she appears obsessed with Marlene Dietrich's lesbianism; throughout Bob Thomas's biography of Harry Cohn she mocks Cohn's physical size as well as his abuse of power to gain sex; and in a number of books she points to what she sees as the imperfections of women's bodies (e.g., Rita Hayworth in *Citizen Cohn*: "bad knees"; Hedy Lamarr in her own memoirs: "knock-knees"). Given Brooks's association with sex (ambiguous or no), such comments are not surprising.

More interesting are her notations regarding money matters, the common myths concerning the shift from silent to sound film, and the very manner in which many of these histories are narrated. Thus, in Lamarr's *Ecstasy and Me*, she approximates Lamarr's earnings over

9 Louise Brooks publicity still.

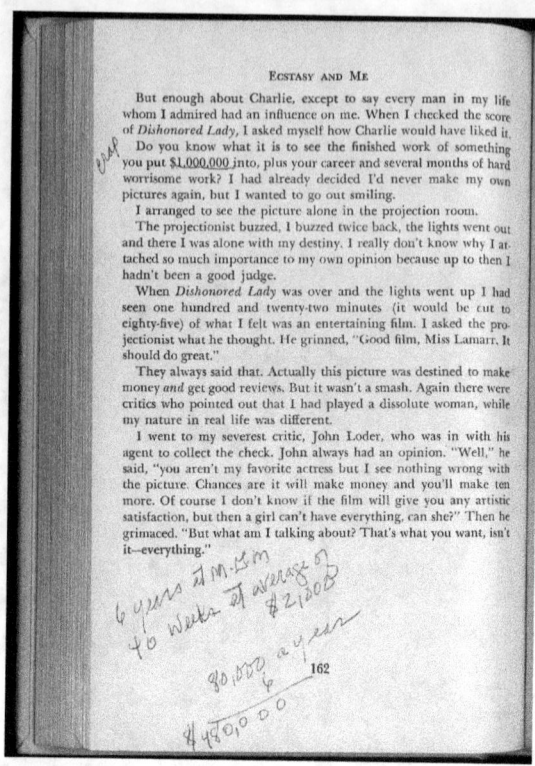

10 Louise Brooks's marginal comments in Hedy Lamarr's *Ecstasy and Me*. Image courtesy of the George Eastman House.

six years, seemingly to disprove her claim that she "put $1,000,000 into" the film *Dishonored Lady* (to which Brooks has responded "crap" in the margins); through her own calculations, Brooks estimates $480,000 at the bottom of the page.[85] On the following page she notes Greta Garbo's salary to refute Lamarr's claim that she was the "highest-priced and most important star in Hollywood." In several books, especially producer Cohn's biography, Brooks repeatedly disputes the accepted myth that many actors could not make the transition to sound because of poor voice quality. Thus, regarding the oft-maligned John Gilbert's voice, she writes, "Gilbert's voice rose in pitch through sound men by orders of Mayer to get out of $1,000,000 contract."[86] Regarding the general shift to sound, she notes, "It was the producers, writers and directors who could not provide material and direction for actors—They panicked—got stage directors—blamed actors voices."[87] As in her own memoirs, Brooks reveals herself as desperate to set the historical record straight. But for whom are these notes intended?

Often the notes seem to be for Brooks herself. As such, they display the process of her education, as well as the critical eye that she has developed over time as a writer. Her comments therefore include discussions in various compact and sometimes scathing forms concerning the narrative process: who wrote what, what can be told, what should be told, what is invented, what is a faithful scene. In Lamarr's book, for instance, Brooks frequently comments on both the "vulgarity" and the infidelity of the author's stories, suggesting that "[King] Vidor never talked like this in his life" or that "this book is 60% padding—mostly invented dialogue."[88] She also speculates that the author was a man rather than Lamarr,[89] in part because of the writer's obsession with and particular description of women's breasts. Her comments within the margins of Herman Weinberg's biography of Josef von Sternberg are similarly concerned with what is true or not in his reporting, as well as who is the source of the included material. On the opening page Brooks speculates, "Weinberg's text about 18,000 words—the rest compilation."[90] She complains frequently throughout her reading of *King Cohn*, especially when it comes to descriptions of Cohn and various actresses but also in relation to the recounting of certain anecdotes. With regard to the termination of Herman Mankiewicz—after a snide comment about Cohn's narcissistic sense of power—Brooks jots "Ridiculous." She follows with, "Every goddamned book on a Cohn, a Warner, a mayor [sic] is loaded with these supposedly deadly strokes of tyranny—if producers were such fools they would be operating an empty lot."[91]

Brooks finds intolerable those accounts that mythologize the power ubiquitous in Hollywood. She abhors what she sees as invented dialogue and fictional padding in so-called historical accounts. She also considers what stories cannot be told. Thus, she flags the following passage in Weinberg's study of Stroheim: "Even the intellectuals, who ought to know better, like to hear about the pretensions, the extravagances and the vulgarities." Brooks responds, "This stopped my film articles—My fact and truth were rejected for the dullest, silliest shit."[92] And she offers a more thoughtful response in the frontispiece of Francis Steegmuller's biography of Jean Cocteau:

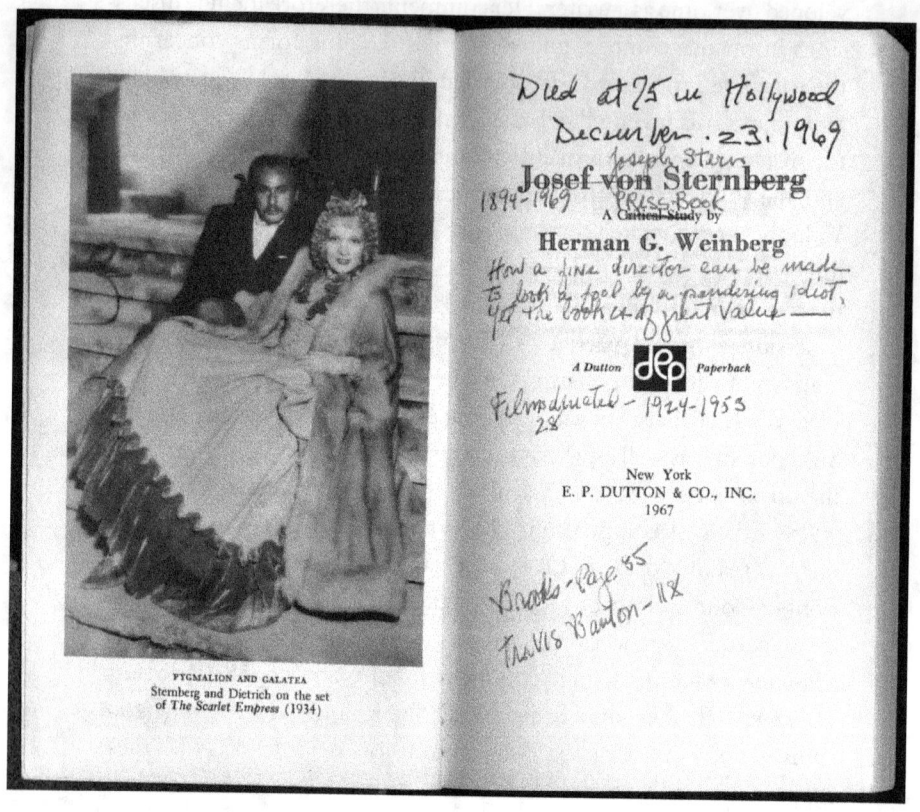

**11** Louise Brooks's marginal comments on the frontispiece to Herman Weinberg's biography of the director Josef von Sternberg. *Image courtesy of the George Eastman House.*

16 January 1972
> This brilliantly written book proves what I feared, yet questioned. I cannot write about Garbo until she is dead (if I outlive her). To write of her without the root of her mystery and genius—her lesbianism totally masculine is a futile attempt to build a structure without foundation. Steegmuller opens with Cocteau's homosexuality from childhood from which he plots and explains his genius.
>
> Yet I feel that Garbo craves to be exposed, to escape from her female coffin. She looks and dresses like a handsome old gentleman. She cultivates friendships with famous and gossipy writers whom she does not read or understand or enjoy. No, it is not she, now frankly referring to herself as "Him," who keeps the lid on her cruel, aggressive, male character. It is the publishers who will not lift the lid for fear of libel and slander suits.[93]

This notation is one of the most complicated and informative of Brooks's marginalia; it depicts what Paris calls her "lifelong appreciation-deprecation of homosexuals" in that she seems at once in awe of Garbo and off-handedly contemptuous. But the passage also offers a rumination on what Brooks feels comfortable writing about, particularly regarding sexuality, and how these particular details about a person can and should inform how we understand her or him. In this way, her penned comments are an outline toward future written work.

Though her usual tone is pretty snarky, sometimes Brooks's reading is more contemplative. This is the case in her marginal comments in Mary Astor's memoirs. Here she underlines and refers to passages that resonate with her emotionally and as a writer, as in the following case:

> <u>The past was finally past. Written down, examined, and discussed—and discharged, deprived of energy</u>. . . . I could feel and know with blessed certainty <u>that I could never again act under the dynamics, the forces of old habits, the caprice of infantile drives, the reactions to former conditioning. Interesting enough</u>, but what else? I had evaluated my past life, and it had been painful of course; but I begin to realize at an accelerating pace that that is not the only purpose of psychotherapy. It is also <u>re</u>-education.[94]

Regarding the underlined passages, Brooks simply writes: "No-Alas." In cases such as this, she uses her reading and writing practices to re-

*the critic* 149

# COCTEAU see page 14

14 January 1972 —

This brilliantly written book proves what I feared, yet questioned. I cannot write about Garbo until she is dead (I'll outlive her). To write of her without the root of her mystery and genius — her lesbianism totally masculine — is a futile attempt to build a structure without foundation. Steegmuller opens with Cocteau's homosexuality from childhood from which he ~~to~~ plots and explains Cocteau's genius.

Yet I feel that Garbo craves to be exposed, to escape from her female coffin. She looks and dresses like a handsome old gentleman. She cultivates friendships with famous and gossipy writers whom she does not read or understand or enjoy. No, it is not she ~~who~~, now frankly referring to herself as "Him," who keeps the lid on her cruel, aggressive, male character. It is the publishers who will not lift the lid for fear of libel and slander suits.

12  Louise Brooks's marginal comments on the frontispiece to Francis Steegmuller's biography of Jean Cocteau. *Image courtesy of the George Eastman House.*

flect on how one's memory might function and how one might design a life history based on memory, experience, and observation. Indeed, the dual processes of reading and writing might function for Brooks, as psychotherapy does for Astor, as a form of reeducation. Unfortunately, these moments of rethinking are somewhat rare for Brooks, as she remains often entrenched in the inflexible role of the teller of truths, or as the natural Lulu.

Alongside those historical and theoretical writings and documentary films that sketch Brooks as a reliable witness, her marginalia reveals her to be conscious of performances in and of sexuality, modernity, and the cinema. In his introduction to *Lulu*, William Shawn stresses Brooks's position not only as an observer but also as a conscious constructor of an image: "Yet it was Louise Brooks, in silence and out of her own person, who created the fundamental, the only Lulu."[95] I would add to this comment that it was Louise Brooks, through her writings and discussions of her image, who created the fundamental image of Louise Brooks: an image, moreover, that speaks, looks, performs, and possibly deceives.

Considering all of these issues, it is almost impossible not to reflect on how they bear on theories of auteurism and authorship. Thus, I will close by looking at two anecdotal discussions that forge speculative links between Brooks and auteur theory. First, in his astute essay "Brooks and the Bob," Peter Wollen conjectures on a historical link between Brooks and the emergence of *les politiques des auteurs* in France. He begins the essay by quoting two written passages, one by Howard Hawks on Brooks and one by Brooks on Hawks. He then notes, "Without Hawks, we might never have heard of Louise Brooks," as it was upon viewing Hawks's *A Girl in Every Port* that Pabst made the decision to cast her as Lulu. But he goes on:

> But there is a twist to the story. After all, it is equally true that without Louise Brooks we might never have heard of Howard Hawks. Even now, people are often surprised that he should be considered one of the great directors, his Hollywood films the touchstone of what cinema should be. Why Hawks? The answer is simple. Henri Langlois, who became the founder and director of the Paris Cinématèque, went out of his way to collect and preserve Hawks' films and, as a result, the young critics of *Cahiers du cinéma* were able to see them and learn from them. . . . But why did Langlois make such an effort to collect Hawks in the first place?[96]

The answer to the last question is, of course, because of his fascination with Brooks. And as Wollen hints, the screening of Hawks's films at the Cinémateque enabled the production of les politiques des auteurs, writings by French critics that sought to elevate film to a serious art form with the director at the helm as artist. This fortuitous connection might lead one to imagine that Brooks herself was indirectly responsible for the development of theories of auteurism, though of course she is still responsible as *image* (that with which Langlois was so fascinated) rather than as *author*.

Over a decade after Langlois's sixty-year celebration of film at the Cinémateque at which James Card was present and at which hung an enormous portrait of Brooks, Brooks directly commented on these theories. Her commentary was in the form of a letter to Andrew Sarris, generally known as the primary importer (and modifier) of what he called "auteur theory" in the United States: "The Bazin translation . . . took me two hours and three dictionaries to get through. Mind, I am no intellectual judge, but it did seem a lot of fancy words . . . to get to the simple fact that 'the *politique des auteurs*' is 'the negation of the work to the profit of the exaltation of its *auteur*.' Ever since the beginning of films, writers and directors have been jealous of the actor's glory, trying to find some way of wiping them off the screen with words." In what has become a typical gesture in relation to Brooks, Sarris printed these comments next to a picture of the star in the next issue of *English Cahiers du Cinéma*. Paris relates that Brooks continued to pursue these issues. For instance, in a letter she wrote to Herman Weinberg shortly after the publication of these comments, she declared, "If I could write in profound generalities I would set up, in opposition to the *auteur* theory, the *acteur* theory."[97]

Brooks's thoughts about the auteur and acteur are significant on a number of levels. First of all, it is unusual for a star to be immersed in academic theories and histories of film. Second, and not unsurprisingly, she emphasizes the role of the actor in the artistic production of a film; with her words, she re-places the actor on the screen. Third, the associations she proffers make possible a number of theoretical links. One might argue, in fact, that even Brooks could be considered an auteur. If one substitutes "star" for "director" (and "her" for "his"), she appears to fit the characteristics that Sarris himself delineates in "Notes on the Auteur Theory in 1962": "the technical competence of a director as a criterion of value," "the distinguishable personality of the director as a criterion of value," and an "interior meaning" that is "extrapolated from the tension between a director's personality and his material."[98] At least, these are all the sorts of terms that writers frequently use to describe Brooks.

But although she might well fit Sarris's conception of the auteur, we don't need Brooks to revive auteur theory (indeed, I'd argue, we don't need to revive traditional auteur theory at all); rather, considering how Brooks is an *author* in her own right, we might utilize her case to rethink auteur theory and to rethink the ways that film history—including the history of authorship itself—is written. Judging from all accounts, Brooks is indeed an author and a critic of how she is perceived in history, however indeterminate that may be; she is also an author of her image, however retrospectively she may have penned it. Finally, along with the convergence of image and word, it is through such indeterminacy, retrospection, and introspection that Brooks is defined.[99]

Suffice it to say that the discourse that circulates around Brooks, and that has been generated in great part by her, does offer an interesting model to examine and learn from. Simply put, it's tremendously useful to recognize other voices in film history and film theory, particularly voices of women who have been seen otherwise as contributing only an image, only a body or sexuality, to film culture and film history. At the same time, however, we might also recognize the inherent problems with a consistent, and often unquestionable, reproduction of such voices or writings. In the case of Brooks, her reputation as a woman known for her intelligence is often traded for her reputation as one known for sexual exploits and her knowledge about things sexual. Thus, knowledge produced by her and about her often becomes primarily a sexual knowledge. So, the discourse surrounding Brooks is indeed economical (as it circulates within a closed system), but that is part of the problem: it is *too* economical and therefore limiting, particularly when it reproduces a logic that suggests we can know one primarily through sex. The focus on Brooks's "indeterminate" sexuality might confirm a belief in the deceptive nature of sexuality (and subjectivity) itself, but it potentially closes off other issues concerning women's collaborative roles in the understanding of their images and, thus, in the writing of film history and film criticism.

In thinking about Brooks's role as a critic, therefore, we need to account for the limits she sets for herself and for her readers about what she will reveal and what is defined as the truth. Her own practices as a reader are particularly informative to conclude, however tentatively, on her work as a critic. Her irritation registered in the margins of her books, her accounting for stars' finances as well as narrative facts, her exegeses on what a writer may or may not reveal in constructing a history of a life—are not these the same kinds of notes the scholar makes today as she reads? This form of compatibility might seem superficial, but it's also a very concrete way in which contemporary writers are like the subjects they study. Brooks studied Hedy Lamarr's, Herman Weinberg's, and Mary Astor's texts in a way not completely disparate from how I study her own texts. Of course, her activity as a student is not the ultimate proof of her work as a critic: that testament is made when we become students of Brooks, collaborating with her in our understanding of who she was and how that affects our own writing of history.

# 4

## THE EXPERT

### *celebrity knowledge and the how-tos of film studies*

> My preference is to turn to history for a context prolonging the life of the ephemeral item or "case": saturating with detail an articulated place and point in time, a critical reading can extract from its objects a parable of practice that converts them into models with a past and a potential for reuse, thus aspiring to invest them with a future.
> —MEAGHAN MORRIS, *Too Soon, Too Late: History in Popular Culture*

> It's not what I know, it's the way that I know it.
> —MAE WEST, "That's All Brother"

The tense of advice comprises a complicated temporality, intersecting the past, present, and future in the briefest moment of time. Our parents, teachers, friends all tell us how to do things: this telling is based on past experience of the expert who advises, but it also always gestures toward the future in its second-person and present-tense command form. In *Grapefruit: A Book of Instructions and Drawings*, Yoko Ono gives directions for various "pieces" her readers ostensibly might perform. For "Echo Telephone Piece," she suggests, "Get a telephone that only echoes back your voice. Call everyday and talk about many things."[1] Offering advice on "Cooking" in *Marlene Dietrich's ABC*, which was published three years after the composition of "Echo Telephone Piece," Dietrich suggests "What to do when": "When your cake won't come out of the mold: Leave it face down and wrap a wet towel around the mold. The cake will slide out in no time."[2] Detailing how to make divinity, Zasu Pitts begins her instructions as follows: "In a heavy three-quart saucepan, blend sugar, corn syrup, water, and salt. Cook and stir over low heat till sugar is all dissolved. Then boil mixture to hard-ball stage. If you use a thermometer, it should read 250° F. Remove from heat, being careful not to disturb the syrup lest it crystallize."[3] In each instance, the writer uses the command form of the present tense (though Dietrich combines it with the transitive), which in effect asks the reader to perform in the future. These future actions, presumably, will also be repeated: "Echo Telephone Piece" is explicitly about repetition (as well as, of course, solipsism); even the best bakers will make cakes that get stuck in their pans; and who wouldn't want to make candy more than once (it's actually the only way to get it right)!

These works therefore point to a time when they will be read, when the performance they describe (and have presumably rendered already themselves) will be repeated by the reader once and then potentially again. They assume an expertise on the part of the writer and an acceptance of that expertise on the part of the reader as she or he follows the advice the writer has offered. And as readers follow the writer's advice, they not only accept the expertise of the author, but ultimately begin to embody it through their shared experience performing the suggested action (and then again if they share the same advice with someone else). With their particular temporal framework, these kinds of advice books, however diverse, offer an epistemological blueprint and a model of the relationship between the subject of historical inquiry and the scholar who seeks to understand her or him. That is, we might see these works as a springboard for multiple epistemological and material forms of production. Each advice book, how-to manual, and cookbook assumes a future moment of production, but not only do they tell us how to make art pieces, candy, money, domestic pleasure, or better bodies, they also instruct us in the production of film criticism and history.

Looking at a wide range of writings, categorized largely under the rubric of the how-to manual, this chapter is the clearest indicator of the overlap of all the roles women have played in their writings and collections. The women I discuss in this chapter are experts in a variety of fields; as they share their expertise, they also sketch histories, offer critiques, and point to the collections they amassed. They are, moreover, experts in how they perceive themselves and how they have been perceived on-screen: they are thus expert critics of photographic and cinematic representation. In my consideration of the autobiographical nature of these works and the ways they reveal women's expertise outside of their roles in film production, I look to how these works extend the conventional images of stars like Mary Pickford, Colleen Moore, and Zasu Pitts and how they also extend our experience of them. It is indeed through works like *Candy Hits by Zasu Pitts* that we—as readers, fans, scholars—can embody those women whose works we study, collect, and consume.

This examination of how-to manuals comprises the most miscellaneous set of works in this study but also perhaps the most metonymic. In some ways an odd group of texts—including spiritual manuals, financial guides, cookbooks, workout books and exercise memoirs, performance art instruction, and self-analysis—such works are more common than one might imagine. In fact, they offer insight through their advice on daily, even mundane activities as well as, implicitly, through their increasingly ordinary status. Though an atypical form of discourse in film history, these sorts of texts were (and, today, are) not wildly uncommon. Some, like silent star Mae Marsh's *Screen Acting* (1921), Frances Marion's *How to Write and Sell Film Stories* (1937), Adela Rogers St. Johns's *How to Write a Story and Sell It* (1956), and Edith Head's *The Dress Doctor* (1959), offer advice based on the writer's area of expertise in the industry, such as acting, screenwriting, journalism and fiction, and costume design.[4] But those I am interested in span a wider reach. One of the earliest such works, Mary Pickford's *Why Not Try God?* (1934), is a short religious tract; Mae West's *Mae West on Sex, Health, and ESP* (1975), also a spiritual guide of sorts, covers rather the opposite spectrum. In the form of a reference book, *Marlene Dietrich's ABC* offers advice on subjects such as cooking and love and philosophy about stardom and glamour; Moore's *How Women Can Make Money in the Stock Market* functions as a financial manual. Cookbooks like *Candy Hits by Zasu Pitts*, themselves advice or how-to manuals, also figure in this study, as they, too,

*the expert* 157

reveal expertise that goes beyond film work. Works by contemporary celebrities, such as *Jane Fonda's Workout Book* and Christy Turlington's *Living Yoga: Creating a Life Practice*, implicitly about women's representation on-screen and in print, turn the celebrity into a physical fitness expert. Isabella Rossellini's books on photographs of herself are instructive in ways of looking, especially forms of self-reflection, and Yoko Ono's playful *Grapefruit* offers suggestions for performance pieces and, indeed, ways of approaching life and art. Although some of the works are less technical than, for instance, Colleen Moore's *How Women Can Make Money in the Stockmarket* or Sophia Loren's cookbook *Sophia Loren's Recipes and Memories*, all offer advice, information, and historical detail in the tradition of nineteenth-century conduct manuals by women and twentieth-century advice and how-to books.[5] In these ways, the advice manual and the cookbook can function as models for our understanding of these figures as both celebrities and historians or cultural critics and for the very way we study them. They are, in other words, instructive to the reader on several counts, offering implicit instructions on how we "do" film history and criticism. As do the collectors, moreover, these writers help us to expand our understanding of the historiographical archive and its future construction. Indeed, in my move in this chapter into an excavation of contemporary volumes alongside those by Pickford, Moore, et al., I hope to consider how these histories and these futures are always in the present making.

## CONDUCT IN HISTORY

Sarah Newton explains that conduct books for women in the United States were initially written by English authors, and "the first true American conduct book for women" was Cotton Mather's 1692 volume *Ornaments for the Daughters of Zion*. As the title and author readily show, most of the early works were written by men, and most also employed Christian rhetoric and ideology to sketch women's proper roles. The demand that "virtuous" women exercise "industry" in the home was commonplace in these volumes and lasted well into the nineteenth century. Yet, as Newton points out, Mather suggested that women also engage in "surprisingly broad intellectual training"; she cites him as follows: "Besides a good skill at her Needle, as well as in the Kitchen, she acquaints her self with Arithmetick and Accomptantship, (perhaps also Chirurgery) and such other Arts relating to Business, as may enable her to do the Man whom she may hereafter have, Good and not evil all the Days of her Life." This focus on education, albeit alongside "the assertion of the woman's intellectual inferiority," remained in conduct books throughout the eighteenth and nineteenth centuries.[6] In the eighteenth century, Newton shows, conduct book writers actually encouraged women's education in the fields of history, biography, religion, geography, and possibly literature by Shakespeare and Milton.

At the same time, however, there was anxiety that too much knowledge would make a woman too "masculine":

> If these contradictory messages to the woman—read and educate yourself but do not cross the invisible line of "learned" and "pedantic"—set up a tension in the female reader, conduct literature sets out to resolve it. One solution is for the woman to confine herself to studying only those topics and areas considered fit and appropriate for her, such as biography and religion. By respecting carefully defined intellectual boundaries, she engages no risk of stepping beyond appropriate female knowledge (and thus behavior).[7]

Such boundaries were actually intensified in the nineteenth century, argues Newton, as education was tied too much to independence, and independence was associated with the evils of the emerging industrial society. Therefore, conservative conduct book writers of the age reemphasized women's place in the domestic sphere: women's education was (re)centered around domestic knowledge. As Newton asserts, "Thus are domesticity and married life seen quite literally as women's business."[8]

Women's business remains the focus of many celebrity how-to manuals, even while they vary wildly from one to the next. For instance, Mary Pickford's *Why Not Try God?* obviously follows the party line of many early works in terms of spiritual guidance, and the volumes by Mae West and Marlene Dietrich narrate a certain knowledge about domestic life, yet the works by female stars in the twentieth century unsurprisingly also advocate other forms of knowledge that would be considered heresy in the preceding centuries. In great part, the expertise they bring to their conduct, or advice, manuals coincides with their images as stars. In this way, their written words and their images are conjoined through these texts, as the writers work with our

*the expert* 159

knowledge of them as stars. But their writings also work against our knowledge of them and the ways that they have been historically and fictionally imagined. Thus, the words themselves extend their images. They add another layer to our understanding of the figures: especially in older age, they become also women who write and women who *know*.

Mary Pickford's role as a writer necessarily raises additional questions about authorship in and around the film industry and film history. These questions concerning the construction of not only histories but fictions might also help frame our understanding of the advice manuals written by some of her relative contemporaries. Pickford published a number of works under her name: a newspaper column called "Daily Talks," which appeared five times a week from 1916 to 1917; another column for the *New York Journal* in 1938; *Why Not Try God?* (1934) and the follow-up to it, *My Rendezvous with Life* (1935); a play called *The Demi-Widow* (1935); and her autobiography, *Sunshine and Shadow*, in 1956. However, as Cari Beauchamp, the biographer of Frances Marion, and Eileen Whitfield, the recent biographer of Pickford, note, Pickford did not write all the works published under her name. Screenwriter Marion penned the "Daily Talks" column for Pickford for almost two years until "Frances's collapse" after the suicide of her sister Maude.[9]

Whitfield, too, emphasizes that Marion wrote the actual "Talks," but she also remarks that the screenwriter was neatly able to capture Pickford's own voice: "Much of 'Daily Talks' reads like a cross between Louisa May Alcott (as presented in the column, Little Mary bore a striking resemblance to Alcott's Polly in *An Old-Fashioned Girl*) and a fan magazine. Still, some anecdotes from Mary's own life ring true and, especially in answers to readers' queries, a bit of Pickford's tartness sparks off the page." Interestingly, Whitfield goes on to describe such answers as if Pickford herself did pen them: "Pickford scolds," writes Whitfield, and, "In a fit of guilt, Pickford tore a strip off the [letter] writer."[10] Whitfield's particular characterization of these writings is telling on a couple of levels. First of all, her links between Pickford and Alcott suggest an important connection between such advice columns and traditions of nineteenth-century women's writings, as I have also tried to lay out. Second, her consolidation of persons and personas—the screenwriter and author of the columns Frances Marion, the silent film star Mary Pickford, and the persona of the columns' author Mary Pickford—into, simply, "Pickford" both belies the origins of the columns and suggests the power of the star's name. In this case, Whitfield implies, because Pickford's name appeared on the columns at the time, we might continue to see the writings as penned by her, in spite of our knowledge to the contrary.[11] It is difficult to wrestle Pickford's actual name from the columns, as her name signifies the persona they helped to construct.

In this way, as in the case of star memoirs and other works ascribed to celebrity authors, Pickford's name carries with it an "author function." That is, her name as author is a function of discourse. As Foucault writes, the author function "is not formed spontaneously through the simple attribution of a discourse to an individual. It results from a complex operation whose purpose is to construct the rational entity we call an author."[12] Concerning Pickford, as well as some of the various other figures I discuss, this author is also a star. As such, each author is formed through a set of intertexts and discourses. The position, or role, of the author is dependent also on the position of the woman as star or celebrity. Moreover, each one's writings as author refer back to her filmic output as actress. Together these various roles and the various texts attributed to each construct a multilayered figure.

Considering this conglomeration of discourses and figurations, one might well ask of what importance it is whether or not these women penned their own works. I suggest that it is of some importance, of course, in order for us to parcel out historical facts and fictions. As I have suggested throughout, all of the examples I have been discussing exhibit additional illustrations of role-playing in which the stars were engaged. That is, texts like "Daily Talks" represent Pickford as an author as well as a film star and fictional character. Is this very role-playing another fiction or not? Surely, it is fictional in some ways, as any performance is. As such texts seek to conjoin the stars' words to their cinematic images, they are at least affected, if not infected, by fiction. At the same time, however, these works are also autobiographical: they tell authentic stories of the women's lives, and the knowledge they inscribe therein is based on the women's lived experiences and beliefs.

The short tract *Why Not Try God?* also lends to the simultaneous fictional and real construction of Pickford's star persona, especially as a diligent, moral, and even cheerful force in the face of adversity.

Yet, writes Beauchamp, Pickford was not the actual writer of this little booklet either: Pickford "resorted to her first face-lift and tried her hand at writing, this time turning to Adela [Rogers St. Johns] to pen *Why Not Try God?* Laced with the Christian Science teachings they both found comfort in, it became a best-seller."[13] Suggestively, Beauchamp distinguishes here between "writing" and "penning." At least, she implies that one can "try writing" without performing the actual labor of putting pen to paper. Hence, the production of this religious tract, as with the "Daily Talks" before it, depended on the collaboration between Pickford and a professional writer. Pickford's voice might well appear in the texts, but it's a voice that is, at least in part, constructed by another woman. Because of the collaborative nature of the works, I would not label them simple impersonations of Pickford by either Marion or St. Johns, but the texts surely also offer evidence of performance and role-playing. While Marion and St. Johns almost seamlessly perform in writing as "Pickford," Pickford herself simultaneously plays the role of the writer. And just as her name—and performances—sold countless tickets to films, here her name sold a manifold number of books.

Of course, the labor involved in these various performances is a bit different, and distinctions between the performances become even more complex when we take into account how the writings themselves mirror Pickford's image off and on the screen. As Whitfield notes, for instance, in the case of *Why Not Try God?*, Pickford combines the teachings of Christian Science with "her own think-positive, chin-up creed."[14] Seemingly as indebted to a watered-down version of Descartes' philosophy as anything else, the book does indeed focus around the power of thinking: "What is the primary fact of existence? Why, thought, of course. The power of thinking. Take that away and man is nothing. Your mind knows that you are and that makes you. Your thinking is the medium through which everything comes to you."[15] Significantly, here Pickford takes on the metasubject of every advice manual: the act of thinking that inherently leads to knowledge itself. Although nineteenth-century advice manuals often had peculiar relations to women's education, all how-to books in some form are intrinsically connected to knowledge: the sharing of one person's personal or collected knowledge with the reader.[16] This excerpt from Pickford's text embodies this spirit. And it does so through marking Pickford herself as a model for thinking as well as accumulating knowledge. Her performance as a thinker is not merely superficial; Pickford was well-known as a shrewd businesswoman from a very young age (and certainly she was not one of the founders of United Artists in name only). "Thinking" here neatly emphasizes the celebrity's expertise derived from the combination of intelligence and experience.

This experience and expertise are developed reciprocally between the writer and the reader. The work is concentrated around such issues and their relation to God, or spirituality, and it depends not only on Pickford's knowledge of Christian Science teachings but also, inevitably, on readers' knowledge of Pickford's stardom. Indeed, Pickford uses facets of her stardom as lessons in how to overcome adversity through thinking spiritually:

> Unlike most women, I have never been able to work out my intimate problems in private. I have to do it in front of the whole world, for the world knows what is happening to me professionally, domestically and personally almost as soon as I do myself. And so, in a way, I become at times more or less of a target for flying rumors and counter-rumors, hasty judgments and thoughtless gossip. . . . The more difficult the problem the harder I try to find the God-element, or the good-element, in people and things, and the more I try to think about others as I would have them think about me.[17]

Here Pickford is able simultaneously to pass judgment on those who spread rumors and gossip about her and to emphasize that she can overcome others' "hasty judgments" about her. With this sort of reference to gossip, surely a staple of some fan magazines, *Why Not Try God?*, like other stars' advice manuals that come after it, trades on the author's image as a star and our knowledge about her stardom. At the same time, the little religious tract might work to defray other knowledge fans would have about Pickford and her family members: her brother Jack's drug addiction and the ugly circumstances surrounding the death of his wife, Olive; Pickford's divorce from Fairbanks; her alcoholism and that of her family members.[18] But of course, these situations cannot be referred to directly. Indeed, the book begins to come to a close with these words: "Back of the glamour that motion pictures have thrown around me, I am just an average, hopeful, prayerful woman."[19] As Richard DeCordova and others have shown, this sort of alliance between the star and the average person has been a necessary element in the success of star images and the star system overall. Here, too, it seems key for the success of Pickford and St. Johns's book, yet in the sense that part of our alliance with the star is based on a recognition of and an exchange of knowledge.

Mae West, a writer before, during, and after she was a film star, also centers on the power of thinking in her book *Mae West on Sex, Health, and ESP*. West published her autobiography, *Goodness Had Nothing to Do with It*, in 1959; *Mae West on Sex, Health, and ESP*, published in 1975, could be read as falling somewhere between being volume 2 of her memoirs and an advice manual.[20] Essentially, West draws on her own autobiographical experience to offer advice to men and women on the promised subjects. For instance, as West remarks in the chapter "For Men Only!" (a primer on sexual performance), "Since experience makes the best teacher, I'm going to put on my professor's hat." Though here she jokingly equates knowledge with academics, throughout the volume she earnestly stresses the importance both of experiential knowledge and of thinking in general. For instance, in the same chapter, West tells an anecdote about having sex with the same partner twenty-six times in just over twelve hours. As she tells it, the man explained this prolific performance by claiming that he'd been thinking only of West for months. Writes West in response, "That just may be a lesson in the power of positive thinking."[21] (Of course, West's own abundant endurance needs no explanation!)

As in Pickford's text (though in a very different way), a focus on "positive thinking" in West's book is threaded throughout. West particularly emphasizes this aspect of her belief system in her section on ESP. A blend of Eastern and Western religious thought, West's version of ESP is essentially based on the notion that if one is self-confident, one can accomplish anything: "ESP can be very helpful to you in everyday life by releasing you from the dreadful bondage of destructive emotions. Once you are able to be a positive person, think and feel positively, you are on the right road to a better understanding of yourself and other people. You will begin to accomplish things you never thought you could. Self-confidence, again, is most important. Say, 'I can do it!' "[22] This assertion of self-confidence was a trademark of West's performance style. Writes Ramona Curry, "Her complex, witty wordplay, the tone of her singing and speaking voice, her dominance in dialogue exchanges, and her pacing . . . all communicated intelligence, confidence, and control."[23] In this way, here and throughout the book, West's advice depends both on what readers know of her and what she herself "knows" from experience. Indeed, these two things are inseparable: because West's performances were always based around her own avowed sexual knowledge (often asserted through puns for her "knowing" audience), what we know about West is that she herself *knows*. This may seem tautological, but it actually goes to the heart of West's star persona. Moreover, this aspect of West—always the experienced, knowing woman—reveals precisely why she is the perfect writer of an advice manual: she has knowledge, and she's willing to share it.[24]

With the exception of some of her claims about ESP, West's advice on most matters in the book is linked to her notorious sexual knowledge. Hence, when she counsels readers on diet and health, she usually also couples the topics with sex. Her chapter entitled "Sex in the Kitchen," for instance, enlightens readers about what foods can increase or decrease sexual drive:

> When it comes to sex, I've always had a very healthy appetite.
>
> I think it's due partly to the way I was born, and partly by the way I live. It is impossible to have a good sex life unless you protect your health and your body by getting regular rest, proper exercise, and by avoiding the wrong foods and eating the right ones.
>
> I've detailed my feelings on health in other chapters, and I believe that if you follow them, you'll have no problem when it comes to sex. There are, though, some people who need a little push—and I'd like to shove them in the direction of the kitchen.[25]

This passage not only reiterates West's sexual image upon which the acceptance of her advice might be dependent for some readers; it also reiterates her performance style, so often drawn from her own writings. Her pun on sexual "appetite" and her wordplay around mapping out her particular rules to follow are characteristic of her rhetorical style. Even the choppy paragraphs, omnipresent throughout the book, mirror the pacing of much of her spoken delivery.

Her turn to the kitchen is an interesting one, for it follows the traditional, domestic line of many advice manuals popular with women in the nineteenth and twentieth centuries. However, though West might be concerned about women's lives in the domestic realm, certainly the "conduct" she advocates in the kitchen (and elsewhere in domestic and public spaces) is decidedly unlike that encouraged by her eighteenth- and nineteenth-century predecessors. Indeed, while she delineates the proper diet for proper sex in the section devoted to "Sex" in the volume, eating is a primary focus in her section on "Health."[26] For instance, in the chapter called "Name Your Poison," she includes a long list of healthy and unhealthy foods. And for those who might have trouble digesting, she also includes a chapter, "Clean Livin'," on colonic cleansing. Thus, West draws on her image as a confidently sexual subject throughout the volume, but she links this image both to traditional women's domestic practices (and, indeed, are not the kitchen and the boudoir two rooms of one house?) and to less traditional—or, at least, less well-known—spiritual ones. These concerns illustrate how *Mae West on Sex, Health, and ESP* both reproduces and extends West's persona and, indeed, her autobiographical text.

Like Pickford's and West's books, *Marlene Dietrich's ABC* is also an autobiographical text of sorts, as it is based on the star's knowledge gained from lived experience. In fact, in the preface to the new edition of the book published in 1984, Dietrich calls it a "version of my beliefs and emotional experiences."[27] Surely, the same could be said of the respective works of Pickford and West. But what sets Dietrich's volume apart from the others is that it is structured like a reference book. Each section is centered around one letter of the alphabet and contains entries that begin with that letter. The topics of the entries range from film stars and directors, to more abstract notions associated with film stars (and Dietrich especially), to advice on housework and her convictions about a range of other miscellaneous subjects and objects. In other words, *Marlene Dietrich's ABC* captures both the extraordinary knowledge of a celebrity and the ordinary knowledge of a housewife.

It is, in fact, this self-promoted image of Dietrich, as one whose glamorous sexuality is not incompatible with a sort of (glamorous) domesticity that I focus on here. Although she does not advocate sex in the kitchen in the same sense that West does, Dietrich does at least illustrate that she is experienced in both domains. Interestingly, of course, West and Dietrich were situated as rivals in the 1930s, each signaling a different form of femininity. In her work on West and camp, Pamela Robertson cites a *Photoplay* article that marks West as "Queen of Curves" and Dietrich as "Queen of Glamour," pitting one against the other.[28] Yet, in their later years—and through these advice manuals especially—they might appear to be more like two sides of the same coin: both women are experts on a variety of domestic pleasures. In fact, the entry on West herself, wedged between "Weltschmerz" and "Western Union," demonstrates at least one aspect of Dietrich's expertise nicely: "A milestone, a catchword, sex with its tongue in its cheeks."[29] Hence, Dietrich's knowledge about sex is here illustrated by her knowledge about West.

At the same time, Dietrich reveals less cheeky knowledge; for instance, only a few entries earlier, Dietrich includes an entry "Wein Chaud D'eau," which is a recipe for the rich egg custard. In West's volume, the same recipe would in all likelihood take into account the aphrodisiac qualities of the egg, but in Dietrich's reference book the entry has nothing overtly to do with sex (though, because of its richness and its European origins, readers might at least associate it with Dietrich's glamour). Instead, she simply describes the ingredients for the dish and the proper way to blend and cook them. Unlike West, then, Dietrich does not explicitly merge the domestic arts of cooking and sex; rather, her interest in these various fields is signaled by the inclusion of the sheer variety of entries throughout her volume.

She does, however, often paint a picture of a kind of domestic glamour. This appears in individual entries as well as across entries. In her entry "Apron," for instance, Dietrich includes the following: "A woman in an apron invites hugging. The apron of a woman flung over a kitchen chair is a wonderful still life. And the pockets of that apron, harboring sticky unwrapped candies, crumpled bits of paper, newspaper ads hastily torn out, pennies and nickels and a ribbon stuck to a band-aid, a baby's sock and a bottle cap, should be food for poets who are so easily tempted to linger on the treasures in a little boy's pants pocket."[30] Kathleen McHugh suggests that domestic manuals often functioned paradoxically to make middle-class white women's domestic labor invisible: "The invisibility of such women's work mystified class difference by constructing appropriate femininity as apparently unlabored, affective, and spiritual."[31] The same claim could be made about Pickford's work (even as she shows how one must labor to practice a spiritual identity), and West's and Dietrich's works display the necessary labor to practice various forms of femininity (and sometimes hide the traces of that labor); yet Dietrich also maps how the image of the domestic woman is innately beautiful. In her entry "Apron," beauty comes from the evidence of everyday domestic life; the apron is the visible evidence of how such a woman might be loved.

*the expert* 167

This intersection between glamour and domesticity is, of course, typical of how we know Dietrich. As I suggested earlier, Dietrich represents herself throughout the ABCs in much the same way that her star image was always constituted. That is, she is known through seeming contradictions: at once an erotic and identificatory object for both men and women, a femme fatale and a nurturing mother, a worldly sophisticate and a "German hausfrau who likes to cook."[32] Yet, she also merges these various identities through the very range of her knowledge exhibited in the *ABC* book. Hence, she points to how these identities for herself—and, in turn, for other women—are not necessarily so contradictory and might even, in fact, be compatible. Sometimes, for instance, she uses culinary metaphors to describe entries outside of the kitchen; under "Lee, Peggy," she writes, "Honey-dripping singing, timing, phrasing; awakening no memories of other voices but awakening all senses to a unique feast." Not only does she invoke food to describe Lee, but she also evokes a sort of eros that one might ascribe to her bisexuality. As is the case with the volume as a whole, this sensual entry is followed by one that summons instead pure practicality: it is here that her entry "Leftovers" appears: "They are real fun. Take any boiled meat you have. Slice it. Fry onions with tomatoes, mushrooms if you have them, also sliced boiled potatoes, green peppers, plus any bits of cooked vegetables you might have; then add the meat, mix till all is hot, sprinkle with chopped parsley—and you will wish you had leftovers more often."[33] Clearly, the production of leftovers would offer a different sort of feast than would a musical number by Lee, but each still evokes somatic pleasures and each stems from a woman's craft. Dietrich's insistence throughout her volume on the beauty of domestic space—and the seeming beauty of the woman who rules there—repeatedly reveals her consistent merging of the various identities by which she is known. Like West's work, *Marlene Dietrich's ABC* is in part a return to some of the original intentions of conduct and advice manuals for women, but it also extends the fields of knowledge with which women might be associated.

## KNOWLEDGE AND NARRATION

Kathleen McHugh's *American Domesticity: From How-to Manual to Hollywood Melodrama* traces an instructive path from advice manuals to film, showing how the new technologies of visibility further sought to make women's domestic labor unseen. As she contends, "While the explicit, realistic, and widely disseminated visual images of housework available in the cinema might be expected to register forcefully the fact of women's domestic labor, instead the cinema followed the path of nineteenth-century domestic housekeeping manuals." In various celebrity advice manuals, this path follows in fascinating ways, as now the manuals build on film narratives at once to offer an intertextual knowledge about the star-author and to duplicate the narrative structure as a foundation for the advice. Writes McHugh, "Domestic femininity and domesticity entered the cinema not only as narrative content and preferred mise-en-scene, respectively, but also and more important as forms of representation laden with social meanings from which the cinema drew heavily."[34] In the case of Colleen Moore's *How Women Can Make Money in the Stock Market*, both domestic space and classical cinematic narrative form sometimes become the "mise-en-scène" for her advice about the public sphere. Though Moore moves well beyond them, narratives about domestic life thus also appear to invoke those social meanings rendered by film.

Moore's book is a work essentially sprung from the public sphere — the world of economics and finance, and certainly the world of men. Moore's very experience with stock trading initially exemplifies a fluid movement between traditional women's and men's roles vis-à-vis domestic and economic business. She became interested in the stock market by way of her second and third marriages.[35] Her second husband, Albert Parker Scott, was a stockbroker, and her third husband, Homer Hargrave, to whom she was married for almost four decades, was one of the founding partners of Merrill Lynch. Moore herself became the first woman to sit on the board of that brokerage, and she also guided the firm's foray into Revlon Cosmetics.[36] In her advice manual, she readily admits that the stock market has not traditionally been a realm where women have much power, so she wants to guide women specifically to find the know-how to succeed in that space. The volume is thus laden with very practical and very technical counsel.

Thus, Moore's expertise as demarcated in *How Women Can Make Money in the Stock Market* exceeds the arena of stardom, suggesting that the work of writing was not, for Moore, merely a staged performance. Nonetheless, like any proper how-to book writer, Moore does play certain roles throughout the volume to help persuade her reader to follow her advice. She begins the book with the story of her origins as a stock market authority. As she tells it, early in her marriage to Hargrave, she asked her husband to help her invest the money she made as a movie star, but he suggested instead that she learn to invest it herself. She describes her response as follows: " 'But, darling,' I said (very appealing and feminine), 'I can't even balance my own checkbook.' " Her husband responded that she should be ashamed to admit that fact and suggested that she "enter the Hargrave School of Finance." At the end of the introduction Moore asserts, "So this book is my graduation thesis for the Hargrave School of Finance, where I was the first and only pupil, plus the findings of considerable postgraduate research."[37]

This introduction certainly opens up a number of relevant points that are reiterated throughout the volume. First, Moore represents herself as one who trades on her femininity to evade her own financial work (in this case, merely balancing her checkbook). But, as is obvious from her rhetorical construction, this story begins a critique of a commonly held notion that women are incapable of handling economic affairs. She therefore offers a conversion narrative to persuade her audience: if I could do it, so can you. But to persuade her audience, she has to adjust herself to that audience. That is, she must represent herself as like her readers (and vice versa): female, certainly; straight and married, presumably; new to the field of finance but apparently with money to invest (she is, after all, a former movie star). Finally, by following Hargrave's lead in terming the knowledge he gave her as a kind of schooling, Moore emphasizes that she had become an expert through learning. For Moore, then, the processes of knowledge production and attainment have both formal and informal qualities; her book is therefore laden with practical yet highly informative (and at times very detailed and technical) advice. It is offered in a tone that would best suit the audience Moore presumes and hence constructs.

I focus here on Moore's representation of women's relation to finance and what she rhetorically suggests is the best way to teach them how to invest. For in making these suggestions, she sets up provocative links between the marketplace and the arenas with which women are familiar. The second chapter of Moore's volume asks the question "Why the Title 'How Women Can Make Money in the Stock Market'?" She begins to answer by noting, "This book is written, first of all, for the woman to whom the world of stocks and bonds is still unfamiliar territory."[38] She then informally—and at times depending on a very essentialist argument—looks at how women have been constructed as unable to know the world of economics since the days of a caveman she refers to as "Pete Piltdown."[39] She writes:

> Men have been telling women they don't understand business, and finally a lot of women have come to believe it. They furnish and maintain a house; they operate the family economy, clothe themselves and the children, see that the whole family gets proper medical and dental care—all on a budget which, in the early days of a marriage at least, is sometimes less than princely. These women do not understand business, according to their husbands, who are direct descendents of Pete Piltdown. These same husbands, incidentally, have their daily routines managed, their expense accounts worked out, their checkbooks balanced, their phone calls screened, their business correspondence monitored and edited by other women who, according to the husbands, also know nothing about business—or at least nothing important.[40]

Although today's readers may find this argument quite familiar, Moore forged it at a time when feminism was just beginning to make such claims known in mainstream America—and appearing very radical in doing so. Considering Moore's own brand of radical feminism, then, one might be tempted to forgive her later essentialist claim that women have "less natural talent for trading than the average male."[41]

Moore's narration of women as those who know economics but who are also always accused of not knowing the field follows the line of nineteenth-century and early-twentieth-century feminist economists. Her narration also significantly presages claims by late-twentieth-century feminists, like those whose work appeared more than two decades after hers, in the collection *Beyond Economic Man: Feminist Theory and Economics*. In their introduction to this 1993 volume, "The Social Construction of Economics and the Social Construction of Gender," editors Marianne A. Ferber and Julie A. Nelson note both that "men have dominated the community of scholars who have created the discipline" and that "gender also affects the construction of the discipline in terms of the standpoint from which the world is perceived, and the way the importance and relevance of questions are evaluated."[42] The editors and the authors whose work is collected in the anthology seek to understand and argue against these simultaneous constructions.

One way gender certainly affects the construction of the discipline of economics, Ferber, Nelson, and other authors argue, is by understanding the home as outside of the marketplace. Ann L. Jennings points out, "Woman is defined as different from man: woman is 'not man,' just as the family is 'not the economy.'"[43] These are the same distinctions that Moore delineates and decries. And in great part, they are formed through what Diana Strassman outlines in the Ferber and Nelson volume as the ideology of the "marketplace of ideas." Writes Strassman, "In the marketplace of ideas, the 'best' ideas bubble to the top, rising in value according to merit. Ideas are exchanged as in a marketplace, their worth ascertained in the competitive process of bidding and exchange." Economics as a discipline has obviously not been an exception to this rule. One example of the discipline's hierarchical valuation of ideas relates to the role women are seen as playing—or not playing—in the economy. Strassman, like Moore, thus examines how women's household labor traditionally hasn't counted in the national, domestic economy. She notes, too, "Although labor economists have begun to recognize the concept of nonmarket production, the very term 'household production' represents a borrowing from a category formed to describe male activity."[44] Hence, Strassman sees inherent links between different forms of domestic economies—at the household and the national levels.

Colleen Moore recognizes and fashions this and other such links as she draws various analogies and tells short tales to help teach her readers about the stock market. She points to public spaces women know in order to draw connections between her and her audience and to suggest that women are already active in the marketplace—just not usually the marketplace that is the stock exchange. In fact, she originally defines the market for her readers in relation to what she assumes would characterize their familiarity with the term:

> In our time, "market" has come to mean a store or supermarket where there are things to buy, with prices marked on them.
>
> The stock market doesn't carry a supply of securities to be sold, the way a supermarket carries groceries and meats and produce. It is a market in the original sense of the term: a setup where people buy *and* sell and where prices are determined primarily by the law of supply and demand.
>
> A market usually, though not always, has a market place: a physical area where the market activity can be carried on. In the stock market, the market places are called *exchanges*.[45]

Obviously, drawing this analogy between supermarket and stock market suggests that women are, in fact, already almost as familiar with the workings of the market as are those men who trade on the exchange.[46] At least, Moore implies, women already have the groundwork of knowledge to be able to understand this larger economic system.

Throughout the book, she continues to build on women's epistemological groundings. For instance, she describes finding a broker in the same terms one might describe nabbing a lover. Assuring women that, in this case, they have "complete freedom" over their choice of men, Moore advises, "There are sound basic qualifications this man should have" and then enumerates those particular characteristics.[47] In this way, Moore uses women's sense of romance to develop their sense of finance. Moreover, she depends on her audience's presumed interest in narrative. Hence, almost every chapter contains some story, however brief, to grab the reader's attention: she narrates the origins of gender discrimination in business through the fictional character of Pete Piltdown; she recounts in colloquial terms the origins of the New York Stock Exchange; she describes various shifts in economics as plot twists; she offers hypothetical stories about the workings of the market; and she sometimes tells cautionary tales about women and men who didn't invest properly.

This turn to narrative is one of the primary ways Moore depends on the intertextual knowledge her readers would have of her as a Hollywood narrative film star (emphasized, of course, on the book flap). These turns further complicate the path from advice manual to narrative cinema, which McHugh traces, as Moore uses film narratives to back up the advice manual. In fact, she offers a relatively long discussion of the movie industry to illustrate the difficulty of recognizing new products that will become popular. As she tells it, many didn't imagine that the movie industry would be more than a mere fad. Thus, argues Moore, "There were no great losses because of this. There was simply a great deal of money not put into motion pictures—fortunes not made. The people who believed the novelty was here to stay put their money into it and became part of a fabulous industry."[48] This and subsequent references to the film industry prove a very significant connection, if only implied, between women and the economy, which goes well beyond fictional narratives but integrates them simultaneously. That is, not only do women, like men, spend millions of dollars at the movies and thus help to keep that particular economy going, but one needs only to glance at the history of the star system in the United States to see that women are, in fact, very much inside that economy, however much they might have been (or continue to be, in some cases) represented as being outside. To be sure, women have been included in this economy as objects that the movies have, in a sense, traded on; nonetheless, there are women, like Pickford and Moore herself, who have very actively helped to control at least their own economic destinies.

Moore thus reveals (and helps to form) many levels of economic knowledge on the part of women in *How Women Can Make Money in the Stock Market*. She also exemplifies how the gendered spaces of home and economics are necessarily bridged. Certainly her work in Hollywood and her expertise in the stock market illustrate her savvy in financial matters. Her dollhouse reveals the same know-how and suggests another bond between the home and the marketplace(s). Built in great part with the money she made as a star, the dollhouse is a miniature, if excessive, version of how money is invested in the home. Moreover, as we know, the dollhouse itself became a wholly public object, traveling throughout the marketplace of the department store to make money for charity. Indeed, the circulation of Moore's productions provides a provocative solution to Ann Jennings's call for a "cultural reconnection of home, workplace, and polity"—proffered, of course, decades prior.[49]

## CONSUMING THE STAR

Early film production by women often built their public business of filmmaking on domestic models. Alice Guy-Blaché's Solax studio was described in the trade press as a "family"; directors like Guy-Blaché, Lois Weber, and Germaine Dulac collaborated with their husbands; Mary Pickford joined in part with husband Douglas Fairbanks to found United Artists; and Italian filmmaker Elvira Notari's Dora studio, named after her daughter, was modeled on an intersection between private and public spaces.[50] These spheres are interdependent and intersecting, yet individually they also have their limits. But whereas these domestic models helped make possible these women's public productions and public lives, Giuliana Bruno describes how the structure of the city of Naples both allowed Notari to participate in film production and enabled the very disappearance of her history: "Ultimately, I would say that her position was made possible by the *meter-polis*, the mother-city: the passage of a local family enterprise into a film production 'house'; the transference of the internalized female knowledge of 'home economics' into the field of 'manufacturing' films; the *transito* from 'matriarchal' roles to film directing."[51] In advice manuals of the nineteenth and twentieth centuries, women's domestic knowledge is marketed in public; in early filmmaking ventures, women's participation in the public, visible world of filmmaking is marked by their "natural" affinity with the private sphere.

Just as volumes like Moore's stock market book trace a narrative route from advice manual to film and back, it should be no surprise that a staple of the how-to manual shows the public star lodging herself in the home. Indeed, the merging of these gendered spaces is perhaps nowhere more acute than in cookbooks attributed to stars. Over the past century, a range of cookbooks has been produced as direct or indirect merchandising tie-ins with film or television texts. In contrast, the works in which I am interested were not published as tie-ins in a conventional sense. That is, unlike, say, the *Murder, She Wrote*, *Star Trek*, or *Wizard of Oz* cookbooks, to name just a few, these works do not relate to a particular film or television text to attract a community of fans. Nor, like *The Mike Douglas Cookbook* and *Soap Opera Café*, do the works indirectly take on the structure of the texts to which they are tied (which is especially the case of Douglas's book, in which many guest cooks appear). Those sorts of cookbooks build on and enhance our knowledge of diegetic and extradiegetic worlds, extending the narratives and communities of the films and television series that they accompany. They also fit into a certain consumer market. The works I discuss here are, rather, based on a particular star's image; thus, it is the star text itself with which they function as tie-ins. Like other forms of advice manuals, these works complicate not only our knowledge of their authors but also our experiences of them, offering a potential recipe for our own work in historical production.

Celebrity cookbooks, like other how-to manuals, usually function simultaneously as autobiographies. Some are related to the celebrity's image that has circulated in popular culture through film, television, and other star discourse. In these ways, such volumes collate, or collect, what we already may know. At the same time, they raise provocative questions about the relations between domestic production, film production, and historical and epistemological production. And, perhaps more than other how-to manuals, they also speak to reception practices in all of these arenas. In this way, they constitute a limit text of sorts, but one lodged between epistemological and bodily practices. Those I consider here also test the limits of historical boundaries; as the celebrity cookbook has been a relatively popular genre since the silent era, I look at works that traverse eras of production, national boundaries, and, in a sense, contexts of reception. In considering *Sophia Loren's Recipes and Memories*, published in 1998, alongside *Candy Hits by Zasu Pitts*, published in 1963, I push the texts in my study into the future, or at least closer to their present moment of continued (re)production.

Like all how-to manuals, each of these cookbooks activates repetition and recirculation. (Interestingly, however, these types of cookbooks do not have a long public shelf life: they go out of print with regularity.) They teach us through the repetition embedded in cooking and in experience; as the recipes are described and performed by the stars, they allow for a renewed circulation of their images first in the public space of the market and then in the domestic space of the consumer's kitchen.

Published in 1998, for instance, *Sophia Loren's Recipes and Memories* is the actress-author's second cookbook. Her first, *In the Kitchen with Love* (also referred to as *Eat with Me*), was published in 1972. At that time, surely, the book would have accompanied the various films Loren had recently appeared in, but the more recent work is not tied directly to one film or another. Rather, it appears as the culmination of her history in film and her history as a cook. So, although it is structured as a relatively conventional cookbook—it is ordered by types of food, such as antipasti, soup, pasta, desserts—it is also peppered with anecdotes about her family history and her work in film. Most of these anecdotes work together to give the book an Italian flavor, marking Loren's national identity and lending her credibility as a cook. Indeed, she embodies the national culture that she's passing on to her readers through her recipes.

The cookbook is introduced with Loren's description of her experiences with hunger and family during wartime. This intro sets the stage for her focus not only on food, but also on her familial and national identity offered throughout. Then, in each of the various sections of the book are a variety of photos of Loren as well as stories about the recipes she includes. The photos range from family shots (her grandmother, her sons) to publicity photos for films, to stills from films, to contemporary images of her in the kitchen, preparing the dishes in the book. Many of the stories that introduce recipes or that are visually set apart from them merge these various discourses and experiences. For instance, she opens the recipe for fagiolo con le cotiche (beans with pork rind) with a sort of eulogy for Marcello Mastroianni. She then asks:

> Why do I bring him up and talk of the cinema when I should be talking of the kitchen? Because I want to remember his most real and everyday side and because I remember his joyous passion for one dish, which for him excelled those on the most refined menus in the world. . . . This is a dish for peasants, for the poor, a dish to be found in the most humble eateries. Perhaps that is why Marcello, a simple man, a friend of common people, favored it. With that thought, and with happiness rather than grief, I offer this robust and satisfying dish.[52]

With this story are two photos from films in which Loren and Mastroianni appeared together: *Marriage Italian Style* and *A Special Day*. These visual and written recollections together produce a multi-dimensional image of both actors (so typical of star discourse) as glamorous stars and as ordinary Italians who love simple food. And certainly Loren's rendering of her memories here and throughout the book offer the recipes themselves (and potentially the food we would reproduce from them) an added dimension through their association with the star's own experiences.

The broader narrative elements of Loren's cookbook are fairly consistent with a tradition of cookbooks, especially ones by women. Indeed, as various writers have noted, recipes themselves are structured like narratives. Colleen Cotter asserts, for instance, "The temporal structure and sequential presentation in a recipe link it with the more traditional narrative framework."[53] Cotter and others, such as Susan Leonardi, Anne Bower, and Lynne Ireland, show us that recipes tell stories beyond how to make, for instance, beans with pork rind. Community cookbooks, many of these authors argue, tell idealized histories of their authors' communities, and single-author texts (like *The Joy of Cooking*) utilize the personal experience of the author to frame the recipes and the author's knowledge therein. The inherent autobiographical nature of cookbooks is, moreover, illustrative of the form that women's autobiographies often take. According to Anne Bower, who draws on Estelle Jelinek's theories of this genre, "The *form* of the cookbook bears relevance to women's autobiographical traditions," for these works are necessarily fragmentary, mirroring women's perceived and interpellated positions in the world.[54] Autobiographies, like cookbooks, exemplify the ways that women juggle roles, images, and work between various places in social and familial worlds.

The inherent autobiographical nature of cookbooks is also strangely reproduced in the works by scholars writing on cookbooks. Many of the essays collected in *Recipes for Reading: Community Cookbooks, Stories, Histories* boldly use the first-person pronoun as a reminder of the critic-historian's presence. Several also begin with anecdotes or minor autobiographical confessions that display the author's intimate experience with cooking and her personal interest in the matter at hand. Thus, Sally Bishop Shigley begins her essay with the following admission: "When freshman composition papers become too much for me, I read cookbooks. . . . Instead of flinging marginal barbs that are more a product of my own impatience than a student's ineptitude, I put down my pencil and retreat to my chaise lounge with a collection of culinary wisdom."[55] Nina Scott begins her contribution with an anecdote about bringing an Argentine cookbook with her when she traveled as a Fulbright scholar to Buenos Aires. As she confesses her reasons for bringing the cookbook with her, she begins, "I am a passionate cook myself. Metaphors of the kitchen and culinary discourse thus hold a particular attraction for me, as they did for a number of the Spanish American women authors I most admire."[56] As with other such examples, Shigley and Scott direct the reader of cookbooks and culinary scholarship to several important points. Surely, they point to the intrinsic relations between the private sphere of cooking and the public sphere of scholarly production, allowing these critics to make their everyday practices of cooking intersect with their everyday practices of textual analysis and production. They suggest, too, that cooking is a practice that is inherited as well as embodied: it is passed down and therefore shared between generations of women. This form of memorialization and its subsequent recollection is surely also at the heart of Luce Giard's statement, especially as she writes in the first-person as scholar, woman, and descendant of past cooks:

I would like the slow remembrance of your gestures in the kitchen to prompt me with words that will remain faithful to you; I would like the poetry of words to translate that of gestures; I would like the writing of words and letters to correspond to your writing of recipes and tastes. As long as one of us preserves your nourishing knowledge, as long as the recipes of your tender patience are transmitted from hand to hand and from generation to generation, a fragmentary yet tenacious memory of your life itself will live on.[57]

These generational connections exist across familial, social, and historical divides, so that Scott can share a practice and a love with other writers, rather than just her family members. Finally, in enacting the autobiographical tales they study and by emphasizing the knowledge intrinsic to the cookbook and to their authors, these contemporary critics reveal how these texts (and their authors) already function as models for scholars (and scholarship).

Given the storytelling aspects of recipes and cookbooks more broadly, as well as the ways they enact, or *tell* of, women's various roles and epistemologies in the world, the cookbook is a peculiarly appropriate vehicle for a star to tell her autobiography and display her knowledge at once. In turn, the cookbook illuminates and expands our own knowledge of the star through her experience with food. That is, as with Scott and the writers she admires, we can share an experience with the star through her written work and the very materiality both of the volume she has produced and the food she teaches us to make. In this way, our own scholarly practices of textual criticism and historical recollection are not unlike cooking: both are embodied practices passed on from generations of women in different forms.

Loren's volume underscores these very concerns. Influenced by and indebted to her foremothers for her knowledge in the kitchen, Loren dedicates her book to her grandmother and repeatedly links her recipes to her historical roots in war-torn Italy. Therefore, many of her recipes meet the challenges of poverty and the lack of resources in general. Like Marlene Dietrich (also a product of world wars), Loren stresses the importance of leftovers as well as cooking on the fly. Her recipe for penne alla puttanesca (pasta quills, whore style) is preceded by the following: "Some interpretations of the name suggest that this dish is fast enough for a 'working girl' to prepare between assignations; what is certain is that it is as good as it is fast."[58] But

*the expert* 179

of course, like Dietrich, Loren's glamour and sensuality are drawn largely from her maternal or domestic image. The photographs and the stories throughout her cookbook stress this fact. But they also suggest an authenticity to her image beyond her fictional films, an authentic image for which Loren herself is responsible, first through her ingrained and learned knowledge of Italian cuisine and then through her authoring of her own cookbook.

I therefore turn to these works not to reinscribe these women solely in domestic space, but to consider the ways they used this space to practice, display, and mediate knowledge. As Sally Bishop Shigley notes, "Leonardi and other feminists, including myself, do not explore 'traditional' roles in order to reify stereotypes or prove that women are limited. On the contrary, examinations of cookbooks or quilts or other 'female' domains illustrate how women have used the discourses available to them to make profound and effective statements."[59] Sarah Leavitt also responds to such implicit critiques in her study of how-to manuals: "These texts, though they may make both historians and the general public uneasy, can teach us about the way in which the home is a place where national ideologies of class, race, and gender are expressed in *things*, such as bric-a-brac and wicker chairs."[60] She concludes her work by asserting that rather than confining women to the home, domestic advice manuals connect the home to a larger culture: between Hollywood and the home, between the homemaker, the star, and the scholar. These celebrity cookbooks also stand as a medium to explore and expand their images and their work. Indeed, the fact (or at least the representation) of the star's authorship, as I have elsewhere noted, invites us to rethink our understanding of the star as pure image. As the case of Loren illustrates, she moves between images and spaces of work, taking on an active role in the production of and within each.

Certainly she also exemplifies the quality so consistent in star discourse, for as this film star who can cook, she is extraordinary and ordinary at once. At the same time, though, her ordinariness is itself extraordinary — not just because she is a star, but because she's an author of a cookbook. In this way, the ordinariness of the star and the cook is balanced (or countered) by her extraordinariness as the star-author. Admittedly, that authorship is itself possible only because Loren is a bankable name, one who can trade on her image in this new field of production and one with fans willing to consume her image in multiple forms and in multiple ways. Moreover, star-authors like Loren who produce cookbooks are themselves adopting ordinary and even often invisible knowledge and granting it visibility and authority. As Luce Giard notes, "Entering into the vocation of cooking and manipulating ordinary things makes one use intelligence, a subtle intelligence full of nuances and strokes of genius, a light and lively intelligence that can be perceived without exhibiting itself, in short *a very ordinary intelligence*."[61] This "ordinary intelligence" essential to cooking is indeed exhibited, however modestly, in Loren's volume. And, as Giard also emphasizes, it is an intelligence that has been passed on to Loren through generations of women; in this way, Loren displays the "ordinary" labor and knowledge of her maternal ancestors and implicitly transforms it into something both potent and visible. This balance is nicely displayed by the array of images in her cookbook: family portraits, publicity shots and stills from her films, and new photographs in which Loren performs as a cook for her readers. By reading her books and following her recipes, we are consuming her history, her knowledge, and her image (via the stills and our memories of her films), as well as her food.

Though her book is less glossy than Loren's and is also structured less conventionally, *Candy Hits by Zasu Pitts* raises similar questions about the production and reproduction of history, images, and, of course, food. Pitts essentially tells her history in film and television production through her history as a candy maker. In this way, she merges these work spaces and labor practices in significant ways, revealing the multiple roles women play in and outside the home. *Candy Hits*, compiled by Edi Horton and published in 1963, is thus structured in part like a memoir. The recipes are organized historically and in terms of the media she worked in: it begins with "Silent-Screen Days," then "Talking Picture Days," "Stage-Tour Collection," "Television Days," and one category outside the others entitled "Candies for Holidays" (apparently a time she had off from work). Through this arrangement and through the stories she tells in each chapter, Pitts's cookbook, like other how-to manuals by stars, produces an abbreviated history of her work as an actress, but it manages this history through its link to her domestic labor as well.

Like many cookbook authors, Pitts often introduces her recipes with a brief summary of the food and the labor involved in its making, but more often than not, these stories have little to do with her work

*the expert* 181

in Hollywood. Her memories as an actress instead structure the work as a whole both in the chapter organization and in her introductions to each chapter. In her first preamble, to "Silent-Screen Days," she tells the story of how she came to be associated with candy in Hollywood. (In this way, the candy making and her acting are merged from the beginning of both her career and her cookbook. Obviously, she trades on each to aid in the labor of the other.)

> As time went on, my reputation as a candymaker spread, and I rarely went to the studio without my old string market bag bulging with boxes of caramels, panocha, peanut brittle, or chocolate creams. Friends brought me recipes, and I tried them all. Some were more successful than others—like my pictures, I might add.... Soon I discovered that whenever I felt blue or discouraged—for there is no clear sailing in any career—I found comfort and forgetfulness while I was in the kitchen candymaking. One day I whipped up enough candy to supply a whole studio while I tried to forget the greatest disappointment I had experienced since my arrival in Hollywood.[62]

This story neatly enacts the tension between remembering and forgetting that structures these cookbooks (and memoirs and other texts by women in the film industry more broadly). Here Pitts claims that candy making allows her to forget. But in the end, candy making clearly didn't allow her to forget this experience. Instead, the act of cooking itself becomes a part of her memory of disappointment (though reinscribing it as a happier or more comic moment, which indeed leads into the following anecdote). Thus, her various memories—about stardom and candy making—are embedded in this new text, the cookbook, and potentially in the production and reproduction of the recipes therein. In this way, the cookbook works with and against the inevitable ephemerality of memory, of stardom, and, surely, of food itself.

So, what does it mean to consume these works? That is, what does it mean to read the cookbooks and then make a recipe for fudge from Pitts's book? To answer this question, let me turn to a consideration of the food itself—and the acts of making it, eating it, or, in current Hollywood style, of just looking at it—to offer further questions and some speculative conclusions. How does making the food illustrate a new relationship between star and fan (one already textually produced by the books themselves)? Does it, for instance, allow us to "consume" the star herself in a new and almost literal way? Does it allow us to embody the star (as an ordinary person)?

To state the obvious, eating is something we need to do everyday. This means that every bite of food we eat is ephemeral, though the act of eating is itself perpetual. Cooking falls between the ephemeral and the perpetual: it is a task that is never done, though each experience of cooking has a finite span. Following a recipe we know well, we are enacting a peculiar kind of repetition compulsion. In making and remaking the same dish, panocha or penne alla puttanesca, we might be trying to get it right, we might be trying to relive our first experience of it, or we might find comfort in the taste and the recollections it bears with it. In the perpetual repetition that is cooking, we might be staving off the ephemerality of food itself or we might even be marking its coincident ephemeral and reproducible nature. Whatever drives us in this compulsion to repeat—beyond hunger, beyond habit—cooking, like eating, is an embodiment of memory and experience through daily, ritualistic, and inherited practice. The authorship of cookbooks and the act of cooking, unlike the celebrity of the chef, allow women to embody and produce knowledge in a world in which their authority has been institutionally and structurally limited. This labor is a kind of model for scholarly work and historical recollection, each of which is an embodied practice passed on from generations in different forms (including the cookbook itself).

The marketing of the cookbooks seems predicated not only on the desire to become like the star, but also on the desire to know more about the star. This knowledge is often endlessly deferred in publicity materials and elsewhere, as information is offered only in fragments and the reliability of that information is usually suspect, especially given that it is usually tied to a particular fictional text, the film, at the time it appears. But in the case of the cookbook, the status of this information, or knowledge, shifts. Like other advice books or Marlene Dietrich's reference book, this information is indeed still fragmentary, structured in the form of discrete recipes. The fragmentary nature of narration and knowledge is itself telling. Still, with cookbooks, our knowledge of the celebrity author is enabled by experience. For we do grow to embody her knowledge as we make and consume the food; we share, albeit vicariously, a relationship with her based on both a form of identification and also on knowledge. Thus, our acts of consumerism and consumption—we buy the books, we may buy into the images, we make and eat the food—might tie into our own history as well, as fans, perhaps, but also as cooks. (One would probably not buy the books if one were not interested in the star, and one would probably not make the food if one were not already a cook of some sort.) Thus, the labor of cooking is conjoined with a sort of knowledge production and reproduction. And cooking itself is a kind of autobiographical act, a form of self-production, in that knowledge and expertise are embedded in the labor and the results from it.

If cooking is a form of production, then it stands to reason that eating is a kind of reception. As such a practice, what does the act of eating suggest? Certainly food is inherently ephemeral; as with Zasu Pitts's fudge, it offers a temporary sweet experience, and then it is gone. It is in some ways like the experience of watching a film. This temporary, or ephemeral, quality might also be a remark on stardom itself. But with the cookbook, the ephemerality of food and the labor it takes to produce it are traded for reproducibility. That is, the reproducibility of recipes points to a way of maintaining, knowing, and embodying a history. The recipes in these particular works reveal the stars' own responsibility for the authorship, or maintenance, of their histories in the movies and outside of them. And in making the recipes, we begin to embody this knowledge and this history ourselves; this embodiment is itself a reception of history.

Thus, telling the (abbreviated) history of her work in Hollywood through the cookbook (and, in fact, fully prioritizing her work in the kitchen), the star herself is domesticated by this text. But, as with other writers of cookbooks and domestic manuals, this domestication does not need to be a form of confinement. That is, this positioning does not need to confine how we understand her epistemological production and our reception of it; rather, we can be enabled by her domestication. Pitts not only represents herself as having a different form of knowledge—and a different kind of image—but she is also placed in our own home. Through this seemingly new positioning, our knowledge of a star like Pitts or Loren is transformed, as is our experience of them. For one thing, as objects, books are unlike films for readers or viewers, because they are tangible things that we can hold in our hands. Certainly, these cookbooks grant us this tactile experience. As we hold them, they also offer us a sort of ownership of the women's work—and by their "work," I mean not just their books, but also their domestic, artistic, and historical labor. The books themselves can become the stuff of everyday life for us as readers—on our shelves, in our kitchens, offices, and bedrooms—just as the authors inscribe the stuff of everyday life, whether glamorous or mundane. In other words, this tangibility matches the tangible knowledge that the stars reveal and perform: the stuff of everyday life.

## MIRRORS, STAGES

As I noted above, by following the star's cookbook, we embody her knowledge as we make and consume the food she describes and (claims to have) once made herself; we thus engage in a relationship with her based on a form of identification and also on knowledge. Psychoanalytic and ideological film theories have detailed how films construct a singular viewing subject: the individual *you* to the film's *I*. The recognition of oneself as the addressee of the film is also linked to the experience of the mirror stage, so that we are not merely addressed by the film, but also idealized by our relationship with it: this address is, indeed, the location of interpellation. Carolyn Steedman's description of the solitary historian in the archive takes on a similar address, though without the explicit ideological trappings. This historian at times also becomes a kind of voyeur, addressed by the archival texts but as an unintended reader. To comment on the role of the scholar, Steedman first depicts a hypothetical reader who peruses letters not addressed to herself or himself: "The Historian who goes to the Archive must always be an unintended reader, will always read that which was never intended for his or her eyes."[63]

As viewers in the movie house or scholars in the archive, we have a sense of ourselves as engaging in a solitary experience, sneaking a look at something not intended for our eyes or relishing the sense that what we are seeing or reading is for our eyes only. Yet watching movies is almost always a collective experience. Even when we go alone to a movie house, we are normally surrounded by other people; when we watch alone at home we can at the very least unconsciously recognize that others have watched the same movie we are viewing. (Certainly the sense of a collective or familial audience is precisely what television creates.) Though theorized as an experience that is ideologically constructed as singular and subjective, the fact is that movies are designed to be seen by as many people as possible. This viewing experience, in a very broad sense, mirrors the production of films.

Although the director has been theorized and is institutionally understood to be the supreme force behind the making of a film, movies are never produced alone: they are inherently collaborative affairs. The ultimate collaboration is that between filmmakers and viewers. Some films stage such a conversation (via direct address, for instance), yet this kind of collaboration almost always remains only implied in narrative fictional films. Such a dialogue, however, is often more explicit in written works, in which a narrator (or implied author) speaks to an implied reader. As Steedman might note, there are degrees to which the implied reader is intended or unintended by the text. However, an intended reader is indeed produced through the institution of the archive itself: the scholar who studies the historical texts of the past. Moreover, a collaborative relationship preexists the archive in certain textual forms, forms that are often not part of an institutional archive or at least do not play the same roles for historians in the archive. This form of collaboration, or conversation, is perhaps most obvious in a how-to manual, in which an author can expect that a reader will follow her advice, eventually becoming more and more like her. This is a peculiar sort of mirror stage, one in which a reader can see what she might become, idealizing her self of the future.

Many celebrity how-to manuals, especially at the end of the twentieth century and the turn of the twenty-first, are focused on an important element of the female celebrity's labor: her body and the representation of its perfection. Some of these books seem almost to be responding to works like that by Loren and Pitts (all that pasta and candy); at least, they testify to women's complicated relationships with their bodies. My emphasis is not on the often troubling relationship women have to eating (especially, seemingly, in celebrity culture); rather, I consider how these works depict women's physical and intellectual work in the arena of popular visual representation.

In her volume, Mae West expounds on the importance of healthy eating. But her dietary regimen does not mirror what is found in healthy cookbooks designed to retrain and slim down women's bodies, such as Oprah Winfrey's coauthored *In the Kitchen with Rosie* and Marilu Henner's *Healthy Life Kitchen*, both produced in the same decade.[64] An integral part of this trend, of course, is the celebrity workout manual. This trend was especially marked in the early 1980s by *Jane Fonda's Workout Book* and its tie-in video. Each of these works sketches the ambivalent and often contradictory relationship women have to their bodies and expectations of feminine ideals. In "Artemis Aging: Exercise and the Female Body on Video," Margaret Morse analyzes this cultural dilemma in depth, considering the projected agency of the aerobics instructor (such as the celebrity Fonda) and the subsequent position of the woman who follows her steps. With regard to aerobics videos and exercise overall, Morse writes, "Women are no longer a veil over a gap, a sign projected by the onlooker, but a self-production, appropriating and reorganizing existing signs and meanings; she is her own Pygmalion, sculpting her own body." As such, "Femininity is no longer proposed as nature, but is read as cultural, as work, a machinated body produced by a woman's consciousness." However, as Morse argues, there is a limit to this "consciousness" that comes in the form of the inherent mimeticism demanded by the exercise video and class. Concludes Morse, "The cultural form itself is, however, less tolerant of invention, a kind of mimetic learning which postpones access to subjectivity except through matching, embodying, and interiorizing a given and unifying ideal feminine subject. The impossibility of doing makes for endless repetition."[65] Such critical recognition is enormously important in looking at these sorts of texts, especially as the repetition of exercise is at once inherently passive in its compliance and dynamic at once. I am therefore interested in maintaining a sense of this critique but also seeing the models that such works offer as productive, metaphorically certainly but also through a literal application in other fields of thought or vision.

In a sense, works like *Jane Fonda's Workout Book* are like Edith Head's *Dress Doctor*; that is, they are expressly related to the women's jobs as visible celebrities. As Morse suggests, they are also the kind of how-to manuals that show readers how to "be like" their authors. But, though they may not exactly expand our knowledge of the stars, they do lend an authority to them: in each case, she has become an expert in training her own body, and that training, in some cases, is an integral part of her autobiography. The story of her life, in other words, is also the story of her body. To work toward a conclusion, then, I consider two contemporary volumes that display the celebrity's awareness of her image and her epistemological or critical processes at once: Christy Turlington's *Living Yoga: Creating a Life Practice* and Isabella Rossellini's *Looking at Me* (an implicit follow-up to her earlier *Some of Me*). Like celebrity cookbooks, these works sketch an autobiography through a particular facet of the author's life: for Turlington, obviously, this is the practice of yoga, and for Rossellini, this is the two-part practice of being photographed and then reflecting on the images created of her. By enacting a process of research and analysis, each celebrity-author becomes like a student or like a critic.

Turlington's book is a relatively exhaustive review of the history and practice of yoga through its multiple schools and incarnations. She examines various teachings, displays and defines postures (or asanas), and links her practice of yoga to her own life. In particular, she tells the story of her father's experience with cancer, detailing how yoga helped her survive his illness and death, and she also narrates her work as a student. At times almost resembling a collage, the book combines different textual forms: autobiographical narratives; researched descriptions of different schools of yoga (Ashtanga Vinyasa, Iyengar, Kundalini); explanations of particular asanas (from the seemingly simple Baddha Konasana, which appears on the cover of the book, to the slightly more advanced Kukkutasana); boxed definitions of significant terms and symbols (chakras, the lotus flower); and Turlington's own philosophies, developed through practice and research, about compassion, faith, and the changes made possible through yoga practice. With the photographs of Turlington modeling poses throughout, coupled with her own words describing the postures and the spiritual aims of yoga, the text itself exhibits how the work is simultaneously about her body and her knowledge. This convergence makes sense on a number of levels. First, of course, yoga is a physical practice whose goal is to gain self-knowledge. As she writes, "A regular asana practice can also open the door to all the rest that the philosophy has to offer."[66] For Turlington in particular, it seems that yoga stands as a hinge between (or metaphor for) her life as a fashion model and her life as a college and postgraduate student.

Her work as both student and teacher is manifested in a number of ways throughout the volume. First, it is implicit in the research that forms the foundation of the book's discussion of the history, philosophies, and practices of yoga. These roles also ground her authority as a yogi; in an early chapter she writes, "I will do my best to guide you through the many options that this ancient philosophy has to offer. I am merely a student myself, seeking a way that will allow me to explore as many paths as I possibly can within this lifetime." Finally, this work, as student and teacher, is also central to Turlington's narration of her life story. A professional model since her teens, Turlington did not receive a conventional high school diploma, but returned to finish this part of her schooling in her early twenties, when, as she writes, "without that other life, the one I'd practically fled, I felt less interesting and much lonelier." She later balanced her modeling career with the pursuit of a college degree from New York University, completing her B.A. just before she turned thirty. In her chapter entitled "Beauty Is in the Heart of the Beheld," she discusses her experience at the university: "I still wasn't completely sure about what I was seeking from it, which didn't matter anyway because I was enjoying it so much, filling myself with knowledge, continuously stimulated." This chapter thus ruminates on the relation between exterior beauty (which Turlington herself recognizes as impermanent) and knowledge, hinged as the two are through the physical and spiritual practice of yoga. In fact, this chapter is followed by a display and description of Salamba sirsasana (supported headstand), about which Turlington concludes, "For the practitioner, the greatest benefits are perhaps developing the strength and flexibility of the body while stimulating and disciplining the mind, all to achieve inner balance."[67]

As with cooking, repetition is essential to yoga practice and to meditation; Turlington notes, "Sometimes meditation involves repetition, as many yoga practices do begin or end with a simple repetition." This is not a mindless repetition, though it is similar to what Henri Bergson describes as "habit," a form of remembering that becomes embodied as well as lodged in the mind. Turlington stresses, too, that mindful repetition in meditation can lead to further contemplation: "In silence, we can explore the words that we use all the time and contemplate our actions in inaction. . . . Observing these processes that we go through is like acting as a witness to ourselves."[68] She uses the practice of writing (and research) to create intersections across mind and body, across seemingly disparate areas of her life (as a model, as a student, as a yogi), and across ways of understanding her (as a visual object, as a subject with agency over body and mind). This writing and the accompanying images allow for a further practice on the part of the reader—not just to mimetically reproduce Turlington's body or way of thinking but to adapt the physical and contemplative practices in her own way. In the same sense that for Turlington yoga is a metaphor for the bridge between being a model and a student, I think her autobiographical study can function as a metaphor (or even model) for the ways we follow, read, and embody our subjects of study—becoming not only their analysts but also their students.

In both of her autobiographical works, but especially in *Looking at Me*, Isabella Rossellini performs as an analyst of herself, particularly investigating how that self is created through commercial photography. She meditates on this visual production, "acting as a witness" to herself. Her work, moreover, is surely about collaboration, collective labor, and conversation. *Looking at Me*, the 2002 follow-up to *Some of Me*, is an autobiographical analysis of eighty-one photographs that lined what Rossellini deemed the "wall of me" in her apartment. She hopes the project will not be a purely narcissistic one; rather, she writes, "For me as the viewer looking at the 'Me Wall' did not make me wonder, like the bad Queen in Snow White, 'Mirror, mirror on the wall . . . who's the fairest of them all?' In fact, I didn't see myself at all for that matter but instead saw the photographers' work, their ideas, and our working collaboration in capturing fantasies."[69] As a viewer and a writer, Rossellini fills her volume of photographs with brief discussions of each that range from anecdotal or flippant to contemplative and revealing. Though it is a text that reflects more than advises, *Looking at Me* can still act as a kind of model for our own acts of reading and our own understanding of critical processes. Rossellini is therefore as much a critic as she is an expert, attesting to the inevitable and necessary intersections between the categories I've set up. These intersections and Rossellini's critical, reflective expertise are each instructive, particularly as her critical acumen, however flippant at times, is what allows her to be an expert on processes of representation (in still or moving imagery and in history).

As the image herself, or the object that is photographed, Rossellini also sees herself as a collaborator with photographers. She repeatedly describes herself as "working with" photographers such as Dominique Issermann, Miles Aldridge, and André Rau. While she suggests that "my job as a model is to lend my two eyes, one mouth, two hands, two feet and one body to the photographer's lens to create his vision," she also asserts that she is not a mere "objet feminine," but a subject at work with other artists to produce an image by "capturing fantasies."[70] In this way, her work is intellectual as much as it is physical. Moreover, in resisting the Queen's question, Rossellini doesn't see the idealized image of the mirror stage in her own reflection; instead, her acts of looking reflect how the images were produced. Looking at the images gives her the opportunity to recollect the context of their production as well as the larger context of her life and work. These acts of recollection, then, set the experiences in relation to one another through the photos; her remembering gives them shape, and so does her embellishment of them.

Her book, she says, is "about 'fictional' pictures—photos that either reconstruct realities or that represent realities that spring from the fantasy of the photographer." These kinds of fantasies in a sense document a history of photography, too. Rossellini describes a work by Max Vadukul: "What inspires the new generation of photographers like Max Vadukul is not only the fantasy or reality in front of them but also the collective memories—the visual culture established by other photographers before them." Drawing on her own memories, she works through the complicated tangles between reality and fantasy in fashion photography throughout her book. But she also warns us that what she says is not purely truthful (in fact, she refers to *Some of Me* as her "fictional memoirs"). In a discussion of an Iké Udé photograph, she writes, "I love to embellish and color the events in my life until I lose sight of what really happened. . . . Fashion photography lies just like I do. It does not capture reality nor total, exaggerated, impossible fantasy. Fashion photography captures something in between the truth and lies. . . . My lies are just the same—not real, not false, just an enhanced, tinted truth. That might be the reason why fashion photography and I get along so well."[71] Musing thus, Rossellini comments on the work of the writer who captures a memory of fictional production as well as the photographer (or filmmaker) and her or his subject who creates an image that can be remembered. The photographs she analyzes embody stories, and looking at the bodies in the photos (usually, of course, her own), she reveals how these stories are created, often in collaboration between the photographer and the subject in the photograph. Using herself as a model, Rossellini therefore shows us both how to look at women's bodies—the staple of visual pleasure and representation—and to see how those bodies are also at work.

# HAPPY ENDINGS

> I love happy endings. I do.
> —MARLENE DIETRICH, *Marlene Dietrich's ABC*

Can these books do all I am claiming they can do? Of course, I am not suggesting that they replace scholarly work or that we turn a blind eye to them, making our own work devoid of criticism. Rather, I want to recognize our debts to their authors as writers and thinkers who come before us, as subjects from whom we borrow and with whom we collaborate. Their modes of thinking—though perhaps not all of their ideas—are instructive as well for how we conceive of women's authorship in institutional and international contexts. Drawing on these books as I have done also allows me to think about what constitutes an archive for media scholars: what we place there, how that becomes history. In the case of cookbooks, advice manuals, how-to books, and so on, we keep them in our homes, but that, too, is a remark on the archive. Indeed, the house as a space of collection is also a space where history takes place. And all of these works by women—collections, writings, recollections—are places, too, where history and even theory are kept.

The advice manual functions as a kind of limit case for this work. The cookbook especially might serve as a model for or design of historiography, both as it tells stories about women's work and women's lives and in the pattern of productions and consumption that it illustrates. That is, the cookbook points to a particular relationship between the subject of historical recollection and the collector (or re-collector) herself. It is one by which we produce and consume the subjects we look at; we remake her, and she dwells in us. This may seem a peculiar relationship indeed, yet perhaps it is inevitable given the intellectual and affective investment we have in any act of recollection. And it reveals, too—to return to André Bazin's suggestion that an "auteur is a subject to himself [*sic*]," but to make the suggestion through that work that has followed him—how we are also the subjects of our own work as well.

The written and collectible works by the women I have subjected to my own study extend our understanding of them: not only do they perform, but they also write, think, pray, cook, invest, practice, learn, and—most of all—*know*. They were indeed active in the construction of the very epistemological fields in which they have been located. Their expertise, moreover, does not only expand our knowledge of these women; it also expands our experience of them. Although in some ways their films might stand as more ephemeral objects, especially before the days of video and digital projection in the home, their books are more tangible indicators of the stars. And the tangibility of the advice and knowledge contained therein might match the tangibility of the books as objects. The stars' knowledge of spirituality, glamour, domesticity, cooking, finance, and representation can become part of our own understanding. These books thus present the opportunity for readers to perform as the stars performed, but in a different sense than on the screen. And when such activity takes place, these works have perhaps come full circle. Written, inevitably, to display that the stars are like common folk, these books allow the common reader to become like a star by acting like herself. In this way, the labor produced by the stars-writers—as celebrities, as authors, as domestic experts—is as naturalized as a classical Hollywood production. And so, indeed, is their knowledge. Our archive of, and therefore our knowledge and ideas about, stars like Moore and Pitts and Brooks might also shift and hence reformulate and discover anew other ways of knowing. To me, such a revelation about the possibilities of knowledge, though perhaps utopian, is the happiest of endings. And maybe that is because it isn't an ending at all.

# Notes

## Introduction

1 Moore, *Silent Star*, 10, 11.

2 Mulvey, *Fetishism and Curiosity*, 54. See also Tom Gunning's work on early cinema and display, especially, of course, "The Cinema of Attractions."

3 Moore, *Silent Star*, 11.

4 On page 292 of Fred Lawrence Guiles's *Marion Davies: A Biography* (New York: McGraw-Hill, 1972).

5 As Rosa-Linda Fregoso shows in her study of film star Lupe Velez, "fantasy heritage" is a particularly appropriate concept through which to understand the history of cinema (*meXicana Encounters*, 103). I return to this concept in chapter 2.

6 Benjamin, *Reflections*, 53, 60.

7 Bachelard, *The Poetics of Space*, 8.

8 See ibid., 39.

9 This, too, is a paraphrase. He writes, "A house that is as dynamic as this allows the poet to inhabit the universe. Or, to put it differently, the universe comes to inhabit his house" (ibid., 51).

10 The documentary film is clearly not the same as a biopic, but the fictional footage included in the documentary film often takes on the same role as the biopic. See George Custen, *Bio/Pics*.

11 My understanding of the structure of memory in relation to fiction and nonfiction film, as well as to written texts, is informed by a range of works, especially those by Münsterberg and Deren, as well as Henri Bergson, Sigmund Freud, and Walter Benjamin, and more recent film and media scholars such as Ann Cvetkovich, bell hooks, Anne Friedberg, Annette Kuhn, José Munoz, and Maureen Turim.

12 Deren, *An Anagram of Ideas on Art, Form and Film*, 42.

13 Ibid., 5.

14 Her provocative theory is not unlike those ideas forged by Sergei Eisenstein before her and Gilles Deleuze (who was in turn greatly influenced by Eisenstein) well after her.

15 Bazin, *What Is Cinema?*, 1:255.

16 Johnston, "Women's Cinema as Counter Cinema," 26.

17 Bruno, *Streetwalking on a Ruined Map*, 235.

18 Friedberg, "'And I Have Learned to Use the Small Projector,'" 27–28.

19 Though also a departure from it, these ideas are influenced by Philip Rosen's *Change Mummified*.

20 Steedman, *Dust*, 82–83.

21 Diane Negra and Sara Ross have also investigated Moore from different vantage points. In fact, Donald Crafton organized a panel at the 2001 Society for Cinema Studies, "Star 20! The Making and Unmaking of Female Movie Stars, 1919–1929," which focused on Moore. The papers delivered included Amelie Hastie, "Collections and Recollections: Colleen Moore and the Business of Film History"; Sara Ross, "The Flapper Who Wasn't 'It': Ambiguity in the Star Persona of Colleen Moore"; Melanie Nash, "The Last Flap: Colleen Moore and the Fall of the Flapper"; and Diane Negra, "Colleen Moore and the Narrative Energy of Irishness in 1920s Hollywood." See also Diane Negra, *Off-White Hollywood: American Culture and Ethnic Female Stardom* (New York: Routledge, 2001).

## 1. THE COLLECTOR

1 These histories were publicly rediscovered by David Nasaw and are excerpted in an article in the *New Yorker*, "Earthly Delights" (March 23, 1998). Nasaw frequently quotes Moore in his essay; indeed, she appears more than any other source.

2 The first edition does not include the actual date.

3 Stewart, *On Longing*, 152, 151, 131, 136.

4 Ibid., 151.

5 Baudrillard, "The System of Collecting," 8.

6 Benjamin, *Illuminations*, 60.

7 Schor, "Collecting Paris," 255, 256.

8 Baudrillard, "The System of Collecting," 7.

9 Stewart, *On Longing*, 152–153.

10 Cardinal, "Collecting and Collage-Making," 75, 71.

11 Baudrillard, "The System of Collecting," 12.

12 The scrapbooks are primarily from the Margaret Herrick and the University of Southern California collections. The Herrick houses scrap-

books pertaining to approximately thirty-one figures who worked in film production (directors, stars, costumers, set designers, writers, makeup artists, and so on). The largest holdings pertain to the following figures: Mary Pickford (73 total, made up of three collections, with 48, 6, and 19 books, respectively); columnist Louella Parsons (61); star Richard Barthelmess (50); Audrey Chamberlin (46); makeup artist Perc Westmore (42); Colleen Moore (36); and columnist Hedda Hopper (34). The USC collection is somewhat smaller, with more unique examples. It houses, for instance, smaller and more intimate books for the actors Claire Windsor, Norma Shearer, Billie Burke, and Fay Wray.

13 The likely original source was the First National studio itself, as Moore's film *We Moderns* was being prepared for release during this same period. Interestingly, Moore's scrapbooks are divided in terms of "Personal Press Clippings of Colleen Moore" (which are numbered in their own series) and "Reviews of" the movies predominant in the volumes. The stories about terminology appear in a "Personal Press Clippings" volume, but they seem just as appropriate to a book regarding the film. Keeping the controversy in the former, however, suggests a blurred distinction between her personal and professional lives, which were, of course, especially intertwined by the fact that her husband was essentially her publicity agent at First National.

14 Bann, *The Clothing of Clio*, 62–63.

15 For a discussion of the complex discursive makeup of fan magazines, see Studlar, "The Perils of Pleasure?"

16 Interestingly, this subject position shifts in scrapbook 27, which chronicles Parsons's radio show *Hollywood Premiere*. In this book, Parsons herself becomes the celebrity (even as she continues to promote celebrities). The book is also structured very differently from the earlier volumes: usually just one article appears per page, to best display Parsons's role as radio star.

17 This book is number 4 of six in the manuscript collection catalogued as U-6 at the Herrick. Pickford's books are categorized by date of donation as well as by author or type of author.

18 White, "Black and White," 257.

19 Scrapbook 32, like many of the other thirty-six, actually leaps between years—in this case, 1932 and 1935. Here I am focusing on the later dates, as that is when Moore's dollhouse was completed and is the period of threats regarding the castle.

20 *Chicago Tribune*, 9 January 1935.

21 In her memoirs, Moore labels Dietrich as her first big tenant and the best housekeeper that lived there.

22 Deren, *An Anagram of Ideas on Art, Form and Film*, 94.

23 Cardinal, "Collecting and Collage-Making," 78. Roger Cardinal describes such an effect of Kurt Schwitters's work: "Hence an individual col-

lage may either confirm the assumption that collecting thrives on systematic ordering, or draw attention to that assumption through ridicule" (78).

24  Bachelard, *The Poetics of Space*, 8, 39.

25  Boym, *The Future of Nostalgia*, 49.

26  Stewart, *On Longing*, 161.

27  In its deep and complicated relation to fantasy, Moore's dollhouse differs from a contemporaneous dollhouse, Queen Mary's Dollhouse, originally produced in 1921 and now on view at Windsor Castle. Though stunning and enormous, this dollhouse is in many ways more utilitarian than Moore's. In fact, its references are more to the real world (however fantastic when we think of the lives of kings and queens) than to the fairies of Moore's domicile. It contains not only the requisite furniture but also, for instance, a sewing machine, a vacuum cleaner, and children's toys—all functioning miniatures. Queen Mary's Dollhouse is, in effect, simply a very large conventional dollhouse, yet one replete with rooms for royalty, their children, and their household staff. Similar to Moore's, though, it does contain small volumes of books penned by authors of the day, and it is the only other dollhouse in the world to share the same Royal Doulton china pattern. The viewing conditions— the structure is encased in glass and illuminated from above—are similar to that in the Museum of Science and Industry, but it has less of a cinematic ambience than Moore's dollhouse, largely because the room as a whole is lit and because no voices accompany the viewing. The official guide to Queen Mary's Dollhouse describes its various features; it was originally published by Pitkin Unichrome Ltd. in 1992.

28  Moore, *Colleen Moore's Dollhouse*, 6.

29  Moore, *Silent Star*, 236.

30  In Moore's defense, the number in the *Dollhouse* volume appears to include only those involved in the construction of the actual house. Many others were involved in the making of the more than two thousand objects housed in the castle. In fact, most of the newspaper stories included in her scrapbooks, as well as advertisements for its various exhibitions, claim that seven hundred artisans worked on the castle.

31  Although it might be nice to believe that this fact bespeaks the pricelessness of the word, it seems as much or more to suggest the value of fame and celebrity, for many of the tiny books were penned by well-known writers and other luminaries of Moore's day, and the autograph book was signed only by those whom Moore saw as having made a substantial contribution to the world.

32  These ads appear in scrapbook 34, which chronicles "1936 Montreal." The book was apparently a gift to Moore from the department store; it seemed something of a ritual for stores to present Moore with a scrapbook,

so apparently she was known for her collection of scrapbooks as well as her collection of miniatures.

33  Benjamin, "Unpacking My Library," 67.
34  Bachelard, *Poetics of Space*, 173–174.
35  Moore, *Silent Star*, 253.
36  Stewart, *On Longing*, 61–62.
37  Moore, *Colleen Moore's Dollhouse*, 10. As Moore describes it, "I began the project at a low point in my personal life at the suggestion of my father. He couldn't bear to see me unhappy, and he fell back on my childhood penchant for doll houses in an effort to divert me" (ibid.).
38  Jack Zipes, *Fairy Tales*, 5, 6.
39  Steedman, *Dust*, 125.
40  Susan Buck-Morss, *The Dialectics of Seeing*, 273, 274.
41  Ibid., 276, 271.
42  Moore, *Silent Star*, 245. John Elsner makes similar suggestive claims about the architectural models of Sir John Sloane: "As a collection, they become more than collector's items, they become an imaginative world that never existed, a world which collectively they represent and which through imagination they come to embody" ("A Collector's Model of Desire," 169). Interestingly, in Moore's case, the small doll marketed with the castle was designed as if it might appear in the dollhouse. In this way, the doll itself embodies, through one's imagination, the castle as a whole.
43  Bal, "Telling Objects," 99.
44  Benjamin, *Illuminations*, 91.
45  Moreover, the masculine-dominated images complement the books kept in this room, for most were penned by men.
46  The Dining Room is similarly gendered, for the story of King Arthur and the Knights of the Round Table forms its theme. The table is based on that legend, and tapestries hanging throughout the room include scenes from the tale.
47  Moore, *Colleen Moore's Dollhouse*, 52.
48  Hansen, *Babel and Babylon*, 254.
49  Studlar, *This Mad Masquerade*, 166–167. Studlar examines how Valentino's star persona and success fit into the "dance madness" of the time, which was closely associated with "darkly foreign" men. Describing his role in *Four Horsemen of the Apocalypse*, she says, "The film exploited the exoticism of non-Anglo ethnicity as well as the audience's familiarity with deviant forms of dancing masculinity, including the male butterfly and the tango tea gigolo. However, it also works to make Valentino's deviant masculine type acceptable to a wide audience within a xenophobic and nativist culture" (167). (In her memoirs, however, Moore is horribly condemnatory of Valentino's manhood;

her condemnation seems born of both xenophobia and a very conservative view of sexuality. This position makes her decoration of the Prince's bedroom all the more interesting and her acceptance of his gifts to the dollhouse rather hypocritical.)

50  Yet although the mural seems inspired by Rococo style, and hence Perrault's telling of the tale, this painting appears drawn from a Russian version of the same story: a Russian castle stands in the background while Cinderella approaches her pumpkin-coach.

51  Such Cinderella-inspired films include *Desert Flower* (dir. Irving Cummings, 1925), *Her Wild Oat* (dir. Marshall Neilan, 1927), *Sally* (dir. Alfred E. Green, 1925), and *The Wallflower* (dir. Rupert Hughes, 1922). *Ella Cinders* also neatly conflates real life and fantasy in its representation of Moore as a performer. This trope was consistent in other films in which Moore performs as a performer. Some are centered around her character's desire to be a performer; thus, for example, in *Ella Cinders* she plays an actress, in *Twinkletoes* (dir. Charles Brabin, 1926) she plays a budding dancer, and in *Broken Hearts of Broadway* (dir. Irving Cummings, 1923), she works in the theater. In other films, the characters Moore plays put on mini-performances for the benefit of other characters: for instance, in *Little Orphan Annie* (dir. Colin Campbell, 1918) she acts out stories to entertain other children in an orphanage, and in *Lilac Time* (dir. George Fitzmaurice, 1928), she improvises for a group of World War I pilots saddened over a fellow flyer's death. (In fact, *Lilac Time* might seem a very loose adaptation of "Snow White," as Moore plays the French housekeeper to seven pilots—illustrating the presence of fairy tales in her life story.) In each of these films, the character Moore plays is a poor girl who succeeds in some way (economically, emotionally, or simply narratively) through acts of performance.

52  Moore, *Colleen Moore's Dollhouse*, 69.

53  Stewart, *On Longing*, 56.

54  Moore, *Colleen Moore's Dollhouse*, 72.

55  Terry Ann Neff, *Within the Fairy Castle*.

56  Moore consistently acknowledges this labor in both *Silent Star* and *Colleen Moore's Dollhouse*.

57  In an appendix, Neff's *Within the Fairy Castle* offers the contents of many of the books.

58  Quoted in Neff, *Within the Fairy Castle*, 123.

59  Moore, *Silent Star*, 232. Moore also claims, "The Fairy Castle is fantasy throughout. We would say, 'What wouldn't people have?' Dad would say, 'People wouldn't have a drawing-room floor made of rose quartz and jade'" (233–234). These various comments are recalled slightly differently in the *Dollhouse* book, but the content is basically the same.

60 Moore, *Colleen Moore's Dollhouse*, 11–12.

61 Moore, *Silent Star*, 236.

62 Moore, *Colleen Moore's Dollhouse*, 17.

63 Ibid., 85.

64 Bann, "Shrines, Curiosities, and the Rhetoric of Display," 21. In his essay, Bann quotes Erasmus on the tradition of displaying slivers from the True Cross: "Erasmus does indeed bring reason to bear on the apparent irrationality of the cult of relics: one of the two participants in his dialogue says of the 'True Cross' that it 'is exhibited publicly and privately in so many places that if the fragments were joined together they'd seem a full load for a freighter' " (21). Of course, such an observation points to yet another way in which even Moore's history of the castle is forever conjoined with fantasy.

65 Moore, *Colleen Moore's Dollhouse*, 86.

66 Two other essays in *Cultures of Collecting*, "Death and Life, in That Order, in the Works of Charles Willson Peale" by Susan Stewart and "Waxworks and Wonderlands" by Marina Warner, are concerned also, in part, with death and the display of the collection.

67 Benjamin, *Illuminations*, 60.

68 Quoted in Buck-Morss, *The Dialectics of Seeing*, 352.

69 Moore, *Colleen Moore's Dollhouse*, 8.

70 In fact, much of this discourse was, in a sense, a mode of exhibition as well.

71 Moore, *Colleen Moore's Dollhouse*, 6.

72 Moore, *Silent Star*, 234.

73 Donald Albrecht, *Designing Dreams: Modern Architecture in the Movies* (Santa Monica, Calif.: Hennessey and Ingalls, 2000), 111.

74 Quoted in ibid., 120–121.

75 Moore, *Colleen Moore's Dollhouse*, 65.

76 Koszarski, *An Evening's Entertainment*, 9.

77 We might see further connections between the picture palaces, or theaters in general, and the museum where the dollhouse is now lodged. In fact, the room where the dollhouse sits is slightly darkened, lit like a movie theater. Outside the entrance to the room where the castle is displayed are photographs of Moore and a video monitor that plays clips from Moore's silent films, such as *Ella Cinders*; this merging of media tightly represents Moore's visual history.

78 Koszarski, *An Evening's Entertainment*, 23.

79 Moore, *Colleen Moore's Dollhouse*, 11.

80 Koszarski, *An Evening's Entertainment*, 22.

81 deCordova, *Picture Personalities*, 107, 108.

82 Moore, *Silent Star*, 231.

83 Celebrity guests at Hearst's estate were interviewed in the early 1970s about their experiences there. Besides Moore, interviewees included Cary Grant, Frances Marion, Adela Rogers St. Johns, King Vidor, and other players in the film industry who knew Marion Davies and Hearst.

84 Quoted in Mulvey, *Citizen Kane*, 82.

85 Ibid., 16.

86 Ibid., 18.

87 Tapert, "Colleen Moore," 218–221.

88 Moore, *Silent Star*, 232.

89 Quoted in *Columbus Dispatch*, 20 March 1927.

90 Quoted in Buck-Morss, *The Dialectics of Seeing*, 352.

91 For significant analyses of women's relations to the cross-marketing of films and material tie-ins, see Doane, "The Economy of Desire," and Gaines, "From Elephants to Lux Soap."

92 This information is detailed in a *First National News* story of September 15, 1927, which was included in a Moore scrapbook.

93 Thanks to Don Crafton for pointing out this link when I delivered a paper on Moore's dollhouse at the 1999 Society for Cinema Studies conference.

94 *Ella Cinders* itself is therefore a text inscribed by multiple media and material forms. Charles Plumb and his partner, Bill Conselman, wrote the story of Ella as a screenplay that would star Moore, but her production company, First National, initially turned it down. They sought other stars and other companies, but were repeatedly rejected. The writers then bought space in a Los Angeles paper to run a comic strip called *Ella Cinders*, with the eponymous character clearly modeled after Moore. After its successful run for several weeks, they again pitched the story to First National, who then agreed to run it. The comic strip's success far outlasted the film; it ran from 1926 to 1957. Besides the doll manufactured in 1926 and revived in the 1980s, Ella Cinders also appeared in a variety of novels. I am indebted to the historian Joseph Yranski for this information about the comic and its history in relation to the film production.

95 A book that Moore wrote, *The Enchanted Castle* (Garden City, N.Y.; Garden City Publishing Company, 1935), was also marketed alongside the dollhouse. This book tells the tale of two girls, Jean and Bebe, who become four inches tall, meet some fairies, and tour the king's fairy castle. Their journey is actually one through Moore's castle, as the book itself catalogues all the items that are in it (the bed, the staircase with no railings, the prince's bedroom, etc.).

96 With many thanks to Joseph Yranski for these details. Phone conversation, 29 November 2000.

97 Steedman, *Dust*, 79.

## 2. THE HISTORIAN

1 Dietrich, *Marlene Dietrich's ABC*, 53.

2 Steedman, *Past Tenses*, 43-44. Steedman offers a useful distinction between the memoir and the autobiography: "Autobiography is to be distinguished from such *genre* as memoir and reminiscence by the status and function of experience within it. In the form of memoir for instance, it is a series of external factors that is presented as dictating the narrative course. These factors or events may be translated into inner experience, but that inner experience—lived and felt experience—is not its focus, as it is in autobiography" (43-44). Although most of the works I discuss would be classified as memoirs—most have a finite historical span that largely deals with their subjects' film careers—I use the terms interchangeably, recognizing that the memoir is an autobiographical form and also encompasses a sense of "inner experience."

3 J. W. Scott, *Gender and the Politics of History*, 18, 20.

4 This kind of incorporation also structures Alison McMahan's groundbreaking study of Alice Guy Blaché.

5 Memoirs by many women who worked in the silent film industry have circulated in other histories as well. I examine the appearance of Louise Brooks's autobiographical essays in chapter 3, but similar investigations could take place concerning the memoirs of Lillian Gish and Linda Arvidson, especially, who are often quoted in historical and theoretical works about D. W. Griffith. Many other women in the film industry of this period also produced their memoirs, some of which have circulated in scholarly discourse. This group of authors includes stars, directors, and screenwriters such as Marion Davies, Anita Loos, Frances Marion, Colleen Moore, Mary Pickford, Leni Riefenstahl, Nell Shipman, and Gloria Swanson. The majority of the works listed here are authored solely by the women named, though works by Gish and Davies list a second author or editor.

6 Swanson, *Swanson on Swanson*, v.

7 Riefenstahl, *The Sieve of Time*, n.p.

8 Ibid., 179.

9 Swanson, *Swanson on Swanson*, v.

10 Hobart, *A Steady Digression to a Fixed Point*, 3. In *The Poetics of Space*, Bachelard argues that memory is ordered by space rather than time.

11 Shipman, *The Silent Screen*, 2-3.

12 See J. W. Scott, *Gender and the Politics of History*, 16-20.

13 Hobart, *A Steady Digression to a Fixed Point*, 13.

14 Pickford, *Why Not Try God?*, 29, 28.

15 Waters and Samuels, *His Eye Is on the Sparrow*, 1. The authorship is marked as follows: "an autobiography by Ethel Waters with Charles Samuels."

16  Fregoso, *meXicana encounters*, 104.

17  This mix of history and fantasy surely appears in three works that Fregoso discusses: *The Assumption of Lupe Vélez* (dir. Rita González, 1999), *Lupe* (dir. Andy Warhol, 1965), and *Lupe* (dir. Jose Rodríguez-Soltero, 1966). It is also an important component of films about other film stars such as Carmen Miranda (*Bananas Is My Business*; dir. Helena Solberg, 1995), Jean Seberg (*The Journals of Jean Seberg*; dir. Mark Rappaport, 1995), and, to an extent, Rose Hobart (*Rose Hobart*; dir. Joseph Cornell, 1936).

18  Bachelard, *The Poetics of Reverie*, 101.

19  Bann, *The Clothing of Clio*, 7.

20  Lacassin, "Out of Oblivion," 151.

21  Peary, "Czarina of the Silent Screen," 35.

22  Nicholson et al., "Women and the Formal Film," 187.

23  Gerald Peary makes a similar call in the postscript to "Czarina of the Silent Screen": "I am glad of introducing film readers to this most unusual and interesting woman, and hope that there will be more articles building on this one, just as I am indebted to the pioneering essay by Francis Lacassin" (6).

24  See Smith, *Women Who Make Movies*; Beck, *Scream Queens*; Heck-Rabi, *Women Filmmakers*; Quart, *Women Directors*; and Acker, *Reel Women*.

25  Of course, Guy-Blaché's case was hardly an exceptional one. As we know, the vast majority of films made during this period were not automatically preserved. At the same time, I agree with the implication of Nicholson et al. in "Women and the Formal Film" that it is not mere coincidence that the loss of Guy-Blaché's films was the loss of a *woman*'s work.

26  As *The Lost Garden* also proclaims, "Lately, however, there is a renewed interest in her work and people are rediscovering the perennial treasures of this Lost Garden." The most significant work to do so is Alison McMahan's *Alice Guy Blaché: Lost Visionary of the Cinema*. Indeed, McMahan's book is largely an exegesis on the many Guy-Blaché films that she has labored to rediscover and make more accessible for future scholars. In general, the trend of recovery, or trope of loss, essentially ends in the early 1990s, when Guy-Blaché was written into two major studies of early French cinema: Abel, *The Ciné Goes to Town*, and Williams, *The Republic of Images*.

27  Patrick Hutton distinguishes between repetition and recollection in *History as an Art of Memory*.

28  Gilmore, *Autobiographics*, 27.

29  hooks, "In Our Glory," 53.

30  Freeman, *Rewriting the Self*, 47.

31  The word "memoir" (usually plural) springs from the French *mémoire*, the Old French *memoire*, and the Latin *memoria*, all of which mean "memory."

32  However, her memoirs were published posthumously. She died in

1968, and the memoirs were originally published in France in 1976. They were then translated by her daughter, Simone Blaché, and published in the United States in 1986. A subsequent paperback edition came out in 1996.

33  The documentary itself also represents such interminglings through a number of strategies. For instance, Guy-Blaché's daughter-in-law and granddaughter appear as the primary historians of her personal and professional life stories. At times, Guy-Blaché's fictional films stand in for her real life; at others, contemporary experts are garbed as characters from the films. In general, the film itself (and the subsequent history it tells) is structured like a personal act of remembering.

34  Certainly the family itself can function as an institution. In his seminal work on ideological theories and practices, Louis Althusser categorizes the family as an Ideological State Apparatus, in spite of his admission that it also "obviously has other 'functions' than that of an ISA" ("Ideology and Ideological State Apparatuses," 143). Moreover, he notes that the distinction between the public and the private—an opposition that helps to define the family—is one "internal to bourgeois law, and valid in the (subordinate) domains in which bourgeois law exercises its 'authority'" (144). He goes on to note, "It is unimportant whether the institutions in which [ISAs] are realized are 'public' or 'private.' What matters is how they function. Private institutions can perfectly well 'function' as Ideological State Apparatuses. A reasonably thorough analysis of any one of the ISAs proves this" (144). The function of the family as part of an ideological discourse, if not an Ideological State Apparatus, has been closely analyzed in the field of television studies. See, for instance, Joyrich, *Re-viewing Reception*, especially "Tube Tied: Television, Reproductive Politics, and *Moonlighting*'s Family Practice"; Dave Morley, *Family Television: Cultural Power and Domestic Leisure* (London: Routledge, 1988); and Spigel, *Make Room for TV*.

35  Nora, "Between Memory and History," 8–9. Some works in film and television studies make similar distinctions. For instance, in his essay, "Third Cinema as Guardian of Popular Memory: Towards a Third Aesthetic," Teshome Gabriel distinguishes between "official history" and "popular memory": "Official history tends to arrest the future by means of the past. . . . [The written word of history] claims a 'centre' which continuously marginalises others. In this way its ideology inhibits people from constructing their own history or histories"; popular memory "orders the past not only as a reference point but also as a theme of struggle. For popular memory, there are no longer any 'centres' or 'margins,' since the very designations imply that something has been conveniently left out. . . . It is a 'look back to the future,' necessarily dissident and partisan, wedded to constant change" (in Jim Pines and Paul Willemen, eds., *Questions of Third Cinema*, 54). In her essay "From the Dark Ages to the Golden Age," Lynn Spigel similarly draws a distinc-

tion between official history and popular memory. (Although she does not cite Gabriel's work, both seem influenced by Michel Foucault, who discusses "popular memory" in an interview in *Cahiers du Cinema* [nos. 251-252 (1974): 5-15].) Spigel writes, "Popular memory is history for the present; it is a mode of historical consciousness that speaks to the concerns and needs of contemporary life. Popular memory is a form of storytelling through which people make sense of their own lives and culture. In this regard, it diverges from official, professional history (by which I mean those histories deemed legitimate by schools, museums, textbook publishers and other arbiters of social knowledge)" (21). Although I do not pursue the notion of popular memory, I find Gabriel's and Spigel's approaches useful, especially as Spigel begins to work through the hybrids that form between these categories.

36 Jacques LeGoff might argue with this distinction. He contends, "Recent, naive trends seem virtually to identify history with memory, and even to give preference in some sense to memory, on the ground that it is more authentic, 'truer' than history, which is presumed to be artificial and, above all, manipulative of memory" (*History and Memory*, xi).

37 An inspired response to this kind of situation is displayed brilliantly in Giuliana Bruno's *Streetwalking on a Ruined Map*. In this work, Bruno recreates readings of Notari's films and a historiography of the filmmaker through exhaustive research of other extant materials: film summaries in contemporary trade magazines, posters, film stills, production notes, and the like.

38 Marcel Proust, *Swann's Way*, trans. C. K. Scott Moncrieff and Terence Kilmartin (New York: Random House, 1992), 5.

39 Benjamin, *Reflections*, 28.

40 The body of criticism from this time period roughly falls into two categories: those foundational texts that centered only on or largely on Guy-Blaché and, hence, influenced the work that appeared after them; and a number of reference texts that include a chapter or entry on Guy-Blaché. Into the first group would fall Francis Lacassin's 1971 *Sight and Sound* essay "Out of Oblivion," Gerald Peary's 1972 essay "Czarina of the Silent Screen," and Anthony Slide's 1986 edited volume of Guy-Blaché's memoirs, as well as his discussion of her in the 1977 *Early Women Directors: Their Role in the Development of the Silent Cinema* (revised and republished in 1996 as *The Silent Feminists: America's First Women Directors*). Aside from these works, as well as the 1978 *Scream Queens* by Calvin Thomas Beck and an essay by Lis Rhodes and Felicity Sparrow, "Her Image Fades as Her Voice Rises," both of which include relatively lengthy discussions of Guy-Blaché's films, the remaining work on Guy-Blaché in the United States during this period appears in historical and biographical reference texts (in fact, Beck's is also a reference text of sorts). Two of these texts include full chapters on Guy-Blaché: Sharon Smith's 1975 volume *Women Who Make Movies* and Louise Heck-Rabi's 1984 book

*Women Filmmakers.* A third, Barbara Koenig Quart's 1988 *Women Directors*, discusses Guy-Blaché along with Lois Weber and Germaine Dulac in a chapter called "Antecedents." Each of these works also exemplifies the reliance on Guy-Blaché's own writings, or at least the transmission of her words, usually via Lacassin's inaugural essay.

41 It does so through its reliance on actual acts of remembering (by Guy-Blaché's family members and, through the inclusion of clips from an archival television interview, by Guy-Blaché herself); its nonlinear movement between temporal periods and various spaces; and even its use of footage from fictional films to illustrate facets of the filmmaker's real life.

42 Nora, "Between Memory and History," 9, 11–12. For Nora, the rise of historiography and changes in national thinking (and ideas about national histories) have "dissociated" history and memory.

43 Ibid., 15.

44 Freeman, *Rewriting the Self*, 32.

45 LeGoff, *History and Memory*, xi–xii.

46 Gish and Pinchot, *The Movies*, 133.

47 LeGoff, *History and Memory*, 99.

48 See especially Bogle, *Toms, Coons*; Thomas Cripps, *Slow Fade to Black: The Negro in American Film, 1900–1942* (New York: Oxford University Press, 1993); and Ed Guerrero, *Framing Blackness: The African American Image in Film* (Philadelphia: Temple University Press, 1993).

49 Benjamin, *Reflections*, 31.

50 Guy Blaché, *The Memoirs*, 1. I use the English translation of Guy-Blaché's memoirs. Most of the changes in translation to the passages I focus on are quite subtle; I will point out any significant alterations.

51 This is also an important distinction to make, though not necessarily one that has been heeded by those writers who came after Guy-Blaché. Indeed, labeling Guy-Blaché as the "mother" of the cinema, or even as a "foremother" of feminist film theory and history, potentially poses certain limitations on how we perceive the filmmaker and her position in history. There are ways in which her very literal position as a mother helped in the eventual circulation of her history, especially through her daughter's and daughter-in-law's efforts to translate and publish the *Memoirs*. However, labeling any woman as the mother of an institution has the potential to shut down a consideration of her ongoing importance in the field; she may be seen as merely the originator whose duty has already been accomplished. In the case of Guy-Blaché, other connections between her motherhood and her work in film have produced provocative but sometimes limiting considerations of her. For instance, several writers link the birth of her second child to the completion of her new Solax studio. Although this connection might suggest ways the public arena could be structured as a woman's field (that is, like

a family or a home), it also might trap our reading of her work as connected only to familial, private life. It would be interesting to extend this analysis of Guy-Blaché's maternal position in film production and film history and of the role of foremothers in a more general sense through psychoanalytic theories of mother-daughter relations. Doing so might illuminate other reasons for Guy-Blaché's dual loss and recovery in film studies. For an insightful reading of a foremother in film history, see Egger, "Deaf Ears and Dark Continents."

52 For instance, we can see this trope in works from André Bazin's *What Is Cinema? Vol. I* when he draws on metaphors of birth and death to describe early and later film production, to Maya Deren's writings, to Laura Mulvey's "Visual Pleasure and Narrative Cinema." In such cases, as in Christian Metz's work, film is lent an anthropomorphic quality, which may partially account for the burgeoning theories of identification and spectatorship that have sprung from the work of Metz and others.

53 Christian Metz, *The Imaginary Signifier*, 93.

54 These two details might partly account for why he's been such an important figure for feminist film theorists: he suggests he has a built-in empathy for women as well as a desire to masquerade as a woman.

55 Guy-Blaché, *The Memoirs*, 28, ix.

56 As McMahan claims, Guy-Blaché remained a Victorian throughout her life, in many senses.

57 Kelley, *Private Woman*, 111.

58 Ibid., 125, 128.

59 Douglas, *Feminization of American Culture*; Fetterley, *Provisions*, 5.

60 Bann, *The Clothing of Clio*, 66, 67.

61 Guy-Blaché, *The Memoirs*, 67, 29, 42, 76–79. In fact, in her discussion of scientific experiments to display the utility of X-rays, for which she "often lent [her] hands," she declares, "I still have a little burn scar from this" (42). The evidence of her work is thus also written on her body.

62 Ibid., 69.

63 Ibid., 33, emphasis in original.

64 Ibid., 35–36.

65 The apparent insistence on her place in history seems more consistent with a short essay published in *Moving Picture World*, July 11, 1914, 195, which is inevitably quoted by all who write about her. In this piece, Alice Guy-Blaché declares, "It has long been a source of wonder to me that many women have not seized upon the wonderful opportunities offered to them by the motion-picture art to make their way to fame and fortune as producers of photodramas. Of all the arts there is probably none in which they can make such splendid use of talents so much more natural to a woman than to a man and so necessary to its perfection." That particular summons noted that film

production was precisely made for women: "The technique of the drama has been mastered by so many women that it is considered as much her field as a man's and its adaptation to picture work in no way removes it from her sphere. The technique of motion-picture photography, like the technique of the drama, is fitted to women's activities" (129). Such a claim was impossible without Guy-Blaché's precursors in the nineteenth-century fiction industry.

66 Freud, "Screen Memories," in *Standard Edition*, vol. 3, 302.

67 Ibid., 315–16.

68 Ibid., 320.

69 In this case, his screen memory reveals the feelings of hunger and love as attached to another experience.

70 Guy-Blaché, *The Memoirs*, 95, 96.

71 Ibid., 20.

72 Ibid., 76, 78.

73 Ibid., 79. The original French reads: "Le directeur poussa la complaisance jusqu'a m'inviter à m'y asseoir, ce que je fis" (Alice Guy-Blaché, *Autobiographie d'une Pionnière du Cinéma, 1873–1968* [Paris: Denoël/Gonthier, 1976], 124). This line would be literally translated as: "The director pushed his hospitality to the point of having me sit down, which I did." Guy-Blaché's original statement is, thus, more critical than the translation of her claim.

74 Ibid., 124. Guy-Blaché originally wrote that the men wanted to smoke their cigars "en paix" ("in peace").

75 Ibid., 79.

76 Yates, *The Art of Memory*, 6. Writes Yates, "The artificial memory is established from places and images . . . the stock definition to be forever repeated down the ages. A *locus* is a place easily grasped by the memory, such as a house, an intercolumnar space, a corner, an arch, or the like. Images are forms, marks or simulacra . . . of what we wish to remember. For instance if we wish to recall the genus of a horse, of a lion, of an eagle, we must place their images on definite *loci*" (6).

77 Bergson, *Matter and Memory*, 104–105.

78 Münsterberg, *The Film*, 25.

79 Eisenstein, *Film Form and Film Sense*, 49.

80 Guy-Blaché, *The Memoirs*, 79. Perhaps she even takes some of the blame here for the loss of her company; after all, after the invitation, she sat in the chair herself.

81 As I noted earlier, for instance, many works emphasize that no obituary appeared on Guy-Blaché's death. As well, several histories of her repeatedly connect the end of the filmmaker's career with the end of her marriage. Writes Sharon Smith: "It was a time of great personal stress. Just when her company went into a decline, her marriage to Herbert Blaché, who had worked closely with her since the Gaumont days, came to an end" (*Women*

*Who Make Movies*, 3). Louise Heck-Rabi similarly remarks, "Sadly, the marital partnership of the Blachés disintegrated with the collapse of their business and careers" (*Women Filmmakers*, 16). Barbara Quart notes, "After the firm dissolved, the marriage did as well" (*Women Directors*, 19). And Ally Acker claims, "A time of great personal strife ensued. Her company fell into decline and so did her marriage" (*Reel Women*, 10).

82  Gilmore, *Autobiographics*, 107.

83  Gerald Peary discusses "A Solax Celebration" as if it were an actual film, but I have found no evidence to indicate it was a real production.

84  *Moving Picture World*, January 13, 1912, 130.

85  Ibid.

86  In this case, the summary rather resembles the rendering of fictional films as historical evidence in Lepage's *The Lost Garden*.

87  Grieveson, *Policing Cinema*, 156, 154.

3. THE CRITIC

1  Brooks, "Why I Will Never Write My Memoirs," 220.

2  Brooks, *Lulu in Hollywood*, 6.

3  Some history of these publications is in order. The same year Brooks's "Why I Will Never Write My Memoirs" was republished in *Film Culture* (1979), Kenneth Tynan's "definitive, classic Profile of Louise Brooks" (according to William Shawn, publisher of the *New Yorker* and the author of the introduction to *Lulu in Hollywood*) was published in the *New Yorker*. In his "Profile" of Brooks, Tynan significantly mentions that "Why I Will Never Write My Memoirs" was published in *Focus on Film* two years earlier, in 1977. Although I find this apparent original date of publication important, what interests me more is that the essay was (re)printed both at the time Tynan's piece appeared in the *New Yorker* and closer to the time that *Lulu in Hollywood* was published. Considering the amount of time it normally takes to have a book published, the time of Brooks's statement in 1977/1979 becomes even closer to that of the collection of her autobiographical essays for eventual publication in 1983 (in that they were most likely prepared for publication as early as 1981). Furthermore, Shawn's introduction to *Lulu* has a copyright of 1982, collapsing this distance even more.

4  Paris, *Louise Brooks*, 69.

5  See Doane, "The Erotic Barter." Doane does point to some affinities between Pabst's film and classical Hollywood cinema.

6  In discussing Brooks's book, I understand "Hollywood" not simply as a town in California, but as the film industry of Brooks's time. Thus, her exploits documented in *Lulu in Hollywood* take place not only in California

but in other locations as well during the time she was part of Hollywood's industry.

7 Brooks, *Lulu in Hollywood*, 104. Indeed, it's difficult to sort out these two alternatives, as each is described by Brooks. She says that after working with Pabst, she no longer desired to work in Hollywood (though she did make seven more—fairly unsuccessful—films after *Diary of a Lost Girl*), but her refusal to return was represented by the industry as her uselessness in talkies. She notes: "When I got back to New York after finishing *Pandora's Box*, Paramount's New York office called to order me to get on the train at once for Hollywood. They were making *The Canary Murder Case* [a film in which Brooks played in 1929] into a talkie and needed me for retakes. When I said I wouldn't go, they sent a man round with a contract. When I still said I wouldn't go, they offered me any amount of money I might ask, to save the great expense of reshooting and dubbing in another voice. . . . But the whole thing—the money that Paramount was forced to spend, the affront to the studio—made them so angry that they sent out a story, widely publicized and believed, that they had let me go because I was no good in talkies" (104). Tynan also notes that around this time, "the word was out that Brooks was difficult and uppity, too independent to suit the system" ("The Girl in the Black Helmet," 50).

8 Ellis, *Visible Fictions*, 91.

9 deCordova, "The Emergence of the Star System in America," 1, 11.

10 See Hake, "The Continuous Provocation of Louise Brooks." The relationship between the two is discussed at length in Hake's essay. As she also notes, Brooks appears to fulfill what Richard Dyer calls the "perfect fit" between character and star, but in fact she better fulfills what Dyer labels the "problematic fit" (Dyer, *Heavenly Bodies*, 68).

11 The original revitalizing boost to Brooks's image was James Card's short essay, "The 'Intense Isolation' of Louise Brooks," published in 1958 in *Sight and Sound*. Card notes that Brooks was "completely forgotten in the United States" and documents his support of Brooks's writings: "As an historian forever carping about the paucity of film writing with just minimal doses of truth and authenticity, I encouraged Miss Brooks, with her obsession for veracity, to get down in print some of the observations churned up by our post-screening arguments" (243).

12 I was inspired here by Giuliana Bruno's use of the incisive phrase "economics of discourse" (*Streetwalking on a Ruined Map*, 107). Bruno, however, uses it to describe language that neatly and ironically defines economic situations, in this case women who assembled films in the early Italian film industry.

13 Hake, "The Continuous Provocation of Louise Brooks," 59.

14  In Jaccard, *Louise Brooks*, 13. The poem's narrative description of Lulu makes clear that she is also Louise, the Kansas native: "Lulu/face so delicate/once musical/from a tender prairie/and wild fields/your voice/covers our little dreams."

15  Ibid., 19.

16  Those photographs that are not stills are primarily from Brooks's childhood and from her work in the period preceding *Pandora's Box*. Indeed, only four of the photographs of Brooks were taken after 1930: one is from one of her last films, *Empty Saddles* (1937); another is of Brooks in Central Park in 1931; one was taken in Paris in 1958; and the latest was shot in Rochester in 1964. These last two photographs are placed at the end of Lotte Eisner's essay, "A Witness Speaks" (Brooks, *Lulu in Hollywood*, 113–116), which I discuss later. Although Brooks herself briefly mentions the contemporary moment in which she is writing, Eisner's short essay "The Other Side of the Camera" is the only one to discuss Brooks in her life beyond Lulu, as an aging woman.

17  From Frank Wedekind, Prologue to *The Earth-Spirit*, in Sol Gittleman, *Frank Wedekind*, TWAS 55 (New York: Twayne, 1969), 67.

18  Jaccard, *Louise Brooks: Portrait of an Anti-Star*, 18.

19  Ibid., 29, 15–16.

20  Card, "The 'Intense Isolation' of Louise Brooks," 243.

21  From John Lahr, "The Comedienne and the Femme Fatale," *New York Times Book Review*, 30 May 1982, 7–8. In his brief yet insightful essay "Brooks and the Bob," Peter Wollen notes that Brooks's writings aided in the representation of her androgyny (and her cult status): "Despite all her evasions and demurrings, Brooks' androgyny was central to her cult allure. Her piquant autobiographical writings, published from the late 50s through the 60s (many of them in *Sight and Sound*) only added to the confusion of documentary and fiction, making her not only a wicked chronicler of Weimar (and Hollywood) decadence, but also a symbol of its polymorphous perversity." As the title of his essay testifies, Wollen emphasizes that "the most visible and memorable reason for Brooks' instant appeal was simply the way she looked and that the way she looked was primarily determined by her haircut" (24). Although Wollen's piece primarily examines Brooks's status as an image, his remarks concerning her writings neatly point to how Brooks has been represented both as an image and as a chronicler (or witness) of sexual decadence.

22  These theories of performance and sexuality have been greatly influenced by the work of Michel Foucault, as well as by feminist writings on masquerade. Judith Butler's *Gender Trouble*, to which I shall turn shortly, is by now probably the best known of such works. See also Judith Butler, "Imitation and Gender Insubordination" and Carole-Anne Tyler, "Boys Will Be

Girls: The Politics of Gay Drag," in *Inside/Out: Lesbian Theories, Gay Theories*, ed. Diana Fuss (New York: Routledge, 1991); Eve Kosofsky Sedgwick, *Epistemology of the Closet* (Berkeley: University of California Press, 1990); Jill Dolan, " 'Lesbian' Subjectivity in Realism: Dragging at the Margins of Structure and Ideology," in *Performing Feminisms: Feminist Critical Theory and Theatre*, ed. Sue-Ellen Case (London: Johns Hopkins University Press, 1986); and the growing body of work on camp and butch-femme aesthetics.

23 Butler, *Gender Trouble*, 136.

24 Dyer, *Heavenly Bodies*, 25.

25 Tynan, "The Girl in the Black Helmet," 60, 65. The biographer Barry Paris doubts the veracity of this story. It's an interesting one, for it seems as if Brooks's tale might follow a conventional path: as an actress out of luck and strapped for cash, she decides to sell herself. Instead of becoming the clichéd prostitute, however, she decides to become an author and sell her story rather than her body. But even in this story of the aborted memoirs, Brooks conflates issues of sexuality, writing, and even erudition (it's Faust she's quoting, after all): "I sit here naked on my goat and show my fine young body."

26 Brooks, *Lulu in Hollywood*, 6, 7, 46, 98.

27 Ibid., 74, 87, 90.

28 Tynan, "The Girl in the Black Helmet," 60.

29 Ibid. I find it peculiarly relevant that in 1944 and 1945 Brooks got "a couple of jobs in publicity agencies, collecting items for [Walter] Winchell's column"; she thus played the part of a witness in the gossip scene.

30 Although I will be looking at other essays as well (particularly Heide Schlüpmann's "The Brothel as Arcadian Space?" and Sabine Hake's "The Continuous Provocation of Louise Brooks"), Doane's and Elsaesser's essays will form the predominant basis for my analysis. I am particularly interested in these pieces because they center around Brooks's role in Pabst's film and so are directly interested in the issues that more popular, or biographical, essays also raise. Certainly each of these historical contexts served to construct Brooks in one way or another (for instance, her insistence, to Kenneth Tynan and others, that she could not write her memoirs in the 1950s because she couldn't speak openly about her sex life), but through the circulation of Brooks's—and others'—writings, her image did begin to function outside of these contexts. (In fact, two decades later, she continued to insist that she couldn't write the memoirs for the same reason.) Lest I now be misunderstood as repeating certain claims that Brooks herself was timeless, I would like to note that this decontextualization itself produced an image of timelessness. I acknowledge the importance of recognizing historical contexts of production and reception of stars, but my focus is on how, through the circulation

of discourse, Brooks's biography—literally, the writing of her life—has been constructed. In doing so I hope to highlight important relations between film history and theory.

31  Tynan, "The Girl in the Black Helmet," 51, 45–46.

32  Ibid., 51. This interpretation of Brooks's performance ("she is following her nature") is often echoed in other writings. As Wollen notes, "Pabst gave Brooks the confidence to be herself as a performer, to live her part on the set as naturally as she could (and, in the case of *Pandora's Box*, as she points out, her part was one she was familiar with from her own time as a Follies showgirl and rich man's companion, from her own eclectic and impulsive sexual life)" ("Brooks and the Bob," 24).

33  Paris, *Louise Brooks*, 427.

34  Ibid., 493.

35  The Tynan quote does, however, introduce Leacock and Woll's film *Lulu in Berlin* (after the initial clip from *Prix de beauté*).

36  Hake, "The Continuous Provocation of Louise Brooks," 58–59. Hake notes that "images of ambiguity predominate" in classical Weimar cinema. She claims, moreover, that "Brooks can only be understood through her association with Weimar cinema" (59).

37  Weiss, *Vampires and Violets*, 22.

38  For a discussion of Nazimova and European exoticism, see White, "Nazimova's Veils." For a discussion of the intersection between ethnic and national identity in relation to Negri, see Negra, "Immigrant Stardom in Imperial America."

39  White, "Black and White," 228.

40  Weiss, *Vampires and Violets*, 24.

41  Brooks, *Lulu in Hollywood*, 99.

42  Quoted in Tynan, "The Girl in the Black Helmet," 71. In his biography of Brooks, Barry Paris does try to decipher the comment. Noting that this statement was made by Charles Weidman, he says, "What Weidman meant is obscure, but what Louise meant, in frequently quoting it, was that she loved women as a homosexual man, rather than as a lesbian, would love them" (Paris, *Louise Brooks*, 417). And not only did *Brooks* frequently quote the line; it appears, for instance, in Tynan's piece, Paris's book, and Weiss's study.

43  Paris, *Louise Brooks*, 417, 518. This claim is particularly fascinating given my own concern with the relationship between the construction of images and authorship. According to Paris, what Brooks didn't like about homosexuals was less their sexuality than their authorship; it is this dislike that helps to form her "deep ambivalence."

44  Another star who is taken up similarly is Lillian Gish; her book *The Movies, Mr. Griffith, and Me* is frequently quoted in essays on Griffith's work (such as Flitterman-Lewis, "The Blossom and the Bole"). Mae West's

and Roseanne's more recently published autobiographical writings function similarly.

45 Schlüpmann, "The Brothel as an Arcadian Space?," 89.

46 Ibid., 82, 89.

47 Doane, *Femmes Fatales*, 284–285; my emphasis.

48 Though I provide an analysis of the essays here, for a lengthier treatment, please see my "Louise Brooks, Star Witness."

49 Elsaesser, "Lulu and the Meter Man," 33, 32.

50 For a provocative discussion of lesbians and phantoms, see White, "Female Spectator, Lesbian Specter."

51 Elsaesser, "Lulu and the Meter Man," 5.

52 Further recognizing this opposition as essentially the invisible versus "visual (and *literary*)," Elsaesser sketches out a difference between cinematic and written performances. (Of course, as he implies, the theater itself might be considered a space where the written—the "literary"—and the "visual" merge.) Brooks's own written and spoken representations of her roles on- and off-screen at the time reemphasize a link between written and physical performances of identity.

53 Lotte Eisner labels Brooks "enigmatically passive," seeming to illustrate that she would not exactly call her "passive," though she's drawn to the term nonetheless.

54 Hake, "The Continuous Provocation of Louise Brooks," 59.

55 Elsaesser, "Lulu and the Meter Maid," 15. He writes, "Following on directly from this reversibility of attributes seems to be the principal ambiguity that preoccupied critics of Lulu, both in the plays and the film— whether she is a victim or an agent, whether she has a passive or an active role in the event of which she is the centre. Wedekind himself writes: 'Lulu is not a real character, but the personification of primitive sexuality who inspires evil unaware. She plays a purely passive role'" (15).

56 Ibid., 27.

57 Obviously, Elsaesser doesn't completely hide the fact that Brooks is often the source for much of the information in his text, as a reader can quite easily turn to his footnotes—and readers often *do* turn to footnotes (case in point). What I want to stress, however, is not that it's impossible to recognize Brooks as Elsaesser's source but that this source is hidden in the body of the text (through his use of the passive voice, for instance), and it becomes something of a surprise when we do turn to the footnotes and find that it is Brooks writing and not, say, Wedekind speaking.

58 Brooks's indeterminacy as a witness is interestingly linked to Elsaesser's arguments concerning the indeterminacy of Lulu's sexuality; but even the indeterminacy of Brooks's sexuality is subject to Elsaesser's editing, as her lesbianism is never a subject of his discussion. Both Elsaesser and Doane

certainly place some focus on Brooks's (sometimes questionable) sexuality. Patrice Petro notes this fascination of scholars. Regarding the representation of both Marlene Dietrich and Louise Brooks as figures in films of the Weimar period, she comments, "Without a doubt, Dietrich and Brooks remain convenient figures upon which to project a reading of male subjectivity in crisis; as figures of female eroticism, they were typically featured in films where male characters are brought to their doom as a result of their uncompromising devotion to a feminine ideal. Given that Dietrich and Brooks only began their screen careers in the final years of the Weimar Republic, however, this kind of retrospective reading would seem to reveal as much about a fascination exerted by a certain type of woman in contemporary scholarship as it does about the figure of woman in the late Weimar period" (*Joyless Streets*, 160).

59  Doane, *Femmes Fatales*, 150, 156.

60  On the other hand, Brooks could be said to be stuck *in* time as the image of Lulu. On the covers of Paris's biography, Doane's *Femmes Fatales*, and *Lulu in Hollywood* and at the opening of Tynan's article in the *New Yorker*, Brooks is pictured as Lulu, or at least as she was seen as Lulu. Of course, her signature haircut (which became synonymous with Lulu) seemed to lend itself to this permanent imaging, as she wore the "black helmet" for most of her years in Hollywood.

61  Doane, *Femmes Fatales*, 143. Lulu is also a witness to history, for at the end of the film she witnesses Jack the Ripper, already a sexual and certainly transgressive (to say the least) historical figure.

62  Ibid., 162.

63  Correctives have also been made to this position. See, for instance, Renate Bridenthal, Atina Grossman, and Marion Kaplan, eds., *When Biology Became Destiny: Women in Weimar and Nazi Germany* (New York: Monthly Review Press, 1984); Atina Grossman, "*Girlkultur* or Thoroughly Rationalized Female: A New Woman in Weimar Germany?," in *Women in Culture and Politics: A Century of Change*, ed. Judith Friedlander et al. (Bloomington: Indiana University Press, 1986); Petro's *Joyless Streets*; and Ann Snitow, Christine Stansell, and Sharon Thompson, eds., *Powers of Desire: The Politics of Sexuality* (New York: Monthly Review Press, 1983).

64  Doane, *Femmes Fatales*, 149, 143.

65  Card, "The 'Intense Isolation' of Louise Brooks," 243.

66  Hall, "Realism as a Style in Cinema Vérité," 38. Hall actually wields the term "cinema vérité" to describe what others term "direct cinema" in the United States. As she notes in a footnote, "Although Erik Barnouw refers to the French school of the movement as 'cinema vérité' and the North American school as 'direct cinema' in his widely used textbook, most documentary

scholars (e.g., Robert C. Allen, A. William Bluem, Noël Carroll, Stephen Mamber, Bill Nichols, Thomas Waugh) use 'cinema vérité' for both schools as well" (47). The expertise of these critics notwithstanding, it seems important to maintain a distinction between the national movements, which can be easily marked by their respective titles. Although the two movements shared a desire and a claim to represent the truth, they did so by rather different means. Indeed, although his assertions are a little hyperbolic in this instance, Brian Winston maps out some of their differences: " 'Cinéma Vérité' is a style of documentary which deliberately draws attention to the processes involved in the making of the film. It was invented, as its name clearly indicates, in France. All it has in common with the American school of 'Direct Cinema' is equipment. 'Direct Cinema' is the exact opposite of 'Cinéma Vérité.' It seeks more completely than any previous mode of documentary to hide the processes of film-making—to pretend to an unblinking objectivity supposedly similar to that possessed by a fly on the wall" ("Direct Cinema," 238).

67 Jaffe, "Editing Cinéma Vérité," 43.

68 Bachmann et al., "The Frontiers of Realist Cinema," 15, 17.

69 Nichols, "The Voice of Documentary," 260.

70 Winston, "The Documentary Film as Scientific Inscription," 43.

71 Hall, "Realism as a Style in Cinema Vérité," 29.

72 Arthur, "Jargons of Authenticity," 124.

73 Ibid., 122.

74 In 1971, Leacock commented on the possibility of such a role in his interview with G. Roy Levin. Levin asks, "In that interview with Blue, in reference to *Happy Mother's Day*, you say you wanted people to talk about the film—what it was about; you got them together, they talked and it was their discussion. This is obviously hindsight on my part, but in that kind of situation, would you now think of talking to the person directly, and you yourself perhaps becoming a character in the film?" Leacock responds, "I haven't done it. I'm not sure why not. I guess it's usually because I've always been doing the filming and that's enough. I can't. Also, my mind is so full from absorbing what's going on, that I would find it very difficult to" (Levin, *Documentary Explorations*, 216–217).

75 Ibid., 217, 218. Interestingly, as both Jeanne Hall and Brian Winston note, the theories behind direct cinema—and its subsequent history—have been based largely on interviews conducted with the filmmakers in the 1960s and 1970s.

76 Hall, "Realism as a Style in Cinema Vérité," 28.

77 Renov, "History and/as Autobiography," 7, 8.

78 This passage ends the version of "Pabst and Lulu" originally published in *Sight and Sound* 34, no. 3 (summer 1965) and subsequently reprinted

in Ladislaus Vajda et al., eds., *Pandora's Box (Lulu)* (New York: Simon and Schuster, 1971), though Brooks expands the essay for inclusion in *Lulu in Hollywood*.

79  In the end, Clair did not direct the film, Augusto Genina did. In Leacock and Woll's film, Brooks contends that Clair urged her to drop out of the project as well, but her contract did not allow it.

80  Paris, *Louise Brooks*, 73.

81  Eisner, "A Witness Speaks," 107.

82  Ibid., 109.

83  Brooks, *Lulu in Hollywood*, photo near p. 36.

84  See Paris, *Louise Brooks*, 534.

85  Hedy Lamarr, *Ecstasy and Me: My Life as a Woman* (New York: W. H. Allen, 1967), Brooks's notation on p. 162. Brooks's copy donated to the George Eastman House.

86  Bob Thomas, *King Cohn: The Life and Times of Harry Cohn* (New York: Putnam, 1967), Brooks's notation on p. 100. Brooks's copy donated to the George Eastman House.

87  Ibid., 108.

88  Lamarr, *Ecstasy and Me*, Brooks's notation on p. 136.

89  Ibid., 169.

90  Herman Weinberg, *Joseph von Sternberg: A Critical Study* (New York: Dutton, 1967). Brooks's copy donated to the George Eastman House.

91  Thomas, *King Cohn*, Brooks's notation on p. 142.

92  Herman Weinberg, *Stroheim: A Pictorial Record of His Nine Films* (New York: Dover, 1975), xvi.

93  Francis Steegmuller, *Cocteau: A Biography* (Boston: Little Brown, 1970), Brooks's notation on frontispiece. Brooks's copy donated to the George Eastman House.

94  Mary Astor, *My Story: An Autobiography* (New York: Doubleday, 1959), Brooks notation on p. 320, with her underscoring. Brooks's copy donated to the George Eastman House.

95  Shawn, introduction to Brooks, *Lulu in Hollywood*, ix.

96  Wollen, "Brooks and the Bob," 22.

97  Quoted in Paris, *Louise Brooks*, 468, 469.

98  Sarris, "Notes on the Auteur Theory in 1962," 63-64.

99  See Paris, *Louise Brooks*, 469. Brooks even waffled on her views about auteur theory. That is, though she initially championed the actor over the director and the writer, Paris reports that she later altered her views. He notes that Brooks "could never quite resolve" these issues. Thus he writes, "Three years after these forceful attacks on the *auteur* theory, she wrote a French journalist: 'Mr. Pabst made me important. The theatre is shaped by actors: films, by directors'" (469).

## 4. THE EXPERT

1  Ono, *Grapefruit*, n.p. Ono's book has no page numbers; the piece is dated spring of 1964. All of these pieces have dates, which makes the book as a whole akin to a diary as well as an instruction manual. It records the past in a future-oriented form.

2  Marlene Dietrich, *Marlene Dietrich's ABC*, 2nd ed., 48. I will be citing entries from this new edition throughout the chapter.

3  Pitts and Horton, *Candy Hits by Zasu Pitts*, 23.

4  Mae Marsh, *Screen Acting* (Los Angeles: Photostar, 1921); Frances Marion, *How to Write and Sell Film Stories* (New York: Covici, Friede, 1937); St. Johns, *How to Write a Story and Sell It*; Head and Ardmore, *The Dress Doctor*.

5  In recent years, we can see increasing interest in this tradition by stars like Jane Fonda, Marilu Henner, Shirley McLaine, Christy Turlington, and Oprah Winfrey, who offer counsel on subjects ranging from past-life experience to workout and diet regimens. And surely the celebrity cookbook has sustained—or perhaps even increased in—popularity. In fact, chefs and domestic experts have themselves become celebrities (Martha Stewart is the most obvious example here, but this category surely also includes figures like Emeril, Japan's "Iron Chef," and England's "Fat Ladies"). And stars from the rock star Ted Nugent to *The Today Show*'s Al Roker have expanded the range of celebrity cookbooks to include a widening number by men. While the role of *professional* chef has traditionally been held by men, the role of the domestic expert characterized by the popular cookbook has conventionally been held by women. Yet, no doubt, as with the development of the film industry as well, when the cookbook industry was shown to be a profitable one, men have increasingly tried to gain a stronghold in it.

6  Newton, *Learning to Behave*, 63, 65, 74.

7  Ibid., 75.

8  Ibid., 79, 94.

9  Beauchamp, *Without Lying Down*, 64. Writes Beauchamp, "Through Frances's pen, five days a week, Mary dispensed helpful beauty secrets, advice on friendships, and memories of her 'happy girlhood.' Mary was paid a thousand dollars a week and Frances made fifty, but she claimed to 'love the experience.' Her background in advertising helped her know what people wanted to hear and she knew Mary so well it was easy to find her voice. And it was a great excuse to get together at least once a week to review what had been written and discuss future ideas" (53). Beauchamp also notes that Douglas Fairbanks published a monthly column with his byline in *Photoplay* in 1917; though she doesn't note who actually wrote the columns, she strongly suggests it was not Fairbanks himself (77).

10 Whitfield, *Pickford*, 153.

11 It might be somewhat unreasonable to assume that Pickford would be able to write all of these texts herself in any case, given that her formal schooling was very limited. Indeed, most of her education came through her work on stage and then in films.

12 Foucault, *Language, Counter-Memory, Practice*, 286. Regarding Pickford, we might even see the author function as a fetish of sorts. We know she didn't actually pen these works herself, but . . .

13 Beauchamp, *Without Lying Down*, 335–336.

14 Whitfield, *Pickford*, 288.

15 Pickford, *Why Not Try God?*, 17.

16 In her book *American Domesticity*, Kathleen McHugh notes that Lydia Marie Child, for example, was "a collector, not the author or owner, of her information. It is not *her* knowledge or *her* property" (30). Catharine Beecher, on the other hand, was a different advisor from Child in that "she conceives of her subject as a kind of knowledge requiring education and training" (42).

17 Pickford, *Why Not Try God?*, 14.

18 All of these situations are well known, but see especially Whitfield, *Pickford*, 223, 264–268, 351.

19 Pickford, *Why Not Try God?*, 34.

20 Her memoirs, *Goodness Had Nothing to Do with It* (Englewood Cliffs, N.J.: Prentice-Hall), were originally published in 1959. A second edition appeared in 1970.

21 West, *Mae West on Sex, Health, and ESP*, 18, 21.

22 Ibid., 138. West credits Yogi Sri Deva Ram Sukul with originally helping her to discover her psychic powers. She first met him when he cured her of an undiagnosed pain she was having in the early 1930s. She later reacquainted herself with him and eventually studied yoga with him. West writes, "I was so impressed with the remarkable Yogi that Sri and I kept in close contact over the years, and I learned the basics of the Yoga philosophy long before the Hollywood Now Crowd drew attention to the subject" (117). Later in this section, West expounds on connections between ESP and Christianity: "Until I became interested in psychic phenomena and the revelations of ESP, I had very little acquaintance with the Holy Bible. But after it was pointed out to me that the Scriptures were full of psychic doings, and of the spirit forces that were at work guiding and directing the affairs of men, and recognising that these forces were also at work in my own life, I made it my business to know what the Bible is all about" (140). (Considering Madonna's avowed interest in the Jewish mystic tradition of the cabala and in yoga, this connection between West and Madonna might well be added to Pamela Robertson's joining them in her work on feminist camp!)

23 Curry, *Too Much of a Good Thing*, 90.

24 *Mae West on Sex, Health, and ESP*, 110. Suggestively, West even equates positive thinking, ESP, and writing itself:

> I did a lot of my writing in bed, but some of my best lines came to me in another way. I'd have my chauffeur take me for a ride, as far away as I could get from ringing phones and people, and drive up to a quiet part of Griffith Park. He'd park the car, then get out and go several feet away.
>
> I'd sit in the back seat, enjoying myself and the rare chance for total relaxation, and in the peaceful atmosphere I'd just try to put all the pressures of my career as far from my thoughts as I could.
>
> Years later, I learned that this was similar to the method used to develop one's psychic powers — but I'll come to that later on.
>
> At these quiet times, when my chauffeur would stand away from the parked car, I'd find wonderful lines coming into my mind. Sometimes a couple of them would come. At other times, several would fill my thoughts. All of them later became the classics that delighted my fans. (110)

25 Ibid., 57.

26 Ibid., 59. For interested readers, West plots out a day's diet to improve one's sex life. For breakfast, she suggests one cup of ginger tea, one bowl of natural wheat cereal, and two soft-boiled eggs; for lunch, shrimp cocktail, tomato salad, and a broiled steak; and for dinner, caviar on celery sticks, a broiled salmon steak, and a cup of ginger tea.

27 Dietrich, *Marlene Dietrich's ABC*, 2nd ed., vii.

28 Robertson, *Guilty Pleasures*, 38–40. In this section of her book, Robertson traces the rivalry constructed through fan magazines and West's own performances. See also Curry, *Too Much of a Good Thing*, who touches on this rivalry, but primarily focuses her attention on the different ways West and Dietrich represented "sexually transgressive implications" (100, 144–145).

29 Dietrich, *Marlene Dietrich's ABC*, 2nd ed., 172.

30 Ibid., 17.

31 McHugh, *American Domesticity*, 84.

32 Dietrich, *Marlene Dietrich's ABC*, 2nd ed., 49. In fact, one of the pithiest descriptions of these contradictions appears in Shirley Sealy's *The Celebrity Sex Register* (New York: Simon and Schuster, 1982): "Beneath the surface glitter, she sometimes pretends to be just a simple German hausfrau who likes to cook, and her tireless campaigning during World War II helped to fix her image as . . . well, a regular guy."

33 Dietrich, *Marlene Dietrich's ABC*, 2nd ed., 93.

34 McHugh, *American Domesticity*, 84, 82.

35 Marriage was also an entry into business for Joan Crawford, becoming active as a board member and publicity chair of Pepsi-Cola when

she was widowed in 1959. Recently, celebrities have traded on their work in the fields of visual representation to head their own businesses that serve these fields in other ways. Thus, supermodel Iman runs her own makeup line (known as Iman), as does model-actress Isabella Rossellini (Manifesto).

36 Information offered in phone conversation with Joe Yranski, Moore historian and long-time friend (November 1998).

37 Moore, *How Women Can Make Money in the Stock Market*, 1, 2, 3.

38 Ibid., 4.

39 The name, she claims, comes from a story her husband told her (the story begins to make the same argument Moore goes on to delineate).

40 Moore, *How Women Can Make Money in the Stock Market*, 5–6.

41 Ibid., 7.

42 Ferber and Nelson, *Beyond Economic Man*, 2.

43 Jennings, "Public or Private?," in Ferber and Nelson, *Beyond Economic Man*, 122.

44 Strassman, "Not a Free Market," in Ferber and Nelson, *Beyond Economic Man*, 56, 60. This last point could also be made concerning the term "home economics."

45 Moore, *How Women Can Make Money in the Stock Market*, 18–19.

46 Martha Stewart brought her early training as a broker to bear on her unabashed induction of the home in the stock exchange when she took her company, Martha Stewart Living Omnimedia, public in 1999. As Sarah Leavitt writes, "The image of Stewart toasting her initial public offering (IPO) at the New York Stock Exchange with fresh-squeezed orange juice and homemade brioche caught so many people's attention specifically because of the perceived clash between the public sphere of stock trading and the private sphere of the home" (*From Catharine Beecher to Martha Stewart*, 201). Surely it was her very visibility as a powerful link between domestic economies of the home and nation—and as a woman—that drove the subsequent investigation and charges against her for relatively minor illegal trading.

47 Moore, *How Women Can Make Money in the Stock Market*, 64.

48 Ibid., 102.

49 Jennings, "Public or Private?," 126.

50 See Bruno, *Streetwalking on a Ruined Map*, 109–110; see also Stamp, "Lois Weber."

51 Bruno, *Streetwalking on a Ruined Map*, 121.

52 Sophia Loren, *In the Kitchen with Love*, 35.

53 Cotter, "Claiming a Piece of the Pie," in Bower, *Recipes for Reading*, 38.

54 Bower, *Recipes for Reading*, 31.

55 Shigley, "Empathy, Energy, and Eating," in Bower, *Recipes for Reading*, 118.

56 N. Scott, "Juana Manuela Gorriti's Cocina Eclectica," in Bower, *Recipes for Reading*, 189.
57 Giard, "Doing Cooking," 154.
58 Loren, *Sophia Loren's Recipes and Memories*, 76.
59 Shigley, "Empathy, Energy, and Eating," 125.
60 Leavitt, *From Catharine Beecher to Martha Stewart*, 206.
61 Giard, "Doing Cooking," 158.
62 Pitts, *Candy Hits by Zasu Pitts*, 16.
63 Steedman, *Dust*, 75.
64 Rosie Daley, *In the Kitchen with Rosie: Oprah's Favorite Recipes* (New York: Knopf, 1994); Marilu Henner, *Healthy Life Kitchen* (New York: ReganBooks, 2000).
65 Morse, "Artemis Aging," 24, 42.
66 Turlington, *Living Yoga*, 42.
67 Ibid., 23, 162, 163, 167.
68 Ibid., 98.
69 Rossellini, *Looking at Me*, 5.
70 Ibid., 60.
71 Ibid., 8, 79, 77, 92.

Bibliography

Abel, Richard. *The Ciné Goes to Town: French Cinema 1896–1914*. Berkeley: University of California Press, 1994.
Acker, Ally. *Reel Women: Pioneers of the Cinema, 1896 to the Present*. New York: Continuum, 1991.
Althusser, Louis. "Ideology and Ideological State Apparatuses." In *Lenin and Philosophy and Other Essays*, translated by Ben Brewster, 127–186. New York: Monthly Review Press, 1971.
Arthur, Paul. "Jargons of Authenticity (Three American Moments)." In *Theorizing Documentary*, edited by Michael Renov, 108–134. New York: Routledge, 1993.
Bachelard, Gaston. *The Poetics of Reverie*. Translated by Daniel Russell. New York: Orion Press, 1969.
———. *The Poetics of Space*. 1969. Translated by Maria Jolas. Boston: Beacon Press, 1994.
Bachmann, Gideon, Robert Drew, Richard Leacock, and D. A. Pennebaker. "The Frontiers of Realist Cinema." *Film Culture*, nos. 22–23 (summer 1961): 12–23.
Bal, Mieke. "Telling Objects: A Narrative Perspective on Collecting." In *The Cultures of Collecting*, edited by John Elsner and Roger Cardinal, 97–115. Cambridge, Mass.: Harvard University Press, 1994.
Balides, Constance. "Scenarios of Exposure in the Practice of Everyday Life: Women in the Cinema of Attractions." *Screen* 34, no. 1 (spring 1993): 19–39.
Bann, Stephen. *The Clothing of Clio: A Study of the Representation of History in Nineteenth-Century Britain and France*. London: Cambridge University Press, 1984.
———. "Shrines, Curiosities, and the Rhetoric of Display." In *Visual Dis-

*play: Culture beyond Appearances*, edited by Lynne Cooke and Peter Wollen, 15–29. Seattle: Bay Press, 1995.

Barthes, Roland. "The Death of the Author." In *Image/Music/Text*, translated by Stephen Heath, 142–148. New York: Hill and Wang, 1977.

Baudrillard, Jean. "The System of Collecting." In *The Cultures of Collecting*, edited by John Elsner and Roger Cardinal, 7–24. Cambridge, Mass.: Harvard University Press, 1994.

Baudry, Jean-Louis. "The Apparatus." *Camera Obscura* 1 (fall 1976): 104–126.

———. "Ideological Effects of the Basic Cinematographic Apparatus." *Film Quarterly* 28, no. 2 (winter 1974–1975): 39–47.

Baym, Nina. *Woman's Fiction: A Guide to Novels by and about Women in America, 1820–1870*. Ithaca, N.Y.: Cornell University Press, 1978.

Bazin, André. *What Is Cinema?* Edited and translated by Hugh Gray. Berkeley: University of California Press, 1967.

Bean, Jennifer, and Diane Negra, eds. *A Feminist Reader in Early Cinema*. Durham, N.C.: Duke University Press, 2001.

Beauchamp, Cari. *Without Lying Down: Frances Marion and the Powerful Women of Early Hollywood*. Berkeley: University of California Press, 1997.

Beck, Calvin Thomas. *Scream Queens: Heroines of the Horrors*. New York: Collier Books, 1978.

Benjamin, Walter. *Illuminations: Essays and Reflections*. Edited by Hannah Arendt. New York: Schocken Books, 1985.

———. *Reflections: Essays, Aphorisms, Autobiographical Writings*. Edited by Peter Demetz. New York: Harcourt Brace Jovanovich, 1978.

Benstock, Shari, "Authorizing the Autobiographical." In *The Private Self: Theory and Practice of Women's Autobiographical Writings*, edited by Shari Benstock, 10–33. Chapel Hill: University of North Carolina Press, 1988.

———, ed. *The Private Self: Theory and Practice of Women's Autobiographical Writings*. Chapel Hill: University of North Carolina Press, 1988.

Benton, Susan Porter. *Counter Cultures: Saleswomen, Managers and Customers in American Department Stores 1890–1940*. Urbana: University of Illinois Press, 1986.

Benveniste, Emile. *Problems in General Linguistics*. Translated by Mary Elizabeth Meek. Coral Gables, Fla.: University of Miami Press, 1971.

Bergson, Henri. *Matter and Memory*. Translated by Nancy Margaret Paul and W. Scott Palmer. New York: Zone Books, 1991.

Bergstrom, Janet, and Mary Ann Doane, eds. *The Spectatrix*. Special issue of *Camera Obscura*, nos. 20–21 (1989).

Bogle, Donald. *Toms, Coons, Mulattoes, Mammies and Bucks: An Interpretive History of Blacks in American Film*. New York: Continuum, 1993.

Bower, Anne, ed. *Recipes for Reading: Community Cookbooks, Stories, Histories*. Amherst; University of Massachusetts Press, 1997.

Bowser, Eileen. *The Transformation of Cinema 1907–1915*. New York: Charles Scribner's Sons, 1990.

Boym, Svetlana. *The Future of Nostalgia*. New York: Basic Books, 2001.

Bratton, Jacky, Jim Cook, and Christine Gledhill. *Melodrama: Stage, Picture, Screen*. London: British Film Institute, 1994.

Brooks, Louise. *Lulu in Hollywood*. New York: Limelight Editions, 1989.

———. "Why I Will Never Write My Memoirs." *Film Culture*, nos. 67–69 (1979): 216–220.

Bruno, Giuliana. *Streetwalking on a Ruined Map: Cultural Theory and the City Films of Elvira Notari*. Princeton, N.J.: Princeton University Press, 1993.

Brunsdon, Charlotte. *Films for Women*. London: British Film Institute, 1986.

Buck-Morss, Susan. *The Dialectics of Seeing: Walter Benjamin and the Arcades Project*. Cambridge, Mass.: MIT Press, 1991.

Butler, Judith. *Gender Trouble: Feminism and the Subversion of Identity*. New York: Routledge, 1990.

Card, James. "The 'Intense Isolation' of Louise Brooks." *Sight and Sound* 27, no. 5 (summer 1958).

Cardinal, Roger. "Collecting and Collage-Making: The Case of Kurt Schwitters." In *The Cultures of Collecting*, edited by John Elsner and Roger Cardinal, 68–96. Cambridge, Mass.: Harvard University Press, 1994.

Carson, Linda, Linda Dittmar, and Janice R. Welsch, eds. *Multiple Voices in Feminist Film Criticism*. Minneapolis: University of Minnesota Press, 1994.

Caughie, John, ed. *Theories of Authorship: A Reader*. New York: Routledge, 1981.

Cha, Teresa Hak Kyung, ed. *Cinematographic Apparatus: Selected Writings*. New York: Tanam Press, 1980.

Clark, Vèvè, Millicent Hodson, and Catrina Neiman, eds. *The Legend of Maya Deren: A Documentary Biography and Collected Works, Vol. 1, Part 1*. New York: Anthology Film Archives/Film Culture, 1984.

———. *The Legend of Maya Deren: A Documentary Biography and Collected Works, Vol. 1, Part 2*. New York: Anthology Film Archives/Film Culture, 1988.

Cooley, Nicole. *The Afflicted Girls*. Baton Rouge: Louisiana State University Press, 2004.

Cotter, Colleen. "Claiming a Piece of the Pie: How the Language of Recipes Defines Community." In *Recipes for Reading: Community Cookbooks, Stories, Histories*, edited by Anne Bower, 51–71. Amherst: University of Massachusetts Press, 1997.

Creekmur, Corey, and Alexander Doty, eds. *Out in Culture: Gay, Lesbian and Queer Essays on Popular Culture*. Durham, N.C.: Duke University Press, 1995.

Curry, Ramona. *Too Much of a Good Thing: Mae West as Cultural Icon*. Minneapolis: University of Minnesota Press, 1996.
Custen, George. *Bio/Pics: How Hollywood Constructed Public History*. New Brunswick, N.J.: Rutgers University Press, 1992.
Cvetokovich, Ann. *An Archive of Feelings: Trauma, Sexuality, and Lesbian Public Cultures*. Durham, N.C.: Duke University Press, 2003.
deCordova, Richard. "The Emergence of the Star System in America." *Wide Angle* 6, no. 4 (1985): 4–13.
———. *Picture Personalities: The Emergence of the Star System in America*. Urbana: University of Illinois Press, 1990.
Deleuze, Gilles. *Cinema 1: The Movement-Image*. Minneapolis: University of Minnesota Press, 1986.
———. *Cinema 2: The Time-Image*. Minneapolis: University of Minnesota Press, 1989.
Deren, Maya. *An Anagram of Ideas on Art, Form and Film*. Yonkers, N.Y.: Alicat Book Shop Press, 1946.
———. "Cinematography: The Creative Use of Reality." In *The Art of Cinema: Selected Essays*, edited by George Amberg. New York: Arno Press and New York Times, 1972.
Dietrich, Marlene. *Marlene Dietrich's ABC*. Garden City, N.Y.: Doubleday, 1962.
———. *Marlene Dietrich's ABC*. 2nd ed. New York: Ungar, 1984.
Doane, Mary Ann. "The Economy of Desire: The Commodity Form in/of the Cinema." *Quarterly Review of Film and Video* 11, no. 1 (1989): 23–33.
———. "The Erotic Barter: *Pandora's Box*." In *Femmes Fatales: Feminism, Film Theory, Psychoanalysis*, 142–162. New York: Routledge, 1991.
———. *Femmes Fatales: Feminism, Film Theory, Psychoanalysis*. New York: Routledge, 1991.
Doane, Mary Ann, Patricia Mellencamp, and Linda Williams, eds. *Re-vision: Essays in Feminist Film Criticism*. Los Angeles: American Film Institute, 1984.
Douglas, Ann. *The Feminization of American Culture*. New York: Knopf, 1977.
Dreyer, Carl Theodor. "Notes on My Craft." *Sight and Sound* (winter 1955–1956).
Dubois, Phillipe. "Photography *Mise-en-Film*: Autobiographical (Hi)stories and Psychic Apparatuses." In *Fugitive Images: From Photography to Video*, edited by Patrice Petro, 152–172. Bloomington: Indiana University Press, 1995.
Dulac, Germaine. "The Avant-Garde Cinema." In *The Avant-Garde Film: A Reader of Theory and Criticism*, edited by P. Adams Sitney, 43–48. New York: New York University Press, 1978.

———. "Visual and Anti-visual Films." In *The Avant-Garde Film: A Reader of Theory and Criticism*, edited by P. Adams Sitney, 31–35. New York: New York University Press, 1978.

Dyer, Richard. *Heavenly Bodies: Film Stars and Society*. New York: St. Martin's Press, 1986.

Eakin, Paul John. "Fiction in Autobiography: Ask Mary McCarthy No Questions." In *Fictions in Autobiography: Studies in the Art of Self-Invention*, 3–55. Princeton, N.J.: Princeton University Press, 1985.

Egger, Rebecca. "Deaf Ears and Dark Continents: Dorothy Richardson's Cinematic Epistemology." *Camera Obscura* 30 (May 1992): 4–33.

Eisenstein, Sergei. *Film Form: Essays in Film Theory*. Edited and translated by Jay Leyda. New York: Harcourt, Brace, 1949.

———. *The Film Sense*. Edited and translated by Jay Leyda. New York: Harcourt, Brace, 1947.

Eisner, Lotte. "A Witness Speaks." In *Lulu in Hollywood*, by Louise Brooks, 113–116. New York: Knopf, 1982.

Ellis, John. *Visible Fictions: Cinema Television Radio*. London: Routledge, 1992.

Elsaesser, Thomas. "Lulu and the Meter Man: Louise Brooks, Pabst, and 'Pandora's Box.'" *Screen* 24, nos. 4–5 (1983): 4–36.

———, ed. *Early Cinema: Space Frame Narrative*. London: British Film Institute, 1990.

Elsner, John. "A Collector's Model of Desire: The House and Museum of Sir John Sloane." In *The Cultures of Collecting*, edited by John Elsner and Roger Cardinal, 155–176. Cambridge, Mass.: Harvard University Press, 1994.

Elsner, John, and Roger Cardinal, eds. *The Cultures of Collecting*. Cambridge, Mass.: Harvard University Press, 1994.

Erens, Patricia, ed. *Issues in Feminist Film Criticism*. Bloomington: Indiana University Press, 1990.

Fell, John. *Film before Griffith*. Berkeley: University of California Press, 1983.

Ferber, Marianne A., and Julie A. Nelson, eds. *Beyond Economic Man: Feminist Theory and Economics*. Chicago: University of Chicago Press, 1993.

Fetterley, Judith, ed. *Provisions: A Reader from Nineteenth-Century American Women*. Bloomington: Indiana University Press, 1985.

*Film Culture*, no. 39 (winter 1965). Special issue on Maya Deren.

*Film Culture*, nos. 56–57 (spring 1973). Special issue on Leni Riefenstahl.

Flitterman-Lewis, Sandy. "The Blossom and the Bole: Narrative and Visual Spectacle in Early Film Melodrama." *Cinema Journal* 33, no. 3 (spring 1994): 3–15.

———. *To Desire Differently: Feminism and the French Cinema*. Urbana: University of Illinois Press, 1989.

Fonda, Jane. *Jane Fonda's Workout Book*. New York: Simon and Schuster, 1981.

Forrester, John. "'Mille e tre': Freud and Collecting." In *The Cultures of Collecting*, edited by John Elsner and Roger Cardinal, 224–251. Cambridge, Mass.: Harvard University Press, 1994.

Foucault, Michel. "What Is an Author?" In *Language, Counter-Memory, Practice*, edited by Donald F. Bouchard, 113–138. Oxford: Basil Blackwell, 1977.

Francke, Lizzie. *Script Girls: Women Screenwriters in Hollywood*. London: British Film Institute, 1994.

Freeman, Mark. *Rewriting the Self: History, Memory, Narrative*. New York: Routledge, 1993.

Fregoso, Rosa-Linda. *meXicana Encounters: The Making of Social Identities on the Borderlands*. Berkeley: University of California Press, 2003.

Freud, Sigmund. "A Disturbance of Memory on the Acropolis." 1936. In *The Standard Edition of the Complete Psychological Works of Sigmund Freud*, translated by James Strachey et al., 22:239–248. London: Hogarth Press and the Institute of Psycho-Analysis, 1953.

———. "A Note upon the 'Mystic Writing Pad.'" 1925. In *The Standard Edition of the Complete Psychological Works of Sigmund Freud*, translated by James Strachey et al., 21:227–232. London: Hogarth Press and the Institute of Psycho-Analysis, 1953.

———. "Notes upon a Case of Obsessional Neurosis." 1909. In *Three Case Histories*, translated by James Strachey, 15–102. New York: Collier Books, 1963.

———. "Screen Memories." 1899. In *The Standard Edition of the Complete Psychological Works of Sigmund Freud*, translated by James Strachey et al., 3:301–22. London: Hogarth Press and the Institute of Psycho-Analysis, 1953.

Friedberg, Anne. "'And I Have Learned to Use the Small Projector': H.D., Woman, History, Recognition." *Wide Angle* 5, no. 2 (1982): 26–31.

———. *Window Shopping: Cinema and the Postmodern*. Berkeley: University of California Press, 1993.

Gaines, Jane. "From Elephants to Lux Soap: The Programming and 'Flow' of Early Motion Picture Exploitation." *Velvet Light Trap* 25 (spring 1990): 29–43.

Giard, Luce. "Doing Cooking." In *The Practice of Everyday Life*, Vol. 2: *Living and Cooking*, by Michel de Certeau, Luce Giard, and Pierre Mayol, translated by Timothy J. Tomasik, 149–247. Minneapolis: University of Minnesota Press, 1998.

Gilmore, Leigh. *Autobiographics: A Feminist Theory of Women's Self-Representation*. Ithaca, N.Y.: Cornell University Press, 1994.

Gish, Lillian, with Ann Pinchot. *The Movies, Mr. Griffith, and Me*. New York: Prentice Hall, 1969.

Grieveson, Lee. *Policing Cinema: Movies and Censorship in Early-Twentieth-Century America*. Berkeley: University of California Press, 2004.

Gunning, Tom. "An Aesthetic of Astonishment: Early Film and the (In)credulous Spectator." *Art and Text* 34 (spring 1989): 31-45.

———. "The Cinema of Attractions: Early Film, Its Spectator and the Avant-Garde." In *Early Cinema: Space, Frame, Narrative*, edited by Thomas Elsaesser, 56-62. London: British Film Institute, 1990.

———. *D. W. Griffith and the Origins of American Narrative Film: The Early Years at Biograph*. Urbana: University of Illinois Press, 1991.

Guy Blaché, Alice. *The Memoirs of Alice Guy Blaché*. Edited by Anthony Slide. Metuchen, N.J.: Scarecrow Press, 1996.

Hake, Sabine. "The Continuous Provocation of Louise Brooks." *German Politics and Society* 32 (summer 1994): 58-75.

Hall, Jeanne. "Realism as a Style in Cinema Vérité: A Critical Analysis of *Primary*." *Cinema Journal* 30, no. 4 (summer 1991): 24-50.

Hamilton, Marybeth. *"When I'm Bad, I'm Better": Mae West, Sex, and American Entertainment*. Berkeley: University of California Press, 1997.

Hansen, Miriam. *Babel and Babylon: Spectatorship in American Silent Film*. Cambridge, Mass.: Harvard University Press, 1991.

Harris, Susan. *Nineteenth-Century American Women's Novels: Interpretive Strategies*. New York: Cambridge University Press, 1990.

Hastie, Amelie. "Louise Brooks, Star Witness." *Cinema Journal* 36, no. 3 (spring 1997): 3-24.

Hastie, Amelie, and Shelley Stamp, eds. "Women and the Silent Screen: Cultural and Historical Practices." Special issue, *Film History* 18, no. 2 (spring 2006).

Head, Edith, and Jane Kesner Ardmore. *The Dress Doctor*. New York: Macfadden Books, 1964.

Heck-Rabi, Louise. *Women Filmmakers: A Critical Reception*. Metuchen, N.J.: Scarecrow Press, 1984.

Hobart, Rose. *A Steady Digression to a Fixed Point*. Metuchen, N.J.: Scarecrow Press, 1994.

hooks, bell. "In Our Glory: Photography and Black Life." In *Picturing Us: African American Identity in Photography*, edited by Deborah Willis, 43-55. New York: New Press, 1994.

Hutton, Patrick. *History as an Art of Memory*. Hanover, N.H.: University Press of New England, 1993.

Jaccard, Roland, ed. *Louise Brooks: Portrait of an Anti-Star*. Translated by Gideon Y. Schein. New York: Zoetrope, 1986.

Jaffe, Patricia. "Editing Cinéma Vérité." *Film Comment* 3, no. 3 (summer 1965).

Jennings, Ann L. "Public or Private? Institutional Economics and Feminism." In *Beyond Economic Man: Feminist Theory and Economics*, edited by Marianne A. Nelson Ferber and Julie A. Nelson, 111–129. Chicago: University of Chicago Press, 1993.

Johnston, Claire. "Women's Cinema as Counter Cinema." In *Notes on Women's Cinema*, edited by Claire Johnston, 24–31. London: Society for Education in Film and Television, 1973.

Joyrich, Lynne. *Re-viewing Reception: Television, Gender, and Postmodern Culture*. Bloomington: Indiana University Press, 1996.

Karnick, Kristine Brunovska, and Henry Jenkins, eds. *Classical Hollywood Comedy*. New York: Routledge, 1995.

Kelley, Mary. *Private Woman, Public Stage: Literary Domesticity in Nineteenth-Century America*. New York: Oxford University Press, 1984.

Kessler-Harris, Alice. *Out to Work: A History of Wage-Earning Women in the United States*. New York: Oxford University Press, 1982.

Koszarski, Richard. *An Evening's Entertainment: The Age of the Silent Feature Picture, 1915–1928*. New York: Charles Scribner's Sons, 1990.

Kuhn, Annette. *Family Secrets: Acts of Memory and Imagination*. London: Verso, 1995.

———. *Women's Pictures: Feminism and the Cinema*. 2nd ed. New York: Verso, 1993.

Lacassin, Francis. "Out of Oblivion: Alice Guy-Blaché." *Sight and Sound* 40, no. 3 (summer 1971): 151–154.

Leavitt, Sarah A. *From Catharine Beecher to Martha Stewart: A Cultural History of Domestic Advice*. Chapel Hill: University of North Carolina Press, 2002.

LeGoff, Jacques. *History and Memory*. Translated by Steven Rendall and Elizabeth Claman. New York: Columbia University Press, 1992.

Leider, Emily Wortis. *Becoming Mae West*. New York: Farrar, Straus and Giroux, 1997.

Lejeune, Philippe. "The Autobiographical Pact." In *On Autobiography*, translated by Katherine M. Leary, 3–30. Minneapolis: University of Minnesota Press, 1989.

Lesage, Julia. "The Political Aesthetics of the Feminist Documentary Film." In *Issues in Feminist Film Criticism*, edited by Patricia Erens, 222–237. Bloomington: Indiana University Press, 1991.

Levin, G. Roy. *Documentary Explorations: 15 Interviews with Film-makers*. Garden City, N.Y.: Doubleday, 1971.

Loos, Anita. *A Girl Like I*. New York: Ballantine, 1966.

Loren, Sophia. *In the Kitchen with Love*. Garden City, N.Y.: Doubleday, 1972.

———. *Sophia Loren's Recipes and Memories*. New York: GT Publishing, 1998.

Mayne, Judith. *Directed by Dorothy Arzner*. Bloomington: Indiana University Press, 1994.

———. *Kino and the Woman Question*. Columbus: Ohio State University Press, 1989.
McHugh, Kathleen. *American Domesticity: From How-to Manual to Hollywood Melodrama*. New York: Oxford University Press, 1999.
McLean, Adrienne. "'I'm a Cansino': Transformation, Ethnicity, and Authenticity in the Construction of Rita Hayworth, American Love Goddess." *Journal of Film and Video* 44, nos. 3–4 (fall–winter 1992–1993): 8–26.
McMahan, Alison. *Alice Guy Blaché: Lost Visionary of the Cinema*. New York: Continuum, 2002.
McPherson, Tara. *Reconstructing Dixie: Race, Gender, and Nostalgia in the Imagined South*. Durham, N.C.: Duke University Press, 2003.
Mellencamp, Patricia. *A Fine Romance . . . Five Ages of Film Feminism*. Philadelphia: Temple University Press, 1995.
———. *Indiscretions: Avant-Garde Film, Video and Feminism*. Bloomington: Indiana University Press, 1990.
Metz, Christian. *The Imagining Signifier: Psychoanalysis and the Cinema*. Translated by Celia Britton et al. Bloomington: Indiana University Press, 1982.
Moore, Colleen. *Colleen Moore's Doll House*. Garden City, N.Y.: Doubleday, 1979.
———. *How Women Can Make Money in the Stock Market*. Garden City, N.Y.: Doubleday, 1969.
———. *Silent Star*. Garden City, N.Y.: Doubleday, 1968.
Morris, Meaghan. *Too Soon Too Late: History in Popular Culture*. Bloomington: Indiana University Press, 1998.
Morse, Margaret. "Artemis Aging: Exercise and the Female Body on Video." *Discourse* 10, no. 1 (1987–1988): 19–53.
Mulvey, Laura. *Citizen Kane*. London: British Film Institute, 1992.
———. *Feminism and Curiosity*. Bloomington: Indiana University Press, 1996.
———. "Visual Pleasure and Narrative Cinema." *Screen* 16, no. 3 (autumn 1975): 618.
Muñoz, José Esteban. "Ephemera as Evidence: Introductory Notes to Queer Acts." *Women and Performance* 8, no. 2 (1996): 5–16.
Münsterberg, Hugo. *The Film: A Psychological Study*. New York: Dover, 1970.
Nasaw, David. "Earthly Delights." *New Yorker*, 23 March 1998, 66–79.
Neff, Terry Ann. *Within the Fairy Castle: Colleen Moore's Dollhouse at the Museum of Science and Industry, Chicago*. Chicago: Bulfinch Press, 1998.
Negra, Diane. "Immigrant Stardom in Imperial America: Pola Negri and the Problem of Typology." In *A Feminist Reader in Early Cinema*, edited by Jennifer Bean and Diane Negra, 374–403. Durham, N.C.: Duke University Press, 2003.

Newton, Sarah. *Learning to Behave: A Guide to Conduct Books before 1900*. Westport, Conn.: Greenwood Press, 1994.

Nichols, Bill. *Ideology and the Image*. Bloomington: Indiana University Press, 1981.

———. *Representing Reality*. Bloomington: Indiana University Press, 1991.

———. "The Voice of Documentary." In *Movies and Methods II*, edited by Bill Nichols. Berkeley: University of California Press, 1985.

Nicholson, Annabel, Felicity Sparrow, Jane Clarke, Jeanette Iljon, Lis Rhodes, Mary Pat Leece, Pat Murphy, and Susan Stein. "Women and the Formal Film." In *Films for Women*, edited by Charlotte Brunsdon, 186–188. London: British Film Institute, 1986.

Nora, Pierre. "Between Memory and History: *Les Lieux de Mémoire*." *Representations* 26 (spring 1989): 7–25.

Olalquiaga, Celeste. *The Artificial Kingdom: On the Kitsch Experience*. Minneapolis: University of Minnesota Press, 2002.

Ono, Yoko. *Grapefruit: A Book of Instructions and Drawings*. New York: Simon and Schuster, 1970.

Paris, Barry. "Dollhouse Deluxe." *Art and Antiques* 6 (December 1989): 98–102.

———. *Louise Brooks*. New York: Knopf, 1989.

Pearson, Roberta E. *Eloquent Gestures: The Transformation of Performance Style in the Griffith Biograph Films*. Berkeley: University of California Press, 1992.

Peary, Gerald. "Czarina of the Silent Screen: Solax's Alice Blaché." *Velvet Light Trap* 6 (1974): 3–7.

Petro, Patrice, ed. *Fugitive Images: From Photography to Video*. Bloomington: Indiana University Press, 1995.

———. "Historical Ennui, Feminist Boredom." In *The Persistence of History: Cinema, Television, and the Modern Event*, edited by Vivian Sobchack, 187–199. New York: Routledge, 1996.

———. *Joyless Streets: Women and Melodramatic Representation in Weimar Germany*. Princeton, N.J.: Princeton University Press, 1989.

Pickford, Mary. *The Demi-Widow*. New York: A.L. Burt, 1935.

———. *Sunshine and Shadow*. Garden City, N.Y.: Doubleday, 1954.

———. *Why Not Try God?* New York: H.C. Kinsey, 1934.

Pines, Jim, and Paul Willemen, eds. *Questions of Third Cinema*. London: British Film Institute, 1989.

Pitts, Zasu, with Edi Horton. *Candy Hits by Zasu Pitts*. New York: Duell, Sloan, and Pearce, 1963.

Portuges, Catherine. *Screen Memories: The Hungarian Cinema of Márta Mészáros*. Bloomington: Indiana University Press, 1993.

Quart, Barbara Koenig. *Women Directors: The Emergence of a New Cinema*. New York: Praeger, 1988.

Rabinovitz, Lauren. *Points of Resistance: Women, Power and Politics in the New York Avant-Garde Cinema, 1943-71*. Urbana: University of Illinois Press, 1991.

Radstone, Susannah. "Cinema/Memory/History." *Screen* 36, no. 1 (spring 1995): 34-47.

Renov, Michael. "History and/as Autobiography: The Essayistic in Film and Video." *Frame/Work* 2, no. 3 (1989): 6-13.

———. "The Subject in History: The New Autobiography in Film and Video." *Afterimage* 17, no. 1 (summer 1989): 4-7.

———. *Theorizing Documentary*. New York: Routledge, 1993.

Rhodes, Lis, and Felicity Sparrow. "Her Image Fades as Her Voice Rises." In *Multiple Voices in Feminist Film Criticism*, edited by Diane Carson, Linda Dittmar, and Janice R. Welsch, 421-431. Minneapolis: University of Minnesota Press, 1994.

Riefenstahl, Leni. *The Sieve of Time: The Memoirs of Leni Riefenstahl*. New York: St. Martin's Press, 1993.

Robertson, Pamela. *Guilty Pleasures: Feminist Camp from Mae West to Madonna*. Durham, N.C.: Duke University Press, 1996.

Rosen, Philip. *Change Mummified: Cinema, Historicity, Theory*. Minneapolis: University of Minnesota Press, 2001.

Rossellini, Isabella. *Looking at Me: On Pictures and Photographers*. Munich: Schirmer/Mosel, 2002.

———. *Some of Me*. New York: Random House, 1997.

Rowe, Kathleen. *The Unruly Woman: Gender and the Genres of Laughter*. Austin: University of Texas Press, 1995.

Sarris, Andrew. "Notes on the Auteur Theory in 1962." *Film Culture* 27 (winter 1962-1963): 1-18.

Schlüpmann, Heide. "The Brothel as an Arcadian Space? *Diary of a Lost Girl* (1929)." In *The Films of G. W. Pabst: An Extraterritorial Cinema*, edited by Eric Rentschler, 80-90. New Brunswick, N.J.: Rutgers University Press, 1990.

Schor, Naomi. "Collecting Paris." In *The Cultures of Collecting*, edited by John Elsner and Roger Cardinal. Cambridge: Harvard University Press, 1994.

Scott, Joan Wallach. *Gender and the Politics of History*. New York: Columbia University Press, 1989.

Scott, Nina. "Juana Manuela Gorriti's Cocina Eclectica: Recipes as Feminine Discourse." In *Recipes for Reading: Community Cookbooks, Stories, Histories*, edited by Anne Bower, 189-199. Amherst: University of Massachusetts Press, 1997.

Shigley, Sally Bishop. "Empathy, Energy, and Eating: Politics and Power in the Black Family Dinner Quilt Cookbook." In *Recipes for Reading: Community Cookbooks, Stories, Histories*, edited by Anne Bower, 118–131. Amherst: University of Massachusetts Press, 1997.

Shipman, Nell. *The Silent Screen and My Talking Heart*. Boise, Idaho: Boise State University, 1987.

Silverman, Kaja. *The Acoustic Mirror: The Female Voice in Psychoanalysis and Cinema*. Bloomington: Indiana University Press, 1988.

Simmon, Scott. "'The Female of the Species': D. W. Griffith, Father of the Woman's Film." *Film Quarterly* 46, no. 2 (winter 1992–1993): 8–20.

Slide, Anthony. *Early Women Directors*. New York: A.S. Barnes, 1977.

———. *The Silent Feminists: America's First Women Directors*. Lanham, Md.: Scarecrow Press, 1996.

Smith, Sharon. *Women Who Make Movies*. New York: Hopkinson and Blake, 1975.

Sobchack, Vivian. "What Is film history?, or, The Riddle of the Sphinxes." In *Reinventing Film Studies*, edited by Christine Gledhill and Linda Williams, 300–315. New York: Oxford University Press, 2000.

Sommer, Doris. "Not Just a Personal Story: Women's *Testimonios* and the Plural Self." In *Life/Lines: Theorizing Women's Autobiography*, edited by Bella Brodzki and Celeste Schenk, 107–130. Ithaca, N.Y.: Cornell University Press, 1988.

Spigel, Lynn. "From the Dark Ages to the Golden Age: Women's Memories and Television Reruns." *Screen* 36, no. 1 (spring 1995): 16–33.

———. *Make Room for TV: Television and the American Family in Postwar America*. Chicago: University of Chicago Press, 1992.

Stamp, Shelley. "Lois Weber, Progressive Cinema, and the Fate of the 'Work-a-Day' Girl in *Shoes*." *Camera Obscura* 56 (2004): 141–169.

Steedman, Carolyn. *Dust: The Archive and Cultural History*. New Brunswick, N.J.: Rutgers University Press, 2002.

———. *Past Tenses: Essays on Writing, Autobiography and History*. London: Rivers Oram Press, 1992.

Stewart, Susan. *On Longing: Narratives of the Miniature, the Gigantic, the Souvenir, the Collection*. Durham, N.C.: Duke University Press, 1993.

St. Johns, Adela Rogers. *How to Write a Story and Sell It*. Garden City, N.Y.: Doubleday, 1956.

———. *Some Are Born Great*. Garden City, N.Y.: Doubleday, 1974.

Strasser, Susan. *Never Done: History of American Housework*. New York: Pantheon Books, 1982.

Strassmann, Diana. "Not a Free Market: The Rhetoric of Disciplinary Authority in Economics." In *Beyond Economic Man: Feminist Theory and Economics*, edited by Marianne A. Nelson Ferber and Julie A. Nelson, 54–67. Chicago: University of Chicago Press, 1993.

Studlar, Gaylyn. "The Perils of Pleasure? Fan Magazine Discourse as Women's Commodified Culture in the 1920s." *Wide Angle* 13, no. 1 (1991): 6-33.

———. *This Mad Masquerade: Stardom and Masculinity in the Jazz Age*. New York: Columbia University Press, 1996.

Swanson, Gloria. *Swanson on Swanson*. New York: Random House, 1980.

Tapert, Annette. "Colleen Moore: The Original Flapper in Bel-Air." *Architectural Digest* 53 (April 1996): 216-221.

Tompkins, Jane. *Sensational Designs: The Cultural Work of American Fiction 1790-1860*. New York: Oxford University Press, 1985.

Turim, Maureen. *Flashbacks in Film: Memory and History*. New York: Routledge, 1989.

Turlington, Christy. *Living Yoga: Creating a Life Practice*. New York: Hyperion, 2002.

Tynan, Kenneth. "The Girl in the Black Helmet." *New Yorker*, 11 June 1979, 45-78.

Waters, Ethel, with Charles Samuels. *His Eye Is on the Sparrow*. Garden City, N.Y.: Doubleday, 1951.

Weiss, Andrea. *Vampires and Violets: Lesbians in Film*. New York: Penguin Books, 1992.

West, Mae. *Mae West on Sex, Health, and ESP*. London: W. H. Allen, 1975.

White, Patricia. "Black and White: Mercedes de Acosta's Glorious Enthusiasms." *Camera Obscura* 45 (2001): 226-265.

———. "Female Spectator, Lesbian Specter: *The Haunting*." In *Inside/Out: Lesbian Theories, Gay Theories*, edited by Diana Fuss, 142-172. New York: Routledge, 1991.

———. "Nazimova's Veils: *Salome* at the Intersection of Histories." In *A Feminist Reader in Early Cinema*, edited by Jennifer Bean and Diane Negra, 60-87. Durham, N.C.: Duke University Press, 2002.

———. *unInvited: Classical Hollywood Cinema and Lesbian Representability*. Bloomington: Indiana University Press, 1999.

Whitfield, Eileen. *Pickford: The Woman Who Made Hollywood*. Lexington: University Press of Kentucky, 1997.

Williams, Alan. *The Republic of Images: A History of French Filmmaking*. Cambridge, Mass.: Harvard University Press, 1992.

Winston, Brian. "Direct Cinema: The Third Decade." In *New Challenges for Documentary*, edited by Alan Rosenthal. Berkeley: University of California Press, 1988.

———. "The Documentary Film as Scientific Inscription." In *Theorizing Documentary*, edited by Michael Renov, 37-57. New York: Routledge, 1993.

Wolfe, Charles. "Just in Time: *Let Us Now Praise Famous Men* and the Recovery of the Historical Subject." In *Fugitive Images: From Photography to*

*Video*, edited by Patrice Petro, 196–220. Bloomington: Indiana University Press, 1995.

Wollen, Peter. "The *Auteur* Theory." In *Theories of Authorship*, edited by John Caughie, 138–151. New York: Routledge, 1986.

———. "Brooks and the Bob." *Sight and Sound* 4, no. 2 (February 1994): 22–25.

Woodward, Kathleen. "Bureaucratic and Binding Emotions: Angry American Autobiography." *Kenyon Review* 17, no. 1 (winter 1995): 55–70.

Woolf, Virginia. *A Room of One's Own*. New York: Harcourt Brace Jovanovich, 1929.

———. *Three Guineas*. New York: Harcourt Brace Jovanovich, 1938.

Yates, Frances A. *The Art of Memory*. Chicago: University of Chicago Press, 1966.

Zipes, Jack. *Fairy Tales and the Art of Subversion: The Classical Genre for Children and the Process of Civilization*. New York: Methuen, 1983.

# Index

Archive, 4, 14, 185, 192
Arvidson, Linda (Mrs. D. W. Griffith), 16, 74
Auteur, 11-12, 151-153
Authorship, 17, 29, 31-32, 35, 72, 83, 153, 161, 180, 192; auteurism and, 10-14; documentary film and, 135-36; reading and, 141, 144
Autobiography, 2-3, 8, 23, 49, 72, 77, 86-87, 161, 187

Bachelard, Gaston, 6-8, 37, 43, 75, 78
Bann, Stephen, 30, 78, 92
Barthes, Roland, 11
Baudrillard, Jean, 19, 24-28, 31
Bazin, André, 11, 71, 152, 192
Beauchamp, Cari, 160, 162
Benjamin, Walter, 6-8, 24, 26, 37, 43, 47-49, 59, 66, 75, 85, 88, 98-99
Bergson, Henri, 98-99
*Biography of Louise Brooks* (Barry Paris), 106-8, 117-18, 122, 140, 144, 149
Books, 4, 5, 192; cookbooks, 175-79, 183, 192; how-to books, 156-57, 186; library books, 40, 58, 144. *See also* Moore, Colleen: scrapbooks
Bow, Clara, 104-6

Boym, Svetlana, 37
Brooks, Louise, 2-4, 7, 16; "Cult" and, 110, 119, 126; as intellectual, 107-8, 123, 130, 140, 143-44, 153; library books and, 141-44; *Looking for Lulu* and, 107; as "Lulu," 16, 107, 111-13, 126-29, 136-37, 151; *Lulu in Berlin* and, 107, 133,-35, 138-41; *Lulu in Hollywood* and, 104-6, 107-9, 113-15, 119-22, 128, 136, 138, 140-43; *Naked on My Goat*, 114, 140; sexuality and, 107, 112-14, 116-17, 120-26, 144, 151, 153; "Why I Will Never Write My Memoirs," 107-8, 110-12, 114, 118-19
Bruno, Giuliana, 12, 174

Camp Fire Girls, 30, 31
Candy and chocolates, 2, 21-22, 156, 182
*Candy Hits by Zasu Pitts*, 2, 17, 156-57, 181-84
Card, James, 113, 117, 119, 131, 140-41, 152
*Citizen Kane* (Orson Welles, 1941), 64
Collaboration, 5, 9, 18, 186, 190-91
Collectibles, 23, 67
Collecting, definition of, 28, 39

Collector, definition of, 23
Cooking, 183–84
Curry, Ramona, 164

Davies, Marion, 63, 115
deCordova, Richard, 109, 163
Deleuze, Gilles, 8
Deren, Maya, 8, 10, 15, 35, 36
*Diary of a Lost Girl* (G. W. Pabst, 1929), 109–11, 123, 141;
Dietrich, Marlene, 3, 33–35, 72, 120, 127, 167–69; *Marlene Dietrich's ABC*, 2, 9, 17, 156–57, 166, 192
Direct Cinema movement, 131–33, 216 n.66
Doane, Mary Ann, 117, 124–25, 128–30
Domesticity, 165–69, 174, 90–91
*Dress Doctor, The* (Edith Head), 157, 187

Education (and expertise), 159, 164, 170, 188–89, 193
Eisenstein, Sergei, 35, 36, 99, 100
Eisner, Lotte, 141, 143
*Ella Cinders* (Alfred E. Green, 1926), 51, 53, 69
Elsaesser, Thomas, 117, 124–28
*Enchanted Castle, The* (Colleen Moore), 34
Ephemerality, 17, 21, 23, 184

Fairy tales, 39, 46–48, 51–53, 65
Fetterley, Judith, 91
Freeman, Paul, 81, 86
Fregoso, Rosa-Linda, 78
Freud, Sigmund, 24, 94, 96, 98, 101
Friedberg, Anne, 12

Garbo, Greta, 33, 115, 120, 146, 149, 150
George Eastman House, 4, 144, 212 n.16
Giard, Luce, 178, 181
Gilmore, Leigh, 81, 101
*Girl in Every Port, A* (Howard Hawks, 1928), 117–18

"Girl in the Black Helmet, The" (Kenneth Tynan), 106–8, 114, 116–19, 125
Gish, Lillian, 2, 16, 76–77, 87–88, 115–16
*Grapefruit* (Yoko Ono), 155, 158
Grieve, Harold, 55–56, 61, 65
Grieveson, Lee, 102
Guy-Blaché, Alice, 3, 16, 73–74, 76, 79–80, 89–92; Herbert Blaché and, 84, 98, 100, 102; film studies and, 80, 83, 206 n.40; as "foremother," 207 n.51; Gaumont and, 84, 93, 102; *Moving Picture Herald* and, 208 n.65; Solax and, 84, 97–100, 102–3

Hake, Sabine, 110, 126
Hall, Jeanne, 131–32, 134
Hargrave School of Finance, 170
Head, Edith, 157, 187
Hearst, William Randolph, 23, 55, 116, 122; San Simeon estate and, 62, 64
Historiography, 4, 9, 29, 64, 65, 73–74, 83
Hobart, Rose, 75–76
Hollywood, 23, 38, 39, 62
*Hollywood* (Kevin Brownlow and David Gill, 1980), 23, 106
hooks, bell, 81
*How Women Can Make Money in the Stock Market* (Colleen Moore), 2, 23, 157, 169–72, 174

Image, 21, 23, 107, 110–11, 121, 123, 130, 185

*Jane Fonda's Workout Book*, 158, 186–87
Johnston, Claire, 11, 72, 79

Kelley, Mary, 90–92

Langlois, Henri, 117, 119, 126, 128, 141, 151–52
Leacock, Richard, 107, 131, 133–39
Leavitt, Sarah, 180
LeGoff, Jacques, 86, 87

*Living Yoga* (Christy Turlington), 17, 158, 188–89
*Looking for Lulu* (Hugh Munro Neely, 1988), 107
Loren, Sophia, 158, 176–77, 179–81
*Lost Garden, The* (Marquise Lepage, 1995), 79, 82, 85
*Louise Brooks, Portrait of an Anti-Star* (Roland Jaccard), 111–12, 117, 140
*Lulu in Berlin* (Richard Leacock and Susan Woll, 1984), 107, 133–35, 138–41
*Lulu in Hollywood* (Louise Brooks), 104–6, 107–9, 113–15, 119–22, 128, 136, 138, 140–43

Marion, Frances, 4, 157, 160, 162
*Marlene Dietrich's ABC*, 2, 9, 17, 156–57, 166, 192
McHugh, Kathleen, 167–69
McMahan, Alison, 93, 204 n.26
Memory, 6–7; and fallibility, 74; and film form, 8–9, 80, 85, 99; and history, 27, 39, 69, 82, 86–87, 95
Metz, Christian, 89
Moore, Colleen, 3, 16, 173; dollhouse and, 15, 23, 34–59; *The Enchanted Castle*, 34; *How Women Can Make Money in the Stock Market*, 2, 23, 157, 169–72, 174; John McCormick and, 22, 62; and photographs, 19, 71; and scrapbooks, 1–2, 9, 23, 29–31, 34, 36; *Silent Star* and, 1, 23, 39, 40
Morris, Meaghan, 155
Morse, Margaret, 187
Movie houses, 61–62, 68
Mulvey, Laura, 1, 3, 64, 104
Münsterberg, Hugo, 8, 99

*Naked on My Goat* (Louise Brooks), 114, 140
Neff, Terry Ann, 40, 55
Newton, Sarah, 158–59
Nichols, Bill, 132, 138

Nineteenth-century women's writings, 91–92, 160, 162
Nora, Pierre, 82, 86

Ono, Yoko, 155, 158

Pabst, Georg Wilhelm, 107–11, 123–24, 127, 129. 134–38, 140
*Pandora's Box* (G. W. Pabst, 1929), 106–13, 117–30, 136–37
Paris, Barry, 106–8, 117–18, 122, 140, 144, 149
Paris Cinémathèque, 152
Parsons, Louella, 29–32
Photography, 19, 21, 23, 71, 177, 191
Pickford, Mary, 76–77; "Daily Talks" and, 160; scrapbooks and, 29, 31–32; *Why Not Try God?*, 157, 159, 161, 163
Pitts, Zasu, 2, 17, 156–57, 181–84

Queen Mary's Dollhouse, 198 n.27

Recollection, definitions of, 3, 5, 9, 23, 39
Renov, Michael, 135, 138
Riefenstahl, Leni, 74–75
Robertson, Pamela, 166
Rogers St. Johns, Adela, 1, 55, 157. 162
Rossellini, Isabella, 7, 17, 190–91

San Simeon oral history project, 34, 63, 202 n.22
Sarris, Andrew, 152
Schlupmann, Heidi, 123–24
Schor, Naomi, 25–27
Scott, Joan Wallach, 73
Screen memories, 95–96, 101
Shipman, Nell, 3, 15, 73, 75–76, 82
*Silent Star* (Colleen Moore), 1, 23, 39, 40
*Sophia Loren's Recipes and Memories*, 158, 176–77, 179–81
Stardom, 21, 30–31, 35, 62, 66, 107
Steedman, Carolyn, 13–14, 47, 69, 185
Stewart, Susan, 24–25, 27, 30, 38, 45, 48–49, 54

*index* 241

Studlar, Gaylyn, 199 n.49
Swanson, Gloria, 2, 16, 74, 75–76

Turlington, Christy, 17, 158, 188–89
Tynan, Kenneth, 106–8, 114, 116–19, 125

Valentino, Rudolph, 52–55

Waters, Ethel, 2, 16, 76–77
Weber, Lois, 32, 97–98, 100
Wedekind, Frank, 111–12, 119, 125–28, 136
West, Mae, 155, 157, 159, 164–65, 167
White, Patricia, 33, 120
Whitfield, Eileen, 160, 162
"Why I Will Never Write My Memoirs" (Louise Brooks), 107–8, 110–12, 114, 118–19
*Why Not Try God?* (Mary Pickford), 157, 159, 161, 163
Windsor, Claire, 29, 31–32
Wollen, Peter, 151–52
Women's writings in nineteenth century, 91–92, 160, 162

Yates, Frances, 37, 59, 98
Yoga, 188–89, 220 n.22

Versions of some chapters were published previously: chapter 1 originally appeared in part as "Historical Recollections: Colleen Moore's Dollhouse and Film History" in *Camera Obscura*; chapter 2 was largely published as "Circuits of Memory and History: The Memoirs of Alice Guy-Blaché," in *A Feminist Reader in Early Cinema*, edited by Jennifer Bean and Diane Negra (Duke University Press, 2001); chapter 3 was published in part as "Louise Brooks, Star Witness" in *Cinema Journal*; and selections from the introduction were previously published in *Film History*.

AMELIE HASTIE
is an associate professor of film and digital media
at the University of California, Santa Cruz.

*Library of Congress Cataloging-in-Publication Data*
Hastie, Amelie
Cupboards of curiosity : women, recollection, and film history /
Amelie Hastie.
p. cm.
Includes bibliographical references and index.
ISBN-13: 978-0-8223-3676-1 (cloth : alk. paper)
ISBN-10: 0-8223-3676-6 (cloth : alk. paper)
ISBN-13: 978-0-8223-3687-7 (pbk. : alk. paper)
ISBN-10: 0-8223-3687-1 (pbk. : alk. paper)
1. Women in the motion picture industry—California—Los Angeles.
2. Motion picture actors and actresses—United States—Biography.
3. Actresses—United States—Biography. 4. Women motion picture
producers and directors—United States—Biography. I. Title.
PN1995.9.W6H37 2006
384′.80820979494—dc22      2006020437

www.ingramcontent.com/pod-product-compliance
Lightning Source LLC
Chambersburg PA
CBHW070759230426
43665CB00017B/2415